Leaders
and Elites

Leaders and Elites

William A. Welsh
University of Iowa

Holt, Rinehart and Winston
*New York   Chicago   San Francisco   Dallas
Montreal   Toronto   London   Sydney*

Library of Congress Cataloging in Publication Data

Welsh, William A.
  Leaders and elites.

  Bibliography: p. 184
  Includes index.
  1. Elite (Social sciences)   2. Power
(Social sciences)   I. Title.
  JC330.W44   301.44'92   76-41972
  ISBN 0-03-038251-3

Chapter 5 is an adaption from *A Psychological Examination of Political Leaders,* ed. M. Hermann, (New York: Macmillan, 1977).

Table 6.2 is from *Comparative Communist Political Leadership* by Carl Beck, Frederic J. Fleron, Jr., Milton Lodge, Derek J. Waller, William A. Welsh and M. George Zaninovich. Copyright © 1973 by Longman, Inc.

for Greg and Wendy

who understand how much
a few hours can mean

Preface

This book is designed to serve three purposes. The first is to provide information on and analysis of political elites and their leadership behaviors, drawn from a variety of political settings. Pedagogically, the book proceeds from the assumption that it is important for students of politics to overcome their natural parochialism—the limitations imposed by their familiarity only with the political practices and structures of the society in which they live. Similarly, it is assumed that systematic comparison is the basis of all understanding. Thus the book provides comparable data on elites and leadership from the pluralist systems of the United States, certain Western European countries, and Japan; from the developing, transitional systems of Latin America; and from the highly structured systems of the Soviet Union and certain Eastern European countries.

Second, the book undertakes a bit of conceptual housekeeping. Early chapters attempt to clarify the notions of "elite" and "leadership," both as these terms have been used historically, and as they are used in current social science literature. The concept of "elite" has acquired over time an unwieldy amount of implicit terminological baggage, much of it normative in connotation. This has led to considerable confusion in the use of the term. Ambiguities in the use of the concept of "leadership" have stemmed less from the historical evolution of the concept, and more from the fact that it is used in very different ways by social scientists from different disciplines. Thus the sense of "leadership" conveyed in experimental literature in social psychology is identifiably different from the senses in which the term commonly is used by political scientists.

As part of this attempt at conceptual housekeeping, the book reviews a number of major approaches used in the study of political elites and leadership. The focus is on approaches which can be used to study leadership extensively—that is, by studying a relatively large number of leaders, rather than looking intensively at one or a few occupants of high political posts.

Third, this book attempts to illuminate the important relationship between substance and method—between *what* we know and *how* we find out. There is a great deal of lip service paid to the notion that the procedures we use in gathering and analyzing data can vitally affect our conclusions. But too little attention has been given to explicating and illustrating this problem in a way that is meaningful to undergraduate students.

An effort has been made to make this book adaptable to three types of courses. First, it can serve as one of several concept-based books around which an Introduction to Politics course could be organized. Second, the book can be used as a supplementary text in introductory or problem-oriented courses in comparative politics. And third, it can serve as a principal text for upper-division courses in political leadership and elites.

A useful feature of this book is the availability of a computer-assisted learning package keyed to Chapter 4. This package, called COMPELITE, permits the student to pose study questions about political elites, and then to examine those questions by conducting n-way crossclassifications of data from seven nations. COMPELITE was written for the HP 2000F and HP 2000 ACCESS series mini-computers, and is easily adaptable to other mini-computer environments. COMPELITE was developed at the Laboratory for Political Research at the University of Iowa. Information on the use of the package, and the software itself, are available from the Laboratory, 321A Schaeffer Hall, University of Iowa, Iowa City, Iowa, 52242. Both Users' and Instructors' Manuals are available. Instructors at institutions with compatible equipment might find COMPELITE a useful accompaniment to *Leaders and Elites*.

My interest in elites and leadership extends over many years; among other things, this means that I have benefited from the opportunity to gather insights on the subject from a number of colleagues. They are to be held blameless, of course, for whatever insensitivities this book may contain, if only because I have undoubtedly represented their views less than adequately. The names of Peter C. Ludz, Adam Przeworski, Milton Lodge, Frederic J. Fleron, Jr., Arthur M. Hanhardt, Jr., Carl Beck, Jerzy Wiatr, and R. Barry Farrell especially come to mind. Any problems in this book also are less defensible because of the polite but persistent questioning of a number of former students, principally Barcaly Ward and David Pfotenhauer.

The genesis of this book came in conversations with Marian S. Wood and Svein Arber, both formerly of Praeger Publishers. Denise Rathbun of Praeger demonstrated the appropriate blend of patience and ire when deadlines were not met. Portions of the manuscript were typed by Barbara A. Gilbert, Karen Stewart, and Linda Samide. I am especially grateful to Barbara Gilbert for all her help, without which—for many reasons—this book would not have appeared.

Iowa City, Iowa   William A. Welsh

Contents

Leaders
and Elites

Leaders and Elites: Some Classical and Contemporary Notions

The study of political elites and leadership is not new. Plato, Aristotle, and Tacitus, to cite just three notable examples, attached considerable importance to an understanding of the nature of political leadership. Particularly in the context of the societies in which these men lived, a strong interest in the nature of political elites and leadership is easy to understand. The concentration of political power and authority in the hands of a very small proportion of the population was a central characteristic of ancient Rome and Greece, notwithstanding the experiments in "democracy" for which Athens historically is known.

Many contemporary historians conclude that the "democratization" of society has been one of the most important social changes of the last 150 years. Examining the validity of this contention is outside the scope of this book, but it is worth mentioning that this validity depends considerably on what one means by "democracy." For our purposes, it is more significant that, regardless of the extension of *opportunities* for political *participation* to larger proportions of the population, the actual *exercise* of political *power* has remained, in most societies, the prerogative of a small part of the citizenry. *In short, the rise of democracy has not signaled the decline of elites.*

The study of political elites is important for an understanding of any contemporary society. Political elites participate in, or influence the making of, decisions that allocate resources within and among social units. These acts of choice constitute the principal component of the process of governing. The reading of any daily newspaper or any news magazine will make this point forcefully. Contemporary press coverage

emphasizes the activities of persons who hold positions of importance
in societal hierarchies, especially the governmental and political hierarchies. One student of political leadership,[1] for example, discovered no
fewer than 35 major news stories dealing directly with the activities of
political elites in a single day's edition of the *New York Times.*

More generally, much of contemporary history is written with frequent and pervasive reference to "great men" whose tenures in office
are alleged to have shaped entire eras in the histories of nations. In
some cases, relatively long periods of time during which major nations
have undergone enormous social and economic transformations are
characterized simplistically in terms of the names and personal attributes of a small number of political elites. Sometimes the focus is on
a single individual, as in the typical characterization of the period 1924
to 1953 in the Soviet Union as the "Stalinist period." The point is not
to defend this (perhaps excessive) concentration on the activities of
political elites, but rather to stress the extent to which their activities
are perceived to be central to the governing of modern nations.

SOME TRADITIONAL VIEWS ABOUT POLITICAL ELITES

The concept of a political elite has a long history. Development of its
usage over time has had a distinct effect on the way we apply this
concept in understanding contemporary society. It is consequently important to take a brief look at how these traditional conceptions of the
political elite evolved. Our approach will be to emphasize the nature
and evolution of ideas, rather than the identities of the persons who
espoused these ideas. The thinkers whose perspectives on the political
elite best reflect the historical development of the concept are Pareto,
Mosca, Michels, and Marx.[2] But rather than stress the specific points of
view of each of these writers, it seems more useful to attempt to identify
both common and divergent elements in what they had to say.

The Notions of Hierarchy and Inequality

Traditional conceptions of the notion of a political elite were founded
on two concepts: hierarchy and inequality. The concept of hierarchy
implies some sort of ranking system in which people are accorded
varying positions. This ranking system is vertical, implying that there
is a top and a bottom; the people at the top presumably are more
important than those at the bottom. The usual assumption is that social
hierarchies exhibit a pyramidal form; that is, there are relatively large

numbers of persons at the bottom of the hierarchy, and relatively small numbers of persons at the top. This pyramidal distribution has been attributed to different causes by different writers, whose perspectives were influenced by the varying social circumstances at the times at which they wrote.

For example, some people have believed that the pyramidal shape of societal hierarchies is due to the "natural" distribution of attributes within the population. The assumption was that only a small proportion of the population was "fit" to rule. Only they had the requisite attributes—wisdom, foresight, courage—to make important choices that would affect the future of large numbers of persons. Other writers, generally of more recent origin, have assumed that this pyramidal distribution is due to the sheer size and complexity of contemporary societies. Social complexity, scope, and heterogeneity demand organization, which, by its very nature, requires structure. Organizational structures with many chiefs and few Indians simply do not work, it is contended. It is a physical impossibility (and a psychological implausibility) for large proportions of any group of consequential size to be involved directly in making critical decisions on behalf of that group.[3] Here we must set aside the question of how, or whether, those at the top of the hierarchy are kept responsive to those who occupy lower positions. But it seems clear that only a relatively small proportion of the members of any large and complex social structure can participate directly in choice taking.

This basic conception of hierarchy is consistent with our common-sense picture of how political power has been exercised through history. All societies have been characterized by the exercise of political power by a small number of persons at any given point in time. Even if we made the expansive assumption that everyone with an administrative or policy-making position at any level of government, or at any level of major political organizations such as political parties, had a direct and significant influence on choices made on behalf of those governmental or political units, we would discover that not more than 10 percent of the population exerted direct influence on political decision making. (This percentage would hold for highly centralized, extensively bureaucratized systems. For less centralized systems the proportion would actually be smaller.[4]) Further, it is clear that many persons involved in governmental and political administration have marginal, if any, influence on critical choices. Later in this book—especially in Chapter 7— we take up the question of how persons in the political elite are held accountable to those members of society whose interests they are supposed to represent. For now, we wish only to make the point that the size of such political elite groups is very small.

Traditional notions of a political elite also were based on conceptions of inequality. No one doubts that political influence is distributed unequally in all societies. Few would challenge the notion that personal attributes associated with success in arenas of political competition are also distributed unevenly through the population. The ability to articulate ideas, to persuade, to cajole and coerce, to mobilize, to embody and advance symbols to which large numbers of people respond—these characteristics, so frequently associated with competitive political success, clearly are held in varying degrees by different individuals.

Such a position does not necessarily correspond to what some have called the "elite superiority" premise. We can recognize differences in individual characteristics without making normative judgments about these differences. Further, the fact that such differences are "natural" does not mean that laws and institutions must necessarily perpetuate or extend them. Pareto, for example, postulated the "inequality of individual endowment," but recognized that such an argument had no necessary relationship to the question of how societal structures should treat *opportunity of access* to political influence. That is, one can readily recognize the inequality of distribution of politically relevant attributes in a population without necessarily concluding that the structural arrangements of government should institutionalize the natural political advantage that some people may have over their fellow citizens. Indeed, one of the criteria of political organization in society might well be to reduce such advantages.

Thus one can well argue that, in contemporary democracies, the question is not whether there is a political elite or whether there will continue to be a political elite. The more important questions have to do with the arrangements by which these elites are held accountable to the broad mass of the citizenry. The reader will recognize this as nothing more than a statement of the impracticality of direct democracy, and of the inherent difficulties in sustaining meaningful indirect democracy. More important, however, is that what Pareto called the "inequality of individual endowment" bears no necessary relationship to one's point of view about the appropriate societal arrangements whereby citizen access to the political process is structured.

The Dichotomy of Rulers and Ruled

One of the most important characteristics of the writings of Pareto and of Marx was their perception of a wide social gap between the political elite and the nonelite. One of their basic premises was that the concentration of political power in the hands of a small number of individuals was self-perpetuating. Elites do not voluntarily invite nonelites to join their number. Those in power do not voluntarily share that power to any greater extent than is required by the situational circumstances in which they operate. Thus both Pareto and Marx believed that political elites would strive to keep as much functional distance as possible between themselves and nonelite members of society. The disparity of political influence between the two basic societal groups would be guarded and cultivated by the elite.

In such a society, the "circulation of elites" to which Pareto referred would take place on an *individual* and *selective* basis. That is, the political elite would revitalize itself only through the selective recruitment of new members on an individual basis. Some persons from outside the social and occupational groups that usually supply the political elite might occasionally be brought into that august stratum of society, but only in sufficiently small numbers as to facilitate their resocialization into the predominant values of the elite. The possibility of *collective* "circulation of elites" was rejected by Pareto, and was thought by Marx to be possible only as an element of a revolutionary situation. The notion that a distinctly different segment of the social hierarchy—a new social class or occupational grouping—could replace the existing elite was discounted, especially by Pareto.

We should note that Mosca's position on this question was noticeably different from Pareto's. Mosca believed that there existed in most societies a "subelite" that served both as a channel of contact and communication between the elite and nonelite, and as a potential tool for the recruitment, sometimes on a relatively large scale, of new members into the elite. Furthermore, Mosca challenged Pareto's assumption that elite circulation would take place only on an individual basis. Mosca believed that the collective replacement of one social group by another in positions of political power was quite possible. Furthermore, he was not convinced that such a transformation would necessarily involve revolution. Thus Mosca felt that motivations toward "collective social mobility"—the desire for increased societal status and other rewards on the part of a social or occupational group—could provide one of the bases for elite circulation.

The question of the extent of the functional gap between persons in elite positions and persons outside those positions is one of the central issues in contemporary politics. Some political theorists argue that an important characteristic of modern society is the tendency for political elites, even in relatively open, pluralistic systems, to become insulated, and eventually isolated, from the masses of the population. We usually attribute this to the complexity of modern society and to the need for complex hierarchical governmental structures involving widespread delegation of political power. Political elites, it is often argued, are too busy running the government and other political organizations to maintain effective contact with the general population. It is worth noting that most contemporary political theorists tend to discount explanations that would suggest that political elites insulate themselves from outside influence because of inherent personality characteristics of members of the elite, or because the exercise of power is "corruptive" in its own right, as some earlier social theorists argued.

Whatever the origins of these apparent pressures toward elite insulation, the problem seems to be identifiable in most modern societies. It is a problem of such significance that political orders that had for years pressed toward increased governmental centralization—for example, the socialist systems of the Soviet Union and Eastern Europe—have in recent years undertaken steps toward decentralization and toward broadening the scope of political participation by increased numbers of citizens. They are also attempting to bridge the communications gap between elites and nonelites by giving citizens' organizations more direct input into policy making. The inadequacies of industrial and agricultural development in these countries, as well as the persistent uneasiness of important segments of the population, is often attributed to the increased isolation of the political leadership. The circumstances that surrounded the extraordinary resignation of Richard Nixon from the presidency of the United States in 1974 also effectively document the apparent ease with which persons in positions of power can lose contact with the political realities that define the societal context in which they must operate.

Concepts of Minority and Majority

As we have suggested, traditional notions about a political elite also involved conceptions of minority and majority. Obviously, political elites constituted a minority of the population, but exercised a majority (if not a near monopoly) of political power. Historically, the majority of the citizenry has had little influence on political outcomes, and at best has exercised such influence indirectly.

The writings of Pareto and Mosca go beyond this simple and obvious numerical description. They treat the concepts of majority and minority in relation to the dynamics of social organization. That is, one of the explanations for the exercise of preponderant political power by a small minority of the population is held to be the perceived need of the minority for strong organization to combat its numerical inferiority. According to Mosca, "the minority is organized for the very reason that it is a minority."[5] This organizational effort must include both internal structuring within the elite (to achieve cohesion and efficient action) and a structuring of the relationship between elite and nonelite such that the elite is able to maintain that relationship essentially as it chooses. Thus, because minorities are minorities, they organize; because they organize, they achieve and/or sustain political power.

This argument about the central importance of organization to the sustenance of political power has been approached in a slightly different, but complementary and enlightening, way by the American political scientist E. E. Schattschneider. Schattschneider notes that the key to political influence in the United States has always been "the mobilization of bias," i.e., the ability to bring effective organization to the activities of a relatively small number of individuals who have reasonably coherent political interests and goals that they wish to pursue at the expense of relatively large numbers of other persons.[6]

The Mosca argument concerning the central importance of organization also explains the "silence" of what has been called in the United States the "silent majority." It is extraordinarily difficult to organize the principal part of the social order. The larger and more heterogeneous a segment of the population, the more difficult it is to bring to that segment a degree of organization sufficient to permit effective, concerted political action. Thus the majority is disorganized because it is the majority; because it lacks effective organization, its political voice is "silent." This argument seems somewhat oversimplified; it might be more accurate to say that the "silent majority" is a disorganized jumble of overlapping and shifting minorities, and the points of view that it does share are so general and vague that they cannot serve as a basis for effective organization.

Mosca's contentions concerning the central features of minority-majority relations in society also are relevant to what more recently have been called "social marginality" theories concerning the composition and behavior of political elites. These theories argue that there is a tendency in most societies toward the emergence of political elite groups whose personal characteristics are not representative of those of the general population. For example, studies of the political elite in Germany between 1871 and 1945[7] suggest that persons whose personal attributes differ from those of the population in the area from which they come are disproportionately likely to achieve positions of political importance. For example, the southern sections of Germany are predominantly Roman Catholic in religious preference; a majority of the national political elites coming from the south have been Protestants. A similar finding, based on the study of a large number of social background characteristics, has been generated by Moskos in his research on the political elite of Albania between 1935 and 1955. Members of the political elite from different areas of Albania have tended to be in the religious and ethnic minorities in the areas from which they come. Indeed, trends in the ethnic composition of the Albanian political elite usually have been the opposite of those in the ethnic composition of the population as a whole.[8]

Mosca would have no difficulty explaining these apparent anomalies. He would say that persons from minority social backgrounds perceive a stronger need for effective political organization as a basis for combating their minority status. Effective political organization emerges as a much more significant factor in determining political influence than does mere preponderance of numbers in the population. Thus persons with "social marginality"—a term that here means nothing more than numerical minority status with respect to personal attributes—achieve a disproportionate amount of political influence through the use of more careful organizational strategies and tactics.

The Political Elite and the Governing Elite

Mosca, in particular, felt it important to distinguish the political elite from the governing elite. He argued that the political elite is one part of the governing elite, but is not synonymous with it. The political elite (or, for Mosca, the "political class") constituted the "intellectual" element of the governing elite, which includes nonintellectual elements as well. Mosca's position is recognition of the fact that the exercise of political power involves not only the manipulation of ideas and symbols (the "intellectual" element), but also the capacity to maintain structure and order in society—by force or coercion, if necessary.

The late American sociologist C. Wright Mills[9] developed this notion of overlapping, but still distinct, political and governing elites in his controversial book, *The Power Elite*. Mills argued that the United States was under the control of a relatively small number of individuals who came from three overlapping power directorates: the executive branch of government, the military establishment, and the top management of a limited number of corporations. Mills's work led to the coining of the term, the "military-industrial complex." For our purposes, a review of Mills's work is not appropriate; there have been numerous methodological critiques of his research, and collectively they cast considerable doubt upon some of the conclusions to which Mills came. But Mills's work does emphasize that what Mosca called the "political class," or political elite, usually requires alliance with other elements, especially those having access to the means of coercion, in order to sustain its political predominance.

This point, in turn, underscores a characteristic of this book: We are concerned here with political elites and political leadership, rather than with Mosca's broader category of the "governing elite." For example, we shall deal only in passing with relationships among the three societal elements asserted by Mills to constitute the "power elite" in the United States. This focus does not imply that civil-military relations, for example, are unimportant. Rather, the choice reflects the necessity to focus more specifically on one aspect of elites and leadership in modern society.

Personal Attributes and Social Context

In characterizing the political elite, writers have tended to diverge into two distinct groups. The approach of the first has been to characterize political elites as *possessors of certain attributes,* frequently psychological characteristics, that supposedly explain their ascendance to power and their maintenance of positions of importance. The other approach has been to characterize political elites in terms of the *social context* out of which they come and, similarly, as "representatives" of societal interests that are dominant at a given point in time. Pareto's approach centered on elite attributes; Mosca—and others, including Karl Mannheim and Schumpeter—tended toward the social context perspective. Thus a Paretian argument might state that individuals come to, and maintain, positions of political power because they have psychological characteristics of dominance. A counterargument might be that individuals acquire and maintain influence "insofar as the kinds of activity in which they engage become of vital importance to society."[10] This second point of view would suggest that political power is associated with the functional significance of the social groups from which potential competitors for elite positions come.

For our purposes, what is most relevant about this distinction between elites as possessors of attributes and elites as representatives of societal structure is that both perspectives seem important in understanding the selection of political elites in contemporary societies. It would be foolish to ignore either possible explanation for the emergence and maintenance of elite groups in power. Both arguments need to be examined with the most comprehensive data we are able to obtain.

The Concept of Elites and the Concept of Democracy

We have touched on the critical relationship between the existence of political elites and the maintenance of democratic political orders. We should not forget that there are virtually no contemporary societies that do not purport either to be democratic or to seek the realization of democracy as a principal social and political goal. Though the acceptance of democratic principles and symbols is by no means universal, it is probably fair to say that the achievement of something called "democracy" is one of the most pervasive contemporary political motivations. Although the different political practices of various groups that espouse democratic principles make it clear that there is a great deal of disagreement as to what "democracy" really represents, the symbolism of democracy seems to have near-universal significance.

It has been all too common to juxtapose the concepts of democracy and elites. Indeed, some writers divide political systems into categories of "democratic" and "elitist" systems. Democratic systems are said to provide a basis for meaningful citizen access to the political process on the basis of equality and universality. Elitist systems, by contrast, are systems in which the exercise of political control by a small number of persons is institutionalized in the structure of government and political activity. In such a system the broad masses of citizens have no pretense for the exercise of political influence. Thus the existence of democratic political practices and the existence of institutionalized political elites are frequently asserted to be mutually incompatible.

Such an argument seems difficult to defend upon a practical reading of contemporary political life. It seems reasonable to argue that: (a) systems commonly thought to be "democratic" in fact exhibit substantially circumscribed access to political influence for the vast majority of citizens; and (b) the handful of persons in positions of political power in so-called "elitist" systems operate with a far greater range of constraints and limitations than is commonly recognized or acknowledged.

Two American political scientists recently published a textbook, the title of which refers to "the irony of democracy."[11] A principal argument of this book is that democratic systems actually share some of the characteristics that "democrats" tend to attribute to "elitist" systems. In Mosca's terms we would say that the theory of democracy founders in reality on the ubiquity of the need for political organization in all modern societies. The only form in which democracy can exist today is an indirect form. The indirectness of democracy leads to its principal ironies and imperfections, especially to the apparently marginal ability of the average citizen to exert direct influence on political outcomes. Thus the question is not whether a democracy will have a political elite, but rather how cohesive and permeable this elite might be, and what linkages—what extent of accountability—the political elite has to other segments of society.

Reference to the work of Robert Michels, especially his "iron law of oligarchy,"[12] should help to clarify the issue. Michels argues that there is an escapable trend toward oligarchic rule in larger organizations. (He was talking particularly about political party organizations.) Political organizations set up for the purpose of competing in a political arena tend to become increasingly oligarchic *internally*. This point has crucial relevance for democracy, because it seems clear that efficient political organizations are critical to the existence of democracy. The sustenance of democratic political practices depends in considerable degree on the extent to which competitive political organizations, representing a reasonable range of political viewpoints, are able to function. Strong organization is critical to successful political competitiveness; democracy requires intergroup competition. Thus democracy requires strong political organizations, effectively structured.

And yet, according to Michels, any such organization tends to become increasingly oligarchic. The number of persons who influence the postures taken by those political organizations becomes smaller and smaller over time. Democratic systems are therefore caught between the need for intergroup competition and the inevitable tendencies toward oligarchy within those organizations that must sustain political competition. The more meaningful the intergroup competition, the greater the pressures for within-group oligarchy.

It is precisely this apparent contradiction in the political structure of many contemporary Western societies that has led a number of Asian and East European political thinkers to argue for a different relationship between intergroup and within-group political competition. Specifically, the argument has been advanced that political competition may ultimately be facilitated more readily by single-party systems than by multiparty systems. The argument is that eliminating the need for intergroup competition reduces (but does not eliminate) the pressures toward oligarchy within the predominant political group. The conclusion is drawn that a genuinely mass-based single-party system might eventually reflect the concerns of the population more effectively than a multiparty system containing competitive but internally oligarchic party structures.

This argument is not fully consistent with Michels's iron law of oligarchy, since Michels argues that the tendencies toward organizational oligarchy exist independent of the extent to which any given organization finds itself confronted with political competition. Michels contends that pressures toward oligarchy stem from the dynamic of organization itself, rather than from the interaction of any given organization with other groups. Further, it seems reasonable to suggest that oligarchic tendencies have not been successfully combated in existing one-party systems. There are some societies in which meaningful efforts toward eliminating oligarchy within single dominant parties have been made, most notably Yugoslavia. But even there, the concentration of political influence still is substantial.

At least one conclusion seems inescapable: Democracies will always have political elites. What is less clear is whether this fact is as threatening to the concept of democracy as some writers have pessimistically argued. A useful perspective on this question can be gained by contrasting democracy as a *set of conditions* with democracy as a *process and direction of change.* If we see the essence of democratic political practice as a condition of mass sovereignty, i.e., the unfettered participation by large numbers of individuals in the making of political choices, the achievement of democracy seems unlikely. If, on the other hand, we see democracy as a set of procedures through which elites charged with the responsibility for making important societal choices can be called to account by representatives of the population at large, then the realization of democracy seems plausible. Similarly, we might be reasonably optimistic about the possibility that a relatively large number of concerned citizens could at least indirectly influence the basic direction of social and political change, assuming they could agree on the desired nature of such change. This, too, would be descriptive of democracy as a process; it implies that mass action is possible, but only with the existence of consensus on what issues are important and on what should be done about those important problems.

These comments about the relationship between the existence of a political elite and the existence of political democracy need *not* be focused exclusively, or even primarily, on political systems that students of politics in the West have tended to label "democratic." Aspirations toward democracy are articulated by political elites and leaders in nearly every society. The focus of the last few paragraphs is on an issue fundamental to all social orders, namely, the nature of the relationship between the inevitable concentration of direct decision-making power in the hands of a relatively small number of individuals, and the existence of a political order generally asserted to be the most desirable one under which men can live.

SOME METHODOLOGICAL REFLECTIONS ON TRADITIONAL VIEWS OF THE POLITICAL ELITE

As you read this book, undoubtedly you will formulate your own opinions about the extent to which these traditional theories about the development and characteristics of political elites, and about the relationship between political elites and democracy, are supported by contemporary evidence. In fact, one of the principal purposes of the book is to encourage the development of thoughtful opinions about these questions. This kind of critique—bringing the evidence to bear against conventional assumptions—will be developed as the book progresses. However, some brief comments designed to tie these traditional views of political elites into some current methodological issues in political science are appropriate here. Three such methodological reflections seem appropriate at this point.

Normative vs. Analytical Perspectives

One of the most distressing characteristics of traditional writings about political elites has been a tendency to mix three distinct forms of the concept of elite: (1) the normative form; (2) the "ideal types" form; and (3) the descriptive-analytical form. It is important to distinguish among these usages, especially since a good deal of confusion about the study of political elites has involved a confusion of these different ways of using basic concepts.

Much of the writing about political elites has been explicitly or implicitly normative in character. That is, the purpose of the writer has been to make judgments about certain forms of political and governmental organization, or about specific sets of persons who occupied important political positions. More often than not, especially in the last 200 years, the term "elite" has taken on a distinctly negative meaning in this normative literature; the presumption has been that the existence of power concentrations was inconsistent with basic liberal democratic theory, and that the existence of "elites" was therefore undesirable. For many people the term "elite" still has this negative normative implication. It should be pointed out that, for Mosca and Pareto, the elite concept "formed part of a political doctrine which was opposed to, or critical of, modern democracy, and still more opposed to modern socialism."[13] That is, Mosca and Pareto, perhaps the two best-known traditional theorists of political elites, were not supportive of nineteenth-century conceptions of liberal democracy. They also were opposed to Marxian theory. One can interpret a substantial part of Mosca's writing as an attempt to discredit Marxian premises concerning the foundations of social and political power.

The second use of the concept of elite has been what social scientists call an "ideal types" usage. Here the idea is to use the elite concept as a relatively "pure"—in the sense of distinct and readily identifiable— fix point, and then to compare real-world distributions of political power against that explicit, but hypothetical, point of reference. Thus if a simple definition of an elitist system referred to the legal concentration of power in the hands of a small number of persons from the same social and/or occupational stratum, one would compare existing political and social orders against such a "pure" point of reference in an attempt to discover the *extent* to which actual cases were consistent with the hypothetical concept. The ideal types usage of the elite concept can be helpful because of its precision, but it can be misleading because it lends itself to abuse. Specifically there is a tendency to attribute the characteristics of the ideal type to societies that only approximate those "ideal" characteristics, and thus to assume that all empirical (i.e., real-world) examples must fall into one or another of the limited number of ideal types categories. In using the concept of an elitist system as an ideal type, the tendency therefore would be to attribute "pure" elitist characteristics to societies that only approximated such conditions. An implicit ideal types usage is common in traditional literature on political elites, frequently accompanied by the logical carelessness to which such a usage tends to lend itself.

The third way in which the term "elite" may be used is in a descriptive-analytical mode. From the perspective of modern social science, this is the most appropriate usage. In this case our approach is to identify the characteristics of those persons who occupy positions of political power, to study their careers, their values, and their behaviors, and to understand the relationships that exist between these individuals and persons who occupy positions of lesser importance. In short, the descriptive-analytical usage is the basis for building empirical theory about the functioning of political elites. In later sections of this book the term "political elite" will be used with this descriptive-analytical connotation.

Mechanistic vs. Organismic Assumptions

As Searing[14] has pointed out, much of the traditional literature on political elites has been undergirded by either mechanistic or organismic models of man and society. Explicating these two fundamentally different approaches can help us to place in perspective traditional writings about elites. Mechanistic images start from the idea that society and its members have an essentially unchanging nature. The segments of society, including its members, are not naturally integrated, and they frequently work at cross-purposes to one another. This is the source of political conflict. Resolution of political conflict is associated with the achievement of preponderant influence by some segments of society over others. Thus one understands society only through comprehension of the characteristics of those segments that become dominant. Society as a whole is an aggregate, equal to, but no more than, the sum of its parts. Some societal elements are a good deal more important than others. Attention should be focused primarily on those critical elements.

Such a mechanistic rendering of man and society may be found in the writings of Aristotle, of Pareto, and in the atomistic characterizations of human nature found in the work of Hobbes, Locke, and John Stuart Mill. Such a rendering lends itself to what has been called the "great man" interpretation of history, an approach that emphasizes the personal characteristics of elites rather than the social forces that define the environment in which elites behave.

The organismic image, on the other hand, emphasizes an integrative, systemic picture of society. Society as a whole, in its integrated form, is greater than the sum of its component parts. The elements of society —institutions and individuals—are derived from the fabric of the society as a whole. They can be understood and explained only in terms of their fit into the total social fabric. Such an approach is similar to that taken by Plato and by Mosca. This perspective lends itself to explanations of elite origins and behavior based on the determining influence of social factors. It is a contextual approach, emphasizing the extent to which environmental context determines the character of political elites and leadership.

Throughout this book you will encounter different conceptions of contemporary political leadership that correspond to these basic distinctions between mechanistic and organismic approaches. Some contemporary students of political elites and leadership emphasize the personal characteristics of leaders, and the capacity of these individual persons to exert influence on their environment. Other writers proceed from the assumption that the social environment has a determining effect on the characteristics of political elites. Unfortunately, few contemporary social scientists have succeeded in bridging the gap between mechanistic and organismic approaches. Only scattered pieces of research attempt to show that the personal characteristics of members of elites and the social contexts in which these persons behave may well be related to one another in complex but still identifiable ways.

Careless Conceptualization

Writings on political elites frequently have invoked undefined concepts, including but not limited to the concepts of elite and leadership. We have thus far resisted imposing formal definitions of important terms. In part it is difficult to do this because most writers have not bothered to define crucial terms very carefully. In a general sense we know that the concept of elite has been taken to refer to the holding of a position of dominance in a societal hierarchy. Frequently it is assumed that leadership is something exercised by elites; that is, that elitness and leadership are functionally synonymous. We shall suggest in the next section of this chapter that such a point of view is misleading.

In addition, four other concepts frequently find their way into traditional literature on political elites, almost always in the absence of explicit definition: the concepts of *power, authority, legitimacy,* and *charisma.* These concepts refer to things that elites have or that they seek to cultivate, and therefore are phenomena closely associated with the existence of political elites.

We can appropriately spare ourselves an excursion into the enormous variety of definitions that these terms have received during the last 200 years. But some basic understanding of the distinctions among these terms is important before we can proceed to an examination of contemporary studies of political elites and leadership.

Power is a special case of *influence.* A serviceable definition of *influence* would be: a condition in which A brings B to do something that B would not otherwise do. This includes not only situations in which A induces B to undertake an action, but also in which A influences B to go on doing something that B is now doing, and that B would stop doing if it were not for the influence of A. *Power* is a special case of such a relationship; it involves the threat or use of *sanctions.* These sanctions may be positive or negative, but in either case they represent a form of direct inducement. Negative coercion is based on the threat of punishment, whereas positive coercion is based on the prospect of gain.

We may define *authority* as *legitimate power.* Authority is present where the existence of coercive influence is accepted by the recipients of that influence as being proper and desirable. We may speak of the legitimacy of a political administration in terms of the extent to which its actions are accepted as proper by its citizen subjects. Thus *legitimacy* is present when there is agreement with the substance of behavior engaged in by political elites, as well as acceptance of the notion that coercion should be used to enforce the designated public policy if resistance is encountered. Using this definition, it is easy to see that some political power exercised in contemporary society is legitimate and therefore constitutes authority, whereas other political power lacks legitimacy, and thus lacks authority. Indeed, we may argue that one of the basic tasks confronting any political administration is the maintenance of synonymity between power and authority; that is, the cultivation of legitimacy for the political power that it holds.

Perhaps the most troublesome of the concepts traditionally associated with political elites is *charisma.* It has been used in a frustrating variety of ways, almost always without careful definition. Broadly, we say that a political leader is charismatic if he induces a personal follow-ing independent of the substance of his positions on important political questions. It is the leader's personality that leads to his assumption and maintenance of a position of leadership. Charisma is easy to assert, but extraordinarily difficult to prove. The evidence brought to bear to sub-stantiate assertions that a given individual is "charismatic" is often dubious at best. Psychological characteristics of prominent persons are frequently the subject of speculation, but rarely studied carefully at close range. In addition, it usually is difficult to separate the appeal of a leader's issue positions from the appeal of his personality. Neverthe-less, it seems important to delve as much as possible into the interactive psychological dimensions of eliteness and leadership if we wish to understand those phenomena in modern society.

THE CONCEPT OF LEADERSHIP

If a focus on political *elites* characterized a good deal of writing between the middle of the nineteenth century and the middle of the twentieth, a gradual shift to a focus on *leadership* has characterized research and writing in the past two decades. As we shall suggest later in this book, however, the shift has been as much one of semantics as of genuine change in the focus or methods of research. Until very recently, the attention given to the broader implications of the concept of leadership has been manifested as much in lip service as in concrete action.

Not all political elites—holders of high positions in the political and/ or governmental hierarchies—are leaders. Conversely, many leaders are not elites, in that they do not hold elite positions. There is good reason to believe that confusion between these two terms—"leaders" and "elites"—is hindering the development of research in this area of study. Although one senses from a reading of recent social science literature that an author's choice of "elite" or "leader" may sometimes be conscious, the rationale for choosing one or the other is rarely given. Further, the terms are not defined consistently—when they are defined at all. Sometimes the concepts of elite and leader are used interchange-ably.

As we have suggested, eliteness inheres in the hierarchical position occupied by an individual. In a related manner, elites constitute a distinct numerical (and often social and functional) minority. As Polish sociologist Jerzy Wiatr points out, political elites are set apart from the rest of society by their preeminence in political and governmental hierarchies. Elites exist where and when the distribution of valued resources is so markedly unequal that some minorities differ sharply from the rest of society in terms of the high concentration of one or more of these resources.[15] Political elites exist where there is a marked concentration of important political positions in the hands of a small proportion of the population.

Whereas eliteness is defined in terms of hierarchical *position*, leadership is a *relational* term. It describes the most important characteristics of relationships between leaders and followers. Elsewhere[16] I have defined leadership as the ability to mobilize human resources in pursuit of specific goals. Leadership has the additional characteristic of inherent authority. Thus leadership is more than simply having influence or power, or being able to bring someone to do what you want him to do, regardless of his intentions or desires. Leadership involves authority, and authority implies legitimacy.

An authoritative leader is one whose actions in organizing, mobilizing, and allocating resources are accepted by the persons for whom these actions are relevant. The decisions of political leaders are carried out as faithfully as possible, not merely because these decision makers may be powerful, but because it is viewed as appropriate and legitimate that they have been involved in making these decisions. And it is worth emphasizing that authority itself is not an attribute of a leader; rather, it is a characteristic of the relationship that exists between leaders and followers. If the followers attach legitimacy to the acts of a leader, we may speak of the relationship between leaders and followers as one of authority.

Thus the concept of leadership has implied the need to examine patterns of *interaction* among elites, between elites and nonelites, and between elites and potential or nonactive elites. It emphasizes the study of *behaviors,* and the study of the *processes* by which political elites define their relationships with their environment, and through which they seek to perform the *functions* that have been allocated to them, or that they have appropriated. A focus on leadership is a focus on the links between members of groups or organizations, some of whom lead and others of whom follow.

Indeed, the study of leadership inevitably involves the study of leader-follower relationships. The proverbial "general without an army" is not a leader, regardless of the eminence of his own position. Some of the major foci in leadership research have to do with the relationship between the styles used by leaders and the responses engendered in followers. For example, an important question in leadership research concerns the effect of three contrasting styles of leadership—laissez-faire, authoritarian, and democratic—on the performance of tasks by followers. Do democratic or laissez-faire leaders evoke a higher and

more consistent level of performance from followers than do authoritarian leaders? The evidence on such questions is mixed.

A number of writers have argued that leadership is both more univer-
sally observed and more rapidly changing than is "eliteness." All political communities undertake various forms of political, social, and
economic activity. These activities require organization, which involves
the mobilization of human resources. Such activity, as we have said, is
the basis of leadership. Therefore, it is reasonable to suggest that wher-
ever there is human organization for the purpose of goal achievement,
there are leaders. At the same time, the identity of the leaders in any
given political community may vary from time to time, and with the
nature of tasks being emphasized in that community at that time. Similarly, the identity of political leaders may change more frequently than
the identity of political elites; there is no necessary relationship between the occupants of high positions in which formal power is concentrated (the political elite) and the identity of political leaders who
mobilize human resources for task achievement.

According to Wiatr, the existence of a political elite is more problematic than is the existence of leadership. There is a political elite
when and only when: (a) "the distribution of power within the community is markedly unequal, a minority having much greater power than
much of the rest of the community"; and (b) "access to the elite is
restricted in such a way that leaders and followers do not easily change
roles."[17] Thus, in Wiatr's view, all political communities have leaders,
but only in some cases do leadership groups constitute a political elite.
At the same time, persons holding high positions in political and governmental hierarchies may not actually exercise leadership functions,
in the sense of being able to mobilize human resources. In such a
situation a political elite might exist, but it might overlap only marginally with the composition of the political leadership.

It might be noted that Wiatr comes close to equating leadership with
what we have earlier called influence. In Wiatr's words, "leadership is
a relationship which consists of systematically influencing others so that
they behave according to the leaders' desires ... some congruence
between followers' behavior and leaders' desires is the definitional
characteristic of leadership."[18] In Wiatr's view, political leadership can
have either *moral* or *legal* bases. Political leadership rests on moral
bases when leaders command authority among their followers in the
absence of any legal sanctions; this would be the case for the leaders of
political groups that stand in opposition to those in power. The bases for
political leadership are legal when leaders have at their disposal legal
sanctions recognized as legitimate by a sufficiently large majority of the
members of the group or institution.[19]

Wiatr's definition explicitly excludes what he calls "unlegitimized coercion," that is, the function of imposing the will of a minority on a political group exclusively by means of force and threats of force. In other words, Wiatr excludes nonauthoritative power from the category of leadership. The officials of an occupying power may "rule" over conquered territory, and they may occupy elite positions in the administration of that territory. However, it is not reasonable to refer to them as political leaders in that society.[20]

A distinction that is in some respects parallel to that between moral and legal leadership bases is the distinction between *formal* and *informal* leadership. A formal leader is one whose relationships with his followers are based on his official position and on the explicit formal rules on the basis of which the group operates. An informal leader is one whose relationships with his followers are based on his ability to mobilize them to concerted action on behalf of shared goals. An informal leader is a *functional* leader. He is able to accomplish things in the context of group activity because of the nature of his relationships with his followers. In any given group, the formal and informal leaders may be the same, or they may be wholly different individuals. One of the most fascinating areas of political leadership research involves attempting to discern the characteristics of political groups in which formal and informal leaders are not identical. In addition, it seems important to determine the effects of the existence of such "dual leadership" on the long-range functioning of political organizations.

LEADERSHIP ATTRIBUTES AND LEADERSHIP SITUATIONS

Traditional studies of political elites frequently were concerned with identifying the common characteristics shared by a particular elite group. In a similar vein, contemporary social scientists have been trying for some time to discover what personal characteristics—other than the ability to mobilize human resources—tend to be associated with political leadership. Are there personal attributes—perhaps personality characteristics—that are found much more frequently among leaders than among nonleaders? As Fiedler points out, "it is probably fair to say that almost every conceivable personality trait has been related at one time or another to leadership behavior, status, or performance."[21] Fiedler is also quick to note that research focused entirely on the attributes of leaders themselves has not been very useful. If leadership consists of *relationships* between leaders and followers, a focus exclusively on the *attributes* of leaders would tell us relatively little about their functioning in relation to other persons.

Recent research on leadership attributes suggests that we must understand these attributes in relation to two other factors: the attributes of the *group* in which leadership is exercised, and the *situations* in which leaders find themselves. That is, there are group and situational determinants of leadership behavior, and these determinants tend to be more important than the personal attributes of leaders in explaining the nature of leadership activity. As Stogdill summarizes this research, "a person does not become a leader by virtue of the possession of some combination of traits, but the pattern of personal characteristics of the leader must bear some relevant relationship to the characteristics, activities, and goals of the followers. . . . [Further] it becomes clear that an adequate analysis of leadership involves not only a study of leaders, but also of situations" in which leaders must operate.[22] In other words, what determines who will emerge in leadership roles, and/or how effectively leaders will perform, depends very much on the nature of the group within which they are operating, as well as on the specific features of the situations in which they must act.

Fiedler's important work on leadership also has led to the drawing of a distinction between two aspects of leader-follower relations: *relationship-centered* links between leaders and followers, and *task-centered* links. Leaders must be concerned not only with the most efficient utilization of human resources toward the accomplishment of specific tasks, but also with the nature of personal relationships among members of the group. Research tells us that leaders vary a great deal in their emphases on task as opposed to relationship-centered factors. Similarly, groups of followers vary in the extent to which relationship-centered problems affect their ability to perform efficiently the tasks assigned to them. Finally, different kinds of situations require more or less attention to relationship-centered considerations. Members of a group may be more willing, for example, to accept largely task-centered behavior from a leader in a time of crisis, but demand greater attention to relationship-centered elements when they perceive that group activity can be more measured and routine.

2

Approaches and Data in Research on Leaders and Elites

THE IMPORTANCE OF ORGANIZING DATA

The idle accumulation of information without some sort of guiding design is obviously inefficient. Any subject needs a framework into which individual pieces of information can be fitted. Social scientists need such frameworks as a basis for developing theories about relationships among social phenomena. But more generally, every human being requires such frameworks for the organization and integration of information. Our ability to give meaning and importance to events in our lives depends on our ability to relate those events to previous experiences we have had and to knowledge we have assimilated.

As a practical matter, further, it is difficult to know where to start in addressing a new subject unless we have at hand some relatively formal approaches or frameworks by which our study can be structured. Because one of the purposes of this book is to stimulate original research on leaders and elites, it is important that we discuss some of the approaches that have been articulated in recent years by students in this field of study.

The notions of organizing and integrating information imply *comparison*. If we wish to understand the general principles underlying the ways elites and leaders are chosen and behave, it is important that we study them in the broadest possible variety of settings. Focusing our attention on a limited range of cases—e.g., relatively open, democratic societies—would probably lead us to oversimplified, and frequently inaccurate, statements about leadership behavior. There may be some reason to believe that leadership behavior varies when the structure of political and governmental activity is substantially different. And if it does not—if the same basic principles underlie leadership behavior regardless of the political, cultural, and economic context—we cannot establish this fact until we have examined leadership in a number of different settings.

Furthermore, even our understanding of a single political system— our own, for example—is severly limited when we study only that society. To say, for example, that the United States has a *presidential* system, and that much of our leadership behavior can be explained in terms of the fundamental characteristics of presidential systems, implies an understanding of how such systems differ from *nonpresidential* (e.g., parliamentary) systems. Only when we understand how presidential systems are different from nonpresidential systems can we understand why leadership behaviors should be expected to be as they are in our own society.

Consequently, approaches and frameworks for studying leaders and elites should be designed for comparative application. They should be relevant to the broadest possible range of political, economic, and cultural settings. Approaches that are expressly designed for application to one country or to a limited number of countries are not of particular value. As we examine the approaches presented in this chapter, we may come to the conclusion that they vary in their breadth of relevance; the interests of social scientists, like everyone else's, vary. What is important is that we try to identify the senses in which each approach seems more or less generally applicable.

SOME CONTEMPORARY APPROACHES

Five approaches to the comparative study of leaders and elites are presented in this chapter. There are two reasons for giving close attention to these approaches. First, they identify important elements of leadership characteristics and behaviors, and suggest how these leadership elements are related to the group and societal contexts in which leadership is exercised. That is, these frameworks for study suggest possible patterns of relationships that tie elites and leaders to the most salient aspects of their environments. Second, these approaches suggest categories of data that might be sought in doing research on political elites and leaders. In this sense, these approaches can serve as practical guides to conducting research in this field.

Three general comments might be made by way of introduction to these approaches. First, the authors sometimes fail to separate explicitly the concepts of elite and leader. Ideally, as we have suggested, references to positional attributes and nonrelational personal characteristics should be treated as part of the study of elites. References to relationships and interactions between persons of greater and lesser functional importance are appropriately part of the study of leadership. The authors of these approaches have not used these terms consistently, nor do they always use the same definitions presented in this book. We sometimes need to do some informal "translation" of their terminology in order to better understand and compare these approaches.

Second, we should remember that formal approaches to the study of political leadership and elites are relatively few in number. Traditionally, writing in this area has been speculative, impressionistic, and descriptive in flavor. Only in the last 25 years has there been much systematic attention to deciding what data should be gathered on political elites and leaders, and to the way these data should be analyzed. In fact, a considerable part of this more systematic research dates from as recently as 1966. Consequently, the approaches discussed in this chapter appeared initially in an intellectual vacuum, and they are somewhat imprecise because of the essential lack of thoughtful previous literature on which they could be based. These approaches need a good deal of refinement, but they seem useful as organizing frameworks for information.

Finally, these approaches share at least one common feature. Each focuses in one way or another on relationships between the political system as a whole and the system of political leadership. The authors are concerned with how elites and leaders relate to subelites, to potential elites, and to nonelites. And they are interested in the *reciprocal* relationships among changes in socioeconomic structure, in the political system as a whole, and in the political leadership system—for example, what happens to the nature of political leadership as societies become more modern economically, more complex socially, and more participatory politically? This common thread runs through the approaches to be discussed and might serve as a basis for organizing our ideas about them.

Harold Lasswell: The "Genetic" Dimension of Elites

One of the first systematic efforts to identify the kinds of information we should have about political elites came through the efforts of Harold Lasswell, who organized a series of elite studies under the auspices of the Hoover Institution at Stanford University.[1] Lasswell and his colleagues were interested in what they call the "genetic aspects" of elites.

These genetic aspects are certain *internal characteristics of the political elite as a group* that are thought to have strong effects on the behaviors of individual elites, including especially the ways in which they structure their relationships with nonelites. We will not deal with all of the genetic aspects of elites discussed by Lasswell and his colleagues, nor will our treatment of this approach be very detailed. The Hoover Institution Studies were published in the early 1950s, and they have been improved upon by more recent and more comprehensive approaches. However, it seems appropriate to begin with Lasswell's work, since some of his ideas tie in with traditional theories about elites, especially those advanced by Pareto and Mosca.

Personnel Circulation.   Lasswell expands the concept of circulation of the elite by dividing it into "personnel circulation" and "social circulation." Personnel circulation is the turnover rate in membership in elite bodies—what proportion of the members are replaced in each unit of time. Elite bodies with very low rates of personnel circulation are hypothesized to have certain other accompanying characteristics (aside from collective aging, which follows logically). These additional characteristics include increasing isolation from nonelites and a declining inclination to promote social change—even in societies based on revolutionary doctrines, such as the People's Republic of China or the Soviet Union. The leadership of the Chinese Communist party frequently has accused the leaders of the Communist party of the Soviet Union of becoming bureaucratically conservative, and of having lost their revolutionary fervor. However, the Soviet elite has undergone periods of fluctuation in its rate of personnel circulation, and the Chinese attacks on the Soviet leaders do not seem to have varied with the rate of personnel circulation, or with the relative aging or youthfulness of the Soviet leadership. In other words, the Chinese attacks cannot be linked directly with personnel circulation in the Soviet elite. There are other—apparently political and ideological—explanations for the Chinese-Soviet disagreements.

Social Circulation.   Even when personnel circulation is not low, the basic social background characteristics of an elite body may remain much the same. This would occur when new members brought into the elite have essentially the same social and occupational origins as the persons they replace. Only when the social backgrounds of members of the elite change over time is there social circulation of the elite. And if basic changes in *perspective* and *attitude* are believed to stem in part from changes in the social composition of elites, it seems clear that such changes are more likely to accompany high social circulation than high personnel circulation.

Representativeness. The social backgrounds, including education and specialized training, of elites may be more or less similar to those of the population as a whole. The extent to which the political elite is "representative" of the population may be relevant to the likelihood that the elite will be responsive to changing need perceptions on the part of the general population. In the work done by Lasswell and his associates, the evidence gathered usually focused on representativeness of social backgrounds, rather than on similarity of political values and attitudes between elites and nonelites. They tended to assume that attitudinal homogeneity will follow from similarity of social background—and, conversely, that elites "unrepresentative" of the general population in terms of social origins will tend to have unrepresentative political perspectives. Such assumptions are unfortunate; research challenging the assumption of a close relationship between backgrounds and perspectives is sufficient to warrant great caution in offering such a premise, even tentatively. We need to research carefully the background-attitude link, rather than assume its existence.

Subsequent writings have approached the concept of representativeness somewhat differently, and frequently have distinguished between two forms of representativeness different from the dimension identified by Lasswell. For example, Seligman[2] has distinguished between *symbolic* and *instrumental* representativeness. *Symbolic* representativeness refers to the inclusion in the elite of persons of various social and occupational backgrounds as a symbolic gesture to persons of those backgrounds in the general population. It is common in modern, heterogeneous societies to find persons of ethnic and religious minority backgrounds included in political elite groups in part for symbolic reasons; literature on the United States Supreme Court includes frequent reference to a "Jewish seat," for example.[3] The leadership of the Soviet Communist party seems consistently to have "reserved" places on the Politburo for persons from certain non-Russian areas of the Soviet Union, such as Georgia and Latvia. *Instrumental* representativeness, by contrast, refers to the inclusion of particular segments of society (especially occupational strata) that have specific skills and competences needed for effective political leadership. Instrumental representativeness, based on leadership perceptions of the functional significance of various occupational and skill groups in the society, is more directly related to the means by which governance is conducted. Although instrumental representativeness may have more direct impact on the way important political decisions are made, symbolic representativeness can be of great political import as well. It is apparent, for example, that the leadership of the Soviet Communist party believes it can reduce dissidence and promote national unification among non-Russian Soviet citizens by providing visible national party and government positions for prominent non-Russians.

Flexibility.   Lasswell's work suggests that there are two dimensions to the concept of elite flexibility. The first concerns the extent to which the social composition of the political elite responds to *changes* in the *demographic* structure of the population. For example, do increasingly young and/or well-educated populations have increasingly young and well-educated elites? Do increasingly urban societies increasingly select urban elites? The second dimension of flexibility deals with the ability of elites to adjust their behaviors to new and challenging situations imposed on them from without. When conditions of social upheaval, economic depression, or involvement in armed conflict demand a new type of leader, does the existing leadership bring in the sort of people who are needed? Are existing leaders capable of exchanging old methods of governing for new when circumstances demand it? Lasswell and his colleagues suggest that there is a relationship between these two dimensions of flexibility. Elites whose composition has responded over time to changes in the characteristics of a population as a whole are thought to respond more effectively to the often-severe challenges of social disorder than do elites whose composition has failed to respond to changing demographic and economic circumstances in society.

Interlockingness.   This concept refers to the extent to which there is overlapping membership in high-ranking bodies within the political hierarchy and between important political groups and other important societal organizations. Thus interlockingness refers to the holding of membership in numerous elite bodies by a relatively small number of persons. A high degree of interlockingness usually reflects the intention of a dominant political organization or social stratum to consolidate preponderant influence over a broad spectrum of political and other societal activities. Research has shown that interlockingness is pronounced in certain communist-governed societies (especially the People's Republic of China, Bulgaria, and the Soviet Union) and in certain traditional oligarchies (e.g., Spain under Franco, Portugal until 1974, and, periodically, Greece).[4] Certain other genetic aspects of elites—especially the notions of career reorientation and cooptation—constitute important modifications and extensions to the work of Lasswell and his associates. These concepts will be presented later in this book.

Carl Beck and James M. Malloy: Political Elites, a Mode of Analysis

In a paper first presented at the International Political Science Association meetings in 1964, Beck and Malloy advanced a set of categories for the comparative study of political elites. Their approach is based on the concepts of power and control. Thus "political eliteness ... is a measure of the control an individual or group exerts over a decision-making process of a given polity."[5] For Beck and Malloy, the focus for the comparative study of political elites should be on the power they hold (i.e., the ability of elites to bring nonelites to support positions or to engage in behaviors desired by the elites) and the control they exercise (the extent to which decisions actually carried out in society conform to the preferences of the political elite).

Certain aspects of the Beck and Malloy approach are of special interest to us. For purposes of simplifying this approach, we shall slightly reorganize and recast it from its original form. This reorganized version of the Beck and Malloy framework is presented in figure 2-1.

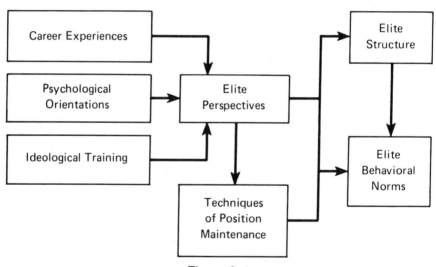

Figure 2–1
CATEGORIES AND RELATIONSHIPS FOR THE STUDY OF POLITICAL ELITES (from Carl Beck and James M. Malloy).

Beck and Malloy suggest that we look at four categories of variables in studying political elites: *elite perspectives, techniques of position maintenance, elite structure,* and *elite behavioral norms and dispositions.* These four categories of information, in turn, permit us to identify and understand the characteristics of the three basic types of *elite system*. These types of elite system may be identified along two dimensions: the dimension of *division/unity* and the dimension of *permeability/impermeability*. An examination of contemporary elites, according to Beck and Malloy, reveals the existence of three basic types of elite: the divided and permeable elite, the unified and impermeable elite, and the divided and impermeable elite. Let us take a closer look at these categories.

Elite perspectives result from the career experiences, psychological orientations, and ideological training and inclinations of the members of the elite. Two dimensions of elite perspectives are important for understanding their impact on elite structure and behavior. One dimension has to do with the way in which the elite *perceives eliteness*, that is, how it perceives its own position in the political and social order, and what significance it attributes to its position of predominant political power. The second dimension concerns the elite's perception of *its constituency*. This can include elements such as the perceived level of interest in politics of nonelites, their perceived inclination to engage in supportive or obstructing behaviors, and the elite's perception of the policy preferences of nonelites. Naturally the relative importance of elite and nonelite preferences varies among societies. In some places the perceptions and preferences of nonelites constitute significant constraints on elite behavior; in others, elites give attention to nonelite concerns largely because they wish to manipulate nonelite thinking as effectively as possible, not because citizen concerns are important inputs to governmental action.

Techniques of position maintenance refer to the methods used by elites to achieve and maintain their predominant positions. These techniques might include, but would not be limited to, competition through structured electoral procedures, the use of mass physical terror, or control over and manipulation of the flow of information.

These two sets of variables—elite perspectives and techniques of position maintenance—are hypothesized by Beck and Malloy to have a determining effect on elite structure and elite behavioral norms. *Elite structure* is defined as the patterned sets of relationships that develop among the individuals and groups who exercise control, as well as the relationships that develop between the elites and nonelites. Elite structure therefore has two dimensions: elite-elite relationships and elite-constituency relationships. Elite-elite structural relationships can be described in terms of their similarity of socioeconomic backgrounds, their similarity of training, skills, and political functions, and their cohesion (the extent to which identifiable cleavages on policy issues exist with the elite). Elite-constituency structural relationships have to do with: (1) the extent to which elite membership is linked to membership in various social and economic categories in the population as a whole; and (2) the extent to which intraelite conflict mirrors conflicts of a social, economic, or cultural nature in society at large.

Elite behavioral norms relate to the basic values that guide decisions taken by elite individuals and groups. These norms, too, can be divided into norms relating to elite-elite relationships and those relating to elite-constituency relationships. Elite-elite norms include the values on the basis of which elites give priority to some social problems over others, and values limiting the means by which intraelite conflicts are pursued. Elite-constituency norms include values concerning the openness and accessibility of government decision making, and values limiting the extent to which elites consciously attempt to mold and manipulate mass opinion and behavior.

Beck and Malloy argue that elite behavioral norms are strongly influenced by elite perspectives and by the techniques used to maintain elites in their positions. The fundamental values regulating elite behavior are assumed to be influenced not only by shared experiences and common ideological commitment, but also by practical issues of how they can maintain their positions. Thus elites who might not otherwise be inclined to turn to force or violence as a basic norm for regulating elite-constituency relationships might nevertheless do so, according to Beck and Malloy, if they perceive that only force and/or violence will successfully maintain their positions. A critical question is whether elites assign a higher value to constitutional limitations on their power or to their own continuance in office. Events in India in 1975, for example, suggest how fragile even a relatively long-standing commitment to democratic practices can be when elites conclude that only force can save their positions of dominance. Prime Minister Indira Gandhi's moves to suspend basic political freedoms, quash political opposition, and neutralize the judiciary transformed a political system thought to operate on essentially democratic principles into a near-dictatorship in a matter of weeks.

When we have mapped the nature of these four variables and their interrelationships for a given society, we should be able to classify that society's political leadership system into one of three elite types: (1) the divided and permeable elite; (2) the unified and impermeable elite; and (3) the divided and impermeable elite. The fourth logically possible elite type—unified and permeable—is considered empirically unlikely by Beck and Malloy. In their view, no strongly unified elite would ever be permeable. A closer look at this classification scheme might suggest why.

Divided and Permeable.   There are a number of competing elite groups in this elite system. Each has some independent basis of power; these bases may overlap in part, but not fully. Thus occupants of official governmental positions as well as leaders of nongovernmental political organizations, including interest groups, exert important influence on the decision-making process. The exercise of political power is linked at least in part to the representation of the interests of significant social groups. There is sufficient political information and vitality in the general population for the behavior of elites to be called into question periodically; this is likely to lead from time to time to the replacement of leading political figures for reasons of perceived inadequate performance.

Another important characteristic of the divided and permeable elite is the "absence of sufficient cohesion among political activists to unite them into a single group dedicated to the management of public affairs and public opinion."[6] The existence of divisions within the elite is of sufficient magnitude and durability that ongoing programs of activity are subjected to constant challenge within the elite itself. Further, there is a high degree of vertical mobility between nonelite and elite in the divided and permeable system. New elite groups have substantial opportunity for penetration into the elite. As Beck and Malloy caution, such opportunities are not unlimited: "This is not to suggest that any individual or group can move into the elite at will. In modern, complex systems the power of individuals and groups is highly circumscribed."[7] But what is critical is that the divided and permeable elite system is structurally organized for, and normatively oriented toward, the penetration of the elite by groups not now in power. Thus persons who can work through groups with the necessary political power potential have a reasonable chance of entering elite positions without resorting to the use of force or coercion. Broadly, "the hallmark . . . of behavioral norms in the divided and permeable type is a condition of open competition."[8]

Unified and Impermeable.   In this second type of elite system, the political elite is highly cohesive. It shares, to a high degree, political experiences and basic ideological perspectives, as well as commitments to certain techniques of position maintenance. These techniques often involve coercion and/or mass manipulation. Such elite systems typically are under the control of a single political organization, from which nearly all members of the elite are drawn, that controls the access of nonelites into the recruitment pool from which elites subsequently will be drawn. There are few independent bases of authority in such a system; it is difficult for persons aspiring to elite positions to use any organizational power base other than the dominant political party.

As with less highly structured systems, a unified and impermeable elite naturally exhibits evidence of political competition and conflict. But in such systems this conflict is best characterized as *factionalism*. That is, the conflict must be pursued by factions within the structure of the dominant political organization, and any other sources of political strength ultimately must be usable within the context of that dominant organization. Thus a powerful official in the police apparatus may derive a great deal of influence from his police position, but only indirectly; he must be able to wield this influence within the dominant political party rather than through the police apparatus itself.

In such a system the boundary between the elite and the nonelite is essentially impenetrable. Mobility from nonelite status to elite status is highly circumscribed. These systems also are characterized by unscheduled and frequently extralegal changes in the occupancy of elite positions. Purges and power seizures take place, often outside the structure of formal laws, and even in conflict with the bylaws governing the dominant political organization. The elite in the unified and impermeable system usually is committed to a high level of mobilization of the population toward explicit goals, most of which are linked expressly to shared ideological postures of the elite. The extent of population influence over the nature of these goals and the means of mobilization is moderate at best.

The description offered by Beck and Malloy of the unified and impermeable elite system illustrates the "ideal types" character of their classification. Even more than is the case with the other two elite system types, the unified and impermeable type probably does not have any contemporary examples. The category may be a useful benchmark against which some contemporary systems can be compared; but these extreme forms of unity and impermeability no longer exist (if they ever did), even in the most highly structured political systems. The emergence of a modest amount of autonomy from the party on the part of some government ministries in the Soviet Union, and the granting of considerable planning and production latitude to the directors of economic enterprises in the communist systems of Eastern Europe, are but two examples of the changes that have moved European communist systems away from the unified and impermeable type. Furthermore, the extent of cohesiveness within the elite in these societies has declined—to different degrees in different communist systems, but generally to the point where it is questionable to refer to these elite groups as "unified." The unified and impermeable category illustrates that the classifications in the Beck and Malloy framework must be viewed as theoretical constructs against which real-world elite systems can be compared. We should not expect that any given elite system will meet precisely the characteristics of any of the categories.

Divided and Impermeable. This elite type roughly corresponds with what often has been described by political scientists as an *authoritarian* elite system. Its principal deviation from the unified and impermeable model is the absence of any single, cohesive elite group that could exert pervasive control over the governmental apparatus. There are numerous centers with autonomous power potential in society, most or all of which are represented to varying degrees within the political elite. These autonomous centers correspond to established institutions in society—in Latin America, for example, they include the aristocracy, large landowners, the military establishment, and the church.

It may well be that elites in divided and impermeable systems share similar socioeconomic backgrounds, and thus develop some commonality of perspective; this third elite type exhibits a greater degree of homogeneity than does the divided and permeable elite. At the same time, policy differences exist within the elite, often because divided and impermeable elites tend to be found in less-developed countries where there is a shortage of, and consequent competition over, basic economic resources. Basic ideological disagreements may exist among elites as well.

The divided and impermeable elite system exhibits a clear line of demarcation between elite and citizenry, together with a low degree of mobility between nonelite and elite sectors of society. Mass involvement in political competition is severely circumscribed, at least through formal structures such as elections. At the same time, the existence of a number of relatively autonomous power centers leads to substantial intraelite political conflict. The absence of structural means for institutionalizing this conflict frequently leads to a relatively high degree of violence and other forms of extralegal behavior. Such societies are frequently characterized by policy immobility, a failure to develop sufficient unity within the elite, or to mobilize sufficient support within the general population, to carry through coherent programs of governmental activity. Political elites in such systems usually do not wish, or are unable, to extend political control over nonpolitical areas of activity. This is in contrast to the unified and impermeable elite system, in which the breadth of societal control exercised by political elites tends to be greater. In divided and impermeable elite systems, significant segments of the social order operate outside direct political control, lending a less highly structured flavor to the character of society.

It is important to stress that Beck and Malloy see a close relationship between the characteristics of the political elite system and the fundamental features of the political order as a whole. Elite structure and elite behavioral norms exert considerable influence on the shape of political activity and on the possible directions and pace of political change. The influence flow between elite and political system is reciprocal, but for Beck and Malloy it is asymmetrical; the elite system is thought to be somewhat more important. They feel that elites affect the nature of the political system rather more than the other elements of the political system constrain the behaviors of elites.

Frederic J. Fleron, Jr.: Political Leadership and Political Change

Fleron's work[9] began as an attempt to "reconceptualize" the political leadership system in the Soviet Union. He was reacting to the overly simplistic distinction between "totalitarian" and "pluralistic" systems that has plagued an understanding in the West of communist-governed systems. Fleron's position had two basic premises: (1) the concept of totalitarianism has carried with it an assumption of all-embracing political control by a cohesive elite, a condition no longer accurately descriptive of any communist system; and (2) the process of change away from a totalitarian mode of governance was not necessarily leading the Soviet Union and other communist systems directly into a condition of competitive pluralism similar to that frequently attributed to the United States and other Western democracies. In short, the process of political change in highly structured systems was being oversimplified by juxtaposing the concepts of totalitarianism and pluralism.

Fleron is also interested in determining how changes in political leadership are related to broader processes of political change. He broadly shares with Beck and Malloy the belief that leadership change has a determining effect on political system change, especially in systems in which citizen political influence is limited. However, Fleron is more prone to recognize the impact on the leadership system of functional changes in the society and economy.

Fleron's approach focuses on two important elements of the political process: (1) the extent and nature of political participation by important groups in society; and (2) the ways in which elites use technical and managerial skills in the process of governing. Using these two basic elements of politics, Fleron derives a typology of four political leadership systems: *monocratic, adaptive-monocratic, cooptative, pluralistic.* According to Fleron, these system types can be arranged on a continuum between monocratic and pluralistic, but they are not necessarily chronologically sequential in the political development process. That is, it is not to be assumed that as a system leaves the monocratic category, it will necessarily move next into the adaptive-monocratic type.

The Monocratic Type. Fleron's monocratic system shares many of the structural characteristics of the divided and impermeable elite system described by Beck and Malloy. In such a system political offices are held only by an elite of professional politicians, almost all of whom belong to a dominant political organization. The influence of any quasi-autonomous political groups that might exist is restricted to the particular sector of society in which they operate, e.g., the cultural or economic sector. Thus such groups do not represent independent centers of political power. Access to the political elite is substantially controlled by current occupants of elite positions, and is structured through the dominant political organization.

For our purposes, the most interesting aspect of Fleron's writings concerns the kinds of political and managerial skills necessary to govern society. According to Fleron, the political elite in the monocratic system, which is frequently traditional and nonspecialized in its education and experience, is in a position of such marked dominance that any skills it believes it needs for the management of society can be obtained from various specialized elites at no political cost. The political elite is able to extract technical and managerial skills without having to offer in exchange any voice in the policy-making process. As societies become more complex and industrially developed there is increased need for these technical and managerial skills in government. This increased emphasis brings with it an increase in the potential functional importance of specialized elites (many of whom may not be committed members of the dominant political organization). With such an increase in power potential, such specialized elites might attempt to trade their skills for some degree of participation in the political decision-making process. If it were to attempt to maintain a monocratic order, the traditional political elite would have to be prepared to use coercion, and perhaps violence, in order to continue to extract needed skills from the specialized elites. As Fleron points out, there is no assurance that such techniques of coercion can be successful over long periods of time. Ultimately such an approach can be self-defeating, by preventing the system from adapting in a satisfactory way to the changing social and technical environment. If this happens, the system might cease to be monocratic and might develop into an adaptive-monocratic type.

The Adaptive-Monocratic Type. This system develops when a monocratic elite does not itself have the skills necessary to make and carry out policy, and is unable to continue to extract such skills from specialized sectors of society without unacceptable cost. In the adaptive-monocratic system the elite does *not* accept the transfer of segments of political power to specialized elites. Rather, the monocratic elite chooses to acquire the needed skills itself, through retraining of its own personnel and through the specialized training of younger members of the monocratic elite who had already been accepted, for ideological reasons, into the traditional political elite structure. In short, the adaptive-monocratic system is characterized by internal functional skill changes within the elite, rather than by specialized elites being brought into the councils of political power.

The Cooptative Type. Another possibility presented to a monocratic elite that does not possess the necessary managerial and technical skills is the cooptative system. Under such an arrangement, the skills are acquired by coopting into the political elite members of the specialized nonpolitical elites, thus giving these specialists direct access to the policy-making process. What distinguishes the cooptation process from recruitment procedures in an adaptative-monocratic system is that coopted specialists have already established professional careers in nonpolitical sectors of society, and thus enter the political elite midway or late in their careers. These individuals may well have substantial bases of influence outside politics. Fleron makes a critical assumption concerning the significance of the established nonpolitical careers of these coopted elites: He assumes that these individuals bring into the political process perspectives on the nature of political governance that are identifiably different from those of the traditional political elite. That is, the coopted specialists frequently are not committed ideologues, and thus tend to see political problems in substantially more pragmatic terms. Further, they have a greater degree of specialized training and experience, which may lead them to seek more complex and sophisticated solutions to economic and social problems. But most fundamentally, their sense of organizational identification is likely to be focused outside the major political organization, perhaps with their nonpolitical professional-vocational group. The possible implications of this cooptation process for political decision making in highly structured and ideologically oriented systems are very great. These may include a decline in the prescriptive importance of ideology, the institutionalization of policy roles for academics, and the routinization of planning and decision procedures.

The Pluralistic Type. The pluralistic type shares many of the characteristics of the divided and permeable elite system described by Beck and Malloy. It is a system in which a high degree of institutionalized, nonviolent competition for political offices and for political influence takes place. There are career politicians, but they do not constitute a self-perpetuating elite. Much of the influence of political figures is based on the extent to which they can obtain support from organized interest groups in society. In such a system, specialized elites have essentially the same opportunity to gain office for themselves as do nonspecialized, more politically oriented individuals. In theory, at least, Fleron suggests that career politicians do not "possess any special privileges or institutionalized advantages—that is they have the same status as any other interest group or specialized elite as far as the possibilities of getting into office are concerned."[10]

While we might see this description of a pluralistic system as somewhat simplified—professional politicians, as a practical matter, do enjoy some institutionalized advantage in office seeking—the basic distinctions between this type and the other three seem clear. And more important, Fleron's formulation suggests a more subtle and meaningful way of looking at the process by which highly structured systems attempt to adapt themselves to the pressures created by industrial development, modernization, and increasing social complexity and heterogeneity.

Lester Seligman: Political Recruitment—Opportunity, Risk, Selection, and Decision Making

Seligman is interested in the way political elites are recruited.[11] He wants to identify the conditions that determine which individuals eventually will be placed in political elite positions, and which individuals will not. More broadly, he is also interested in developing a basis for classifying political systems. Seligman's argument is that the recruitment of elites reflects certain salient features of the political order, and in turn affects the subsequent development of the political system as a whole. Thus Seligman also illuminates relationships between the political elite system and the broader political environment of which it is a part.

Seligman's approach specifies four phases in the political recruitment process: *eligibility, selection, role assignment,* and *role behavior* (especially, decision making). Figure 2-2 summarizes the categories discussed by Seligman.

Eligibility. The eligibility of persons for selection into political elite positions is determined by four basic elements. The first of these is the *formal opportunity structure;* this consists of the electoral laws and other formal rules that stipulate which persons may offer themselves for elite positions, and outline the procedures through which such office seeking can be conducted. The second factor affecting eligibility is the *effective opportunity structure,* or the informal factors that increase the likelihood that certain individuals will consider themselves eligible, and decrease the likelihood that others will so perceive themselves. Some

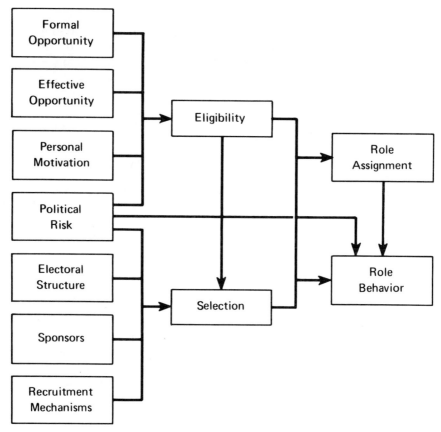

Figure 2–2
CATEGORIES AND RELATIONSHIPS FOR THE STUDY OF
POLITICAL LEADERSHIP (from Lester Seligman).

of the many components involved in the informal opportunity structure
are the process of political socialization, various aspects of the social
structure of society, the extent to which access to financial and other
related resources is distributed evenly in the population, and the extent
to which the prevailing societal norms encourage widespread office
seeking.

A third factor influencing eligibility is the structure of *political risk*.
Seligman has made an important contribution to our understanding of
political elite recruitment by addressing himself not only to what happens to those who are *successful* in their office-seeking efforts, but also
to the fate of those who are *unsuccessful*. He properly argues that the
perception of individuals of the severity of risks they take when they

seek office is a major factor in determining who will seek such positions, and under what conditions. In Seligman's terminology, every society has a system of *cushions* that are used to "break the fall" of those rejected by the operative selection mechanisms. These cushions may include, for example, the awarding of symbolic positions within political party organizations for those who unsuccessfully attempt to unseat veteran politicians from opposition political organizations. Seligman demonstrates that there is great variation among societies in the extent to which cushions exist for persons who fail to achieve political elite positions, or who are unceremoniously removed from such positions.

A fourth factor influencing the eligibility of individuals for elite positions is the somewhat nebulous matter of *personal motivation*. We know that individuals differ substantially in their willingness to expose themselves to public scrutiny in the course of seeking office. Further, people obviously vary in the extent to which they are interested in holding public office. The precise antecedents of these motivations are not yet well-known, but it is clear that an understanding of them will be important to our grasp of the political recruitment process.

Selection.   The selection process through which those persons who perceive themselves to be eligible are narrowed down into a subset of persons who will actually occupy elite positions varies greatly among societies. In some societies there are several stages, involving formal and informal choices within nongovernmental political organizations, such as political parties, followed by a multistage election process. In other societies the selection process is substantially less competitive and less complex. Elite selection may take place entirely within the structure of a dominant political party and consist of a single act of choice, namely, the approbation of a handful of elites at the top of the party structure. Indeed, there appear to be more contemporary societies having circumscribed, closely controlled elite selection procedures than there are societies with open competitive selection mechanisms.

In addition to the importance of formal electoral procedures and the system of risks and cushions to the selection process, two other elements are considered relevant by Seligman. One has to do with the sponsors or agents who stand behind candidates for elite positions, and who participate as organizations in the selection process. The other concerns the mechanisms of choice by which individuals emerge as the candidates of political organizations.

The *agents* of selection may be divided into categories such as political parties, interest groups, subcultures, and the electorate as a whole. Persons who seek elite positions may emerge as the representatives of one or more of these groups. Indeed, depending on the structure of the political system, selection by one of these groups (e.g., a dominant political party) may be sufficient to guarantee entry into a elite position. The *mechanisms* of recruitment identified by Seligman are cooptation, conscription, agency, and bureaucratic ascent. (One can also imagine a hypothetical "self-starting candidate," but practical examples of this phenomenon are infrequent in modern societies. Most potential aspirants for elite positions are linked to some sort of political organization.) Seligman uses the term "cooptation" in much the same way as does Fleron—a process in which persons with high prestige in nonpolitical areas are "coopted" by a political organization to serve as its candidate or representative. The mechanism called "agency" refers to selection based on a perception by leaders of a political organization that an individual would serve as a faithful agent representing the interests of the organization within the political elite. "Conscription" here carries a meaning similar to its use in connection with military service; persons may find themselves in situations in which they cannot refuse an "invitation" from a political organization to serve as a candidate, simply because they are, for reasons of long association or ideological commitment, bound to serve that organization. Conscription is frequently used as a method for selecting candidates who must oppose particularly imposing candidates from other political organizations. Conscripted candidates often have little chance of success; their service is to keep the name of their political organization before the public. Finally, "bureaucratic ascent" is a procedure in which a person rises to a position of candidacy through long service, usually of a bureaucratic or administrative nature, to his or her political organization.

Role Assignment and Role Behavior.   Seligman postulates close relationships between the eligibility and selection phases of political recruitment, and the ultimate behaviors and role perceptions of persons who occupy elite positions. In his view:[12]

> The assignment of individuals to specialized roles in decision-making institutions is the function of political opportunity, risk, and selection. The interplay of these factors influences the distribution of power, the representativeness of elites, elite competence, policy outputs, and the collective norms of elites. The adequacy of decision-making and policy outputs thus tests recruitment.

Seligman sees particularly close relationships between opportunity and selection structures and the degree of openness of political decision making. The relationships he hypothesizes seem quite plausible. He suggests, for example, that systems with a high-opportunity, low-risk eligibility structure, and with highly competitive and open selection procedures, will tend to have open decision-making practices. Such systems would also be characterized by more representative elites, by a broader and more pluralistic distribution of political power, and by policy outputs more generally in tune with the desires of the population. Similarly, Seligman argues that the broader the range of elite sponsorship during the selection process, the more open the decision-making behaviors of elites will be. That is, systems in which there are relatively few sponsors of political candidates, and in which any given candidate is likely to be tied to a specific political organization, will tend to have less open decision making. In such systems political groups will exert direct influence on the governing process through their representatives (agents); this influence frequently will not be subject to public scrutiny. In circumstances in which there is "coalition sponsorship," i.e., sponsorship of a given candidate through the combined actions of several essentially independent interest groups, relatively open decision making will result. The influence of specific interests on policy outcomes in society will be moderated and reduced.

The Research Group on Comparative Communist Political Leadership: Categories for the Comparative Study of Political Leadership

Another set of categories that has been advanced for the study of political elites and leadership was developed by the Research Group on Comparative Communist Political Leadership, which met for a period of several years during the late 1960s and early 1970s under the auspices of the Carnegie Foundation and the Center for International Studies at the University of Pittsburgh.[13] The focus of this group was on the study of political leadership in communist systems, but the conceptual scheme on the basis of which their principal published work was organized is thought to be of general relevance for the study of political leadership. Broadly, the purpose of their work was to arrive at two kinds of explanations: (1) What are the sources of elite orientations, including basic value positions and orientations toward specific political issues?; and (2) What are the impacts of elite characteristics (their backgrounds, their careers, their orientations) on political outcomes in society? Figure 2-3 summarizes the categories suggested by this group.

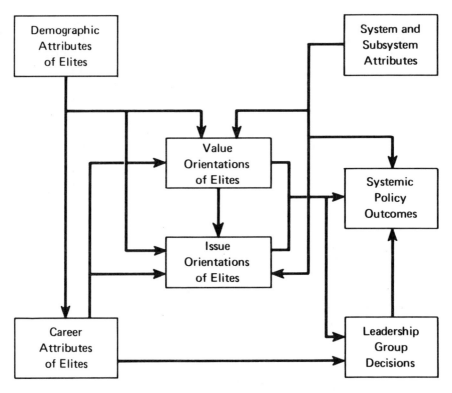

Figure 2–3
CATEGORIES AND RELATIONSHIPS FOR THE STUDY OF
POLITICAL LEADERSHIP (from the Research Group on Comparative
Communist Political Leadership) (Figure from William A. Welsh,
"Introduction," in Carl Beck, *et al., Comparative Communist Political
Leadership,* p. 10).

In general, this approach looks at four individual characteristics of
elites (demographic attributes, career attributes, value orientations,
and issue orientations), one group characteristic of elites (decisional
outputs of leadership groups), and two characteristics of the political
systems in which these elites operate (the economic, social, and cultural
attributes of the society, and the policy outcomes connected with outputs of elite groups). This approach is designed to help students of
political leadership to identify relationships that exist among these
seven sets of variables. For our purposes, the categories of information
suggested by this research scheme should have practical utility, in that
this approach should be useful as a basis for organizing research.

Demographic Attributes.   Demographic attributes of persons are characteristics that describe basic social origins. This approach suggests attention to seven categories of demographic attributes of elites: age/year of birth, ethnic background, character of place of birth and/or locale of early childhood (e.g., along an urban/rural dimension and/or in terms of economic or geographic characteristics), family social background and standing, nature and extent of family political participation, amount of formal education, and nature of any special education or training. The purpose of acquiring information on demographic attributes is not only to provide a basic description of the social origins of elites, but also to provide a basis for discovering if variations in demographic attributes help us to explain the differences we observe in the orientations of elites.

Career Attributes.   Career attributes refer to professional activities and experiences. They can be defined by the following kinds of question: What formal positions have members of an elite held in the government hierarchy, in political parties, or in other political groups? When, at what age, for how long did they hold each position? With what nonpolitical or quasi-political organizations have they been affiliated? What positions have they held in these nonpolitical organizations? In which professional skill areas (e.g., industry, agriculture, communications, science, education, engineering) have they been engaged, and in what sequence, and for how long in each case? What other significant adult political experiences have elites had (e.g., participation in strikes, armed uprisings, detention, emigration)? This approach views career attributes as being influenced by demographic characteristics of elites, and also as exerting influence on the nature of elite values and issue orientations. These career data also provide a basis for developing composite pictures of "career types" for given elite bodies. For example, are propagandists becoming increasingly important in the political elite? Are persons with advanced technical or managerial training and skills becoming more important? Is the police and security apparatus increasingly important as a career channel? Identification of such career trends may provide important clues to future changes in the policies pursued by government.

Value and Issue Orientations.   The basic values held by individuals are not necessarily consistent with the positions they take on specific political issues of the moment. *Values* are viewed as more general and enduring postures defining the relationship between man and his environment. *Issue orientations* are more specific, event-related, and therefore ephemeral. One of the important questions in elite research is why the connections between values and issue orientations of elites vary from place to place and from time to time. Students of political elites would like to be able to identify more precisely the situational factors that lead individuals either to cling closely to fundamental values when taking positions on specific political issues, or to deviate substantially from these basic values. For example, we know that persons apparently committed to open, democratic forms of government not infrequently lend support to the restriction of individual freedoms. Sometimes these seemingly inconsistent positions are easily explained, as in the case of limiting personal freedoms in the face of external threat or aggression. In other circumstances the gulf between values and issue orientations seems more difficult to explain.

We often assume that apparent inconsistencies between fundamental values and specific issue positions are due in considerable part to the complexity of human cognitive and evaluative processes. Any given political issue is likely to be relevant to several fundamental values; further, a given issue may be relevant to different values for different people. When legislators must decide how to vote on an education bill, they will find themselves influenced by several basic value orientations, including feelings about: (1) the value of public education; (2) the proper role of government vis-á-vis nongovernmental institutions in providing education; (3) the appropriate *level* of government at which such services should be provided; (4) the importance of fiscal stability and balanced budgets; (5) their obligations to reflect constituents' feelings about the issue; and (6) the obligations of legislators to follow their party leadership. Obviously, these factors may exert conflicting pulls on their choice, and it seems likely that their ultimate decision on the issue of the moment might well conflict with at least one of his or her basic value postures.

Decisional Outputs of Elite Groups. Here the focus is on identifying the formal prescriptions issued by political leadership groups. We wish to do this not only as an indicator of the nature and results of governmental decision making, but also as a basis for relating the values and issue orientations of elites to their decision-making behaviors. Values and issue orientations are held *individually*, although any given person's orientations are likely to be influenced by the postures taken by close associates. Governmental decision making, by contrast, almost always consists of a series of *collective* acts of choice. (To be sure, the size of the collectivity varies a good deal among societies.) It is important to try to assess the impact of individual value and issue orientations on collective decision-making behavior. To the extent to which differences appear between the aggregated *individual* positions of members of elite groups and the *collective* decisions taken by these groups, we need to ask ourselves what other factors have intervened in the decision-making process. The explanation might be the simple but significant fact that some members of decision-making groups are more powerful than other members. Or it might be that the dynamics of group interaction resulted in a modification of individual positions. If the latter, we would be interested in trying to identify the most salient features of the way in which the decision-making group operates. Another possible explanation for discrepancies between individual preferences and collective choices would be the limitations imposed on group decisions by attributes of the environment in which the group operates; e.g., limitations on resources needed to carry out contemplated decisions.

Systemic Attributes.   A principal intervening factor that influences the relationship between the individual characteristics of elites and their group behavior is the environmental context in which they operate. Environmental factors include: (1) levels and rates of economic development in society; (2) the demographic and social structure of the population, and the spatial distribution of the population; (3) the nature and extent of political participation in the polity; (4) the formal authority structure in the polity; and (5) the extent to which the society for which the elites are acting operates autonomously or, conversely, is influenced by a foreign power. Doubtless other important systemic attributes could be listed. The point is that we now recognize that elite decision-making behavior does not take place in a vacuum. It is conditioned by numerous factors of social, economic, and cultural context that must be analyzed in conjunction with the behaviors of elites if those behaviors are to be fully understood.

Policy Outcomes.   It is important to distinguish the *decisional outputs* of elite groups from the ultimate *policy outcomes* that result from attempts to enforce those decisions. It is axiomatic that in nearly every society there is "slippage" between decision (the selection by authoritative decision makers of a course of action) and policy (the result of interaction between decision and environmental constraints). The members of this research group argue that one of the most important bases for comparing political systems is the extent of slippage between decision and policy. In some societies the actual states of affairs—the actual policy outcomes in the real world—conform closely to what official decision makers have declared. In other societies there sometimes appears to be frustratingly little relationship between the content of official decisions and the content of actual public policy. Sometimes these slippages result from the simple inability of government to enforce its decisions or, relatedly, from concerted opposition by large numbers of citizens. Or decision/policy slippage may result from the failure of political and administrative bodies to communicate effectively the nature of decisions reached to those who must enforce those decisions locally. Finally, slippage may result from the impracticality of governmental decision making, e.g., the positing of unreasonable goals for economic growth and production.

The importance of approaches such as the five summarized in this chapter is that they provide a basis for organizing information about leaders and elites, and for relating the activities of these persons to characteristics of the broader political and social environment in which they operate. As we make use of these approaches we should keep in mind that all such frameworks are simplified and sometimes somewhat abstract. We may well feel that important categories of information for understanding political elites and leaders in a given country are omitted from these approaches. Thus we may wish to modify them as they seem appropriate for our use, and to make them more concrete. In fact, this is a basic characteristic of systematic inquiry: We refine and modify our general approaches as a result of applying them to specific cases in which we are interested.

It may also be that some of these approaches are more or less relevant for general comparisons across categories of different political systems. It may be, for example, that Seligman's work is useful primarily in studying less highly structured, relatively open political systems. Conversely, the work of the Research Group on Comparative Communist Political Leadership may or may not be relevant in looking at less highly structured systems. The test of the breadth of relevance of these approaches must be in their application to a variety of specific cases. They should not be treated merely as abstract statements of political theory.

3

Methods of Analysis in Research on Political Leaders and Elites

Now that we have examined the way studies of political elites and leaders have developed, as well as several frameworks for organizing such studies, it is appropriate that we consider some methods by which data on elites and leaders can be gathered and analyzed. In this book we do not deal with experiment-type methods that would be appropriate for studying leadership in small groups—especially in laboratory situations or through participant observation[1] in the field. This book is oriented toward the study of political elites and leaders whose positions (and personal schedules) make experimental or participant-observation techniques implausible. Thus our emphasis is on the use of indirect research methods, which seem necessary in the study of most political elites and leaders, especially those above the local level of government.

This is not to suggest that persons in positions of political importance are never accessible, for example, to interviewing. In fact, some recent evidence suggests that national elites in several European countries are more accessible to researchers than we had believed,[2] although such accessibility does not seem to extend to involvement in experimental or participant-observation research studies. Research in laboratories, or through the direct participation of social scientists in the activities of groups, can be useful in showing how leadership develops and is used in small-group settings. But these techniques are not practical for the study of most political elite and leadership situations.

A BASIC DISTINCTION:
INTENSIVE VS. EXTENSIVE STUDIES

The literature on political elites and leadership can be divided into intensive and extensive studies. These two strategies of inquiry are quite different, and the contributions they make to an understanding of the subject matter differ correspondingly. Intensive studies focus on a small number of high-ranking elites, or perhaps even a single dominant leader. Such studies attempt to probe, usually rather unsystematically, the motivations, personality characteristics, interpersonal styles, and behaviors of a handful of individuals assumed to have dominant influence over some aspect of the political process. Many of these intensive studies have taken on a kind of psychoanalysis-from-a-distance flavor. This sort of perspective has been especially common in writings about elites in dictatorial systems, as illustrated by the numerous biographies of Hitler and Stalin, and corresponding studies of the Bolshevik leadership in the Soviet Union and the Nazi elite in Germany.[3] Studies from a similar perspective also have examined some leaders from less highly structured political systems, especially persons with strong personalities who held office during periods of crisis—for example, Franklin D. Roosevelt and Winston Churchill.[4]

Although such studies are usually based only marginally, if at all, on concrete data, and thus tend to be speculative and impressionistic, they still may provide insight into the idiosyncratic contributions made by individual leaders to leadership roles in their societies. These intensive studies are perhaps more likely than are extensive studies to highlight "unique" situational factors that may influence the shape and substance of the decision-making process. In short, intensive studies may give us a sensitive understanding of particular times and places and of specific individuals. But they usually are difficult to generalize from, and consequently contribute relatively little to an understanding of leadership behavior as a general political phenomenon.

Extensive studies of political elites and leaders, on the other hand, focus on a much larger number of persons. They are based on aggregated biographic data, usually dealing with most or all of the members of the principal political institutions and groups. Such studies are more useful than are intensive studies for purposes of identifying trends in elite recruitment. They are also more likely to provide a basis for relating changes in the composition of leadership groups to indicators of social and economic development, or to changes in other political system variables, such as intraparty conflict. Although a focus on a large number of individuals places some sense of "distance" between the researcher and his subjects, extensive studies tend to be more reliable and replicable than intensive studies. To use some of the terminology introduced in the preceding chapter, extensive studies permit us to examine a political leadership *system,* not merely the idiosyncratic behavior of one or a few elites. Consequently, extensive studies provide a basis for relating patterns of political leadership to the evolving characteristics of the social, cultural, and economic environments in which political elites and leaders must operate. At the same time, extensive studies are not likely to be helpful in explaining specific events, or the behaviors of specific leaders.

ANALYZING BIOGRAPHICAL DATA

We use the term "biographical data" to refer to information dealing with the social backgrounds and careers of political leaders and elites. Some writers have extended the notion of biographical data to include data on orientations and behaviors; however, this broadens the term beyond its traditional usage. This term usually has referred only to information provided in self-reported biographies of prominent persons, which normally do not include data on political perspectives and behaviors. Thus, in this more traditional and commonly used sense, the notion of biographical data refers only to information on social origins and careers.

We also exclude from the category of biographic data information obtained through interviews with elites, especially information on political orientations or attitudes. The use of interviews to obtain data on leaders and elites is discussed in a subsequent section of this chapter.

Many students of politics have believed for a long time that an understanding of a person's social origins, conditions of upbringing, educational and professional training, and early adult career experiences was important for explaining his political behavior. In chapter 2 we mentioned some examples of kinds of biographical data that are used in studying political elites and leaders. Some of the background characteristics studied are attributes acquired by an individual at birth, including sex, nationality, race, and ancestral origins. Some of these background characteristics refer to conditions of early childhood socialization, such as rural versus urban upbringing, the nature and extent of education, the political involvement of one's family, religious practice in the family, and memberships held in youth organizations by an individual. In addition to these data on attributes and early childhood experiences, numerous data on adult career experiences are also thought to be relevant for an understanding of perspectives toward politics. Indeed, recent research suggests that these career experiences probably are more important than social background factors in explaining the orientations and behaviors of political elites.[5] Notwithstanding the fact that social background attributes, including both characteristics acquired at birth and early socialization, may be of greater utility in understanding the roles of the *mass citizenry* in politics, research on elites is increasingly emphasizing data on recent career experiences.

It must be recognized that biographical data alone are of limited significance to the student of politics. Not only must students of political elites and leadership look at the social origins, backgrounds, and careers of their subjects, but they also must look carefully at the value and issue orientations and the political behaviors of these persons. Furthermore, it is important to relate the backgrounds, careers, attitudes, and behaviors of elites to the organizational and societal contexts in which they operate. Thus characteristics of the political system as a whole, and of the social and demographic structure of society, are likely to influence the characteristics of persons who are elevated to positions of importance. The degree of competitiveness and the risk structure in the polity, for example, may affect the kinds of people who seek power. The economic and occupational characteristics of society may influence elite selection: Largely rural, agricultural societies may tend to have different sorts of leaders from those commonly found in urban, industrialized settings.

Further, characteristics of major political organizations influence not only the kinds of person who are recruited into positions in those organizations, but also the kinds of behavior in which these people engage. We tend to assume that highly structured, hierarchical organizations recruit persons with different points of view and predispositions from those recruited by organizations that are more open and less hierarchical.

In a sightly different vein, we may view the backgrounds of political leaders as indicators of the sorts of values held by influential people in society. Some students of social change have argued that the personal characteristics of political elites become "secondary societal values."[6] According to this view, persons who are elevated to positions of public prominence must have personal characteristics that are respected by the people who put them in such positions. In turn, the mass citizenry tends to develop, over a period of time, an identification between the personal characteristics of existing leaders and more generalized images of political leadership. Existing leaders shape mass images of what future leaders should be like. This tends not only to reinforce the values of dominant societal groups, but also to make it more likely that the personal attributes of political leaders will be emulated by new generations. There is a demonstration effect of elite values on subsequent generations, according to this argument.

Such a view of the self-perpetuating tendencies of leaders' personal characteristics is based on some crucial assumptions. In particular, such a view assumes that public leadership is regarded in a basically favorable way by the general population. The degree to which this is true apparently varies among political systems. We have numerous contemporary examples of widespread public rejection of the values exhibited by prominent political leaders. At the same time, there seems little doubt that characteristics reflected by persons in positions of leadership are highly visible, and thereby acquire at least potential influence on subsequent value formation in society.

The point of offering these examples of possible relationships between leadership characteristics and the broader elements of social change is to emphasize that the study of elites and leaders purely for its own sake is not particularly rewarding. We wish to acquire a better understanding of the origins, careers, perspectives, and behaviors of these individuals in order to improve our understanding of the processes by which important decisions are made for society. We want to know more about the way in which persons at the top of political hierarchies influence the allocation of resources in society. We want to know which elements of the political, economic, and cultural environment exert the strongest influence on the behavior of persons who occupy positions of public prominence and trust. In short, the analysis of biographical data is but one step—albeit a particularly important one—toward a more general understanding of the functioning of contemporary societies.

Most of the studies of political elites and leaders that have appeared in recent years have been based on one or both of two kinds of data-gathering procedures. In relatively open societies, where the interviewing of political elites may be possible, increasing attention has been given to the use of such interview techniques to provide a comprehensive range of data about political leaders. We discuss this technique later in this chapter. Where the character of society, or the importance of the persons being studied, makes direct access to these individuals impractical or impossible, resort typically is made to the accumulation of data from standard biographical dictionaries and directories. Such collections of information are convenient, and therefore tend to be used widely by students of political elites.

Certain problems of data reliability are presented by the use of such sources, however. Biographical data collections usually are based on self-reporting, and most people paint as positive a picture of themselves as they can when providing information for public consumption. Further, some kinds of background and career data may be considered politically sensitive, especially in societies in which there are ideological connotations attached to such things as class background. Thus we know that biographical directories dealing with political elites in several communist systems report that a high proportion of the political leadership comes from proletarian origins, even though Western sources tend to challenge the blanket assertion of proletarian background. A further problem has to do with the difficulty of controlling for the equivalence in different locations of certain social background items. References to level and nature of education provide a serviceable example. The completion of schooling variously referred to as "high school," "gymnasium," "secondary school," or "preparatory school" cannot be assumed to be equivalent in various societies, even though the ages in which individuals attend such schools tend to be relatively similar across nations. In short, it is difficult to compare self-reported biographical data from a number of different cultural settings, since each respective collection of data concerns a single environment, and consequently uses terminology peculiar to that location. This is one of the major problems in cross-national comparative research, and one to which we shall return in other contexts later in this book.

All of the above is not to imply that existing collections of biographical data should not be used, either for single-country studies or for cross-national comparison. Rather, we need to be sensitive to possible inadequacies in such data, and to seek verification from other sources (such as newspaper files) for any categories of data that we believe to be politically or otherwise sensitive in the societies from which they come. And we need to remain sensitive to problems of comparability in categories of data between societies. Our correction for these incomparabilities in data sources will never be perfect, but the necessity of using disparate data, gathered at different times by different individuals for different purposes, requires that we exercise extraordinary care.

One other important point about the handling of biographical data should be made. One of the strongest, and most unfortunate, tendencies in past studies of political leaders and elites has been the inclination to *assume* linkages between demographic attributes and social backgrounds, on the one hand, and values, issue orientations, and behaviors of elites, on the other hand. The tendency has, in fact, been remarkable in studies of political elite groups. When research is of the intensive type, focusing on a single individual or a small number of persons, it is difficult to examine assumed relationships between backgrounds and attitudes or behaviors in a systematic way. Because the research deals with such a small number of subjects, there is not a sufficient amount of variation in either backgrounds or behaviors and attitudes to test effectively the hypothesized relationships among them. Extensive studies have an advantage in this regard, in that they permit us to look at a variety of backgrounds and careers and to attempt to identify patterns in the ways in which these backgrounds and careers are related to attitudes and behaviors.[7] The tendency to assume, for example, that a higher level of education leads to more open-minded and sophisticated handling of policy problems, or that upper-class background predisposes an elite toward socially conservative solutions to pressing social problems, must be subjected to rigorous test. We do considerable harm to our ability to understand the nature of elites and leadership by assuming, rather than researching, such relationships.

CONTENT ANALYSIS OF ELITE COMMUNICATIONS

Content analysis is a data-gathering and analysis method that focuses on the content of communications between individuals. It seeks to understand the characteristics of the communicator and the recipient of communications, as well as characteristics of the flow of communication in society, on the basis of a detailed examination of the flow of such communications.

This book is not a "how-to" research handbook. We will not discuss the actual procedures used in content analysis studies, since there are some excellent handbooks available.[8] Broadly, content analysis involves the use of a "dictionary"—a framework of analysis that contains: (1) the general concepts, or themes, on which the research focuses; (2) a list of specific words and phrases that will be searched for in the communications being analyzed; and (3) explicit rules relating the general concepts to the specific terms. These rules indicate which specific terms index (indicate) the occurrence of which general concepts, and under what conditions (e.g., in conjunction with what other terms). The dictionary is used to "map" the patterns of thought contained in the communications being studied.

This technique seems especially relevant to the study of political leadership. Content analysis focuses on what many social scientists consider to be the central process in all social interaction, communication.[9] Further, communication seems especially important in the management of political affairs. We know that political leaders spend a considerable portion of their time transmitting ideas. In fact, much of the behavior of political leaders in which we are interested involves communication of some kind. Similarly, since leadership is properly viewed as a relationship, the sustenance of relationships involving leaders depends on the ways in which they communicate with followers, and the ways in which followers are able to, and motivated to, communicate with their leaders.

From this perspective, it is easy to understand why a significant part of the available data on political leaders and elites is in the form of communications from, to, or about them. This data pool is essentially untapped in studies of elites and leaders in most countries. The content analysis of political elite communications should provide insight into many important aspects of the political order, including: (1) elite political culture (the values, beliefs, and attitudes of elites); (2) leadership perceptions of how important political situations are developing; (3) the techniques of communication, including propagandizing, preferred by different leadership groups under different circumstances; and (4) the salience of different kinds of events for an explanation of the reactions of elites to their environment, and of their policy preferences.

Content analysis has several advantages as a technique for studying the values, beliefs, and attitudes of political elites. Five of these advantages will be mentioned here.

First, content analysis especially recommends itself in situations in which there is restricted data access, i.e., where direct access to political elites (e.g., interviewing) is difficult or impossible. In these cases, documents constitute the principal data source concerning the positions being taken by political elites. This situation seems to characterize the elite groups in a number of highly structured, relatively closed societies.

Second, content analysis is particularly useful in the study of polities in which there is a positive relationship between the sources of public communication and salience for societal outcomes, i.e., where political elites whose speeches and writings are widely promoted also seem to have decisive influence on public policy. Again, there are numerous relatively closed systems in Asia, Africa, Latin America, and Eastern Europe to which this description applies.

Third, content analysis, especially when done by computer, can be crucial when the researcher feels he must have particularly large samples of communication to insure accuracy of interpretation. For example, researchers who have used content analysis in studying communist elites often have cautioned against drawing samples that are too small. The validity of any given speech or essay as an indicator of the researcher's theoretically relevant concepts may be dubious, given both the verbal ideological overlay found in much political rhetoric, and the eminent flexibility sometimes exhibited by political elites in highly structured systems in redefining events as well as ideological precepts. There is good reason to believe that careful sampling procedures and large samples are necessary in studying the communications of political leaders.

Fourth, systematic content analysis can be particularly helpful when the subject matter under study is burdened either with excessive "conventional wisdom," especially in the form of stereotypes, or with a widely shared normative perspective, or both. For example, it is by now a truism that the post–World War II Western study of contemporary communism has been struggling to free itself both from stereotypes and from feelings of negative affect that emerged from the cold war/ McCarthy era. Perhaps no other area of social science inquiry has required such a substantial amount of conceptual rethinking in the last 15 years. We have progressed with the task, but there seems little doubt that techniques permitting the dispassionate and theoretically relevant examination of the verbal behaviors of communist elites should still have special appeal.

Finally, content analysis seems useful for our purposes even in those cases in which direct access to political elites may sometimes be possible. Here content analysis may serve as a supplementary or corroborative technique. Elite interviewing probably will always be a sensitive mode of data gathering, especially in systems in which political elites are relatively insulated from nonelites. In this regard, content analysis has the advantage of being a "nonreactive" or "unobtrusive" research technique.[10]

Given these advantages, there is reason to believe that the *reliability* of content analysis may actually exceed that of survey research. On the other hand, the *validity* of content analytic techniques may be challengeable. The fact that a given member of a political elite has his or her name associated with a public statement, or even delivers a statement publicly, does not indicate that this person in fact drafted (or even believes) the substance of the statement. Precisely because political elites are busy people, their public statements frequently are written by others. Thus it becomes important to examine a large number of statements by political elites when doing content analysis. Examination of a large volume of communications should make it possible to identify the genuine consistencies and patterns of expression that are associated with the political orientations of elites. We return to a discussion of methodological issues in content analysis in chapter 8.

SURVEY RESEARCH ON POLITICAL ELITES

We have suggested that survey research, when handled properly and when facilitated by openness of the political system and personal accessibility of elites, can be an important method of data gathering. Overall, the amount of survey research done on political elites has been small.

At the same time, those who have had the audacity to undertake such research generally report that the problems of access are not nearly as great as we might expect. Indeed, recent survey research has involved political elites in societies generally thought to be relatively closed, including some single-party states in Africa and two communist-governed societies, Yugoslavia and Poland.[11] Two of the most important of these projects have dealt with Yugoslavia. Research by Zaninovich has contrasted the value orientations of three strata of Yugoslav society—the political elite, the professional elite, and the citizenry. This research seeks to explain intrastratum and between-stratum differences in value orientations by examining demographic attributes, career attributes, and characteristics of the economic and political communities in which people live. The research not only provides a basis for characterizing the political leadership system at subnational levels in Yugoslavia, but also makes it possible to compare the ideas of elites with those of the citizenry. Some important and fascinating contrasts between elite and citizenry are developed in the most recent report of this research.[12] One major finding is that career characteristics tend to be the most effective predictors of the orientations of political elites, but that certain factors of social origin, including nationality, are much more salient predictors of the orientations of the mass citizenry.

Another important project involving survey research on Yugoslav political elites was carried out jointly by researchers at Columbia University in the United States and at the Center for Public Opinion Research of the Institute of Social Sciences in Belgrade.[13] The research involved interviewing more than 500 national and regional leaders in Yugoslavia, including federal legislators, federal administrators, leaders of mass organizations (including the League of Communists of Yugoslavia), economic leaders (including the directors of major economic enterprises, as well as economic planners and consultants), editors and leading journalists in the area of mass communications, and an additional sample of intellectuals (including university professors in the social sciences), and a sample of writers, artists, and film and theater directors.

Survey research on political elites, where it is possible, has the advantage of directness, and the accompanying advantage of being able to pursue interesting issues and/or clarify ambiguous responses. Further, survey research enjoys the obvious virtue of being organized around precisely those topics in which the researchers are interested. This is a major advantage over the use of secondary data sources such as biographic directories or printed communications.

At the same time, there are potential difficulties in doing survey research on political elites, and a great deal of care must be exercised in using this technique. Some of the potential difficulties are ones of *validity;* it is not easy to design questions that elicit meaningful responses from elites without seeming too "sensitive," and that have the same meaning or connotation for the respondent as for the researcher. Other potential problems have to do with *reliability.* Whenever human beings conduct research that involves repeated interaction with a series of others over some period of time, experience shows that it is unlikely that the researchers will perform with a high degree of consistency. Experiences in early interviews affect the way in which later interviews are handled; fatigue and/or boredom may also affect later interviews. More important, the respondents, since they are by definition busy, may be affected by the pressures of the moment; these reactions will probably vary among respondents in a given study. Yet another difficulty is presented by the fact that human beings are not insensitive to the personalities of those with whom they interact; it is unlikely that a given interviewer will have equal rapport with each respondent. Any of these factors may affect the responses given by the elites being interviewed. These difficulties affect not only the reliability of given responses, but also the *comparability* of the responses as a set of data.

Additional methods can be used to gain an understanding of political elites and leadership. These other possibilities include: (1) interviewing persons close to elites, or whose lives are identifiably influenced by elites (which could well involve interviewing a sample of the general population about their attitudes toward elites); and (2) carefully examining archival and other documentary materials dealing with elites and leaders. The three methods we have looked at in this chapter are probably the most commonly used by political scientists today, however.

Each of these methods has both strengths and drawbacks. Where possible, these methods should be used in conjunction with one another —as part of a "multiple-strategy" approach to understanding political elites and leadership. Taken collectively and used thoughtfully, these methods can provide a sound basis for research. When our studies of elites and leaders are based on only one of these methods, or when we do not exercise sufficient care in conducting our research, the confidence we can have in our findings is correspondingly diminished. The "what" of our research—its substantive conclusions—is very much affected by the "how"—the methods used to gather and analyze data. In chapter 8 some related methodological questions will be raised.

4

System Types and Career Types

In the first three chapters we have looked at some concepts and approaches used in studying political elites and leadership. In the second section of this book, we turn our attention to some data that can be integrated into these concepts and approaches. In chapters 4 through 7 we will try to provide some answers to the question: What do we know about the characteristics of political elites and leadership in various kinds of social, economic, and political settings?

Chapter 4 provides some general descriptive distinctions among political leaders and elites in three types of political system, and among persons who have pursued three types of political career. The presentation in this chapter is largely descriptive as opposed to analytical, in the sense that, for the most part, we examine only *frequencies of occurrence* of various background and career characteristics, rather than *relationships among* these characteristics. In the case of system types, we contrast *pluralistic* systems, *highly structured* systems, and *transitional* systems. In the case of political careers, we focus on *executive, legislative,* and *political party* careers. There is no intention of suggesting that either the list of system types or the list of political careers is exhaustive. We focus our discussion in this manner because the research that has been done emphasizes these categories of system and career.

In chapters 5 through 7 we examine more specific data on leaders and elites in each of the three categories of political system. These three chapters are largely analytical rather than descriptive, in that they focus on relationships among background and career characteristics. These chapters focus with greater specificity on elite characteristics, but at the expense of comparability across system types. The data presented in chapter 4 are, with some reservations expressed below, generally comparable across systems. By contrast, the results of the studies presented in chapters 5 through 7 cannot reasonably be argued to be comparable with one another. They do, however, provide considerably greater detail on the nature of contemporary elites and political leadership. In chapter 5 we focus on a particular aspect of leadership activity in Latin America: the persistence of extralegal patterns of political behavior among a relatively large number of elites. In chapter 6 the leadership of several Communist parties is selected as a basis for illustrating patterns of change in leadership in highly structured systems. In particular, we focus on leadership in the Bulgarian and Soviet party organizations. Then, in chapter 7, leadership in pluralistic systems is illustrated primarily with data on the United States, with some supplemental reference to Western European locations, especially including the Federal Republic of Germany.

SYSTEM TYPES

It will be useful to begin with a broad overview of the three categories of system with which this chapter deals. The system characteristics we want to discuss are thought to be important contextual factors that influence the selection of political elites and the characteristics of political leadership.

Our first system type is the *pluralistic* system, in which political power is more widely dispersed spatially, and less consistently located over time, than in the other two system types. Pluralistic systems encompass some important political groups that operate independently of government and of the formal organizations that are currently in political ascendancy (e.g., a dominant political party). Such groups operating in opposition to the government offer candidates and policy alternatives to the electorate, and are able to carry on their activities without undue harassment from those in power. In pluralistic systems there is a high degree of institutionalized, nonviolent competition for political offices and political influence.

A pluralistic system is not necessarily the same as a democratic system. It is possible for the kind of dispersion of bases of political influence described above to exist without anything approximating majority rule, or equal citizen access to the means of political influence. We recognize, of course, that many contemporary political theorists equate pluralism and democracy. It may well be that the elements of pluralism are *necessary conditions* for the sustenance of democracy. In the view presented here, however, it is useful to keep separate two basic dimensions of political activity. One dimension has to do with the extent to which groups independent of government are able to exercise political influence; the second has to do with the means by which, and the *extent* to which, the opinions of a majority of citizens come to be reflected in governmental policy. It is quite possible for a system to exhibit the first characteristic—the basic element of pluralism—without displaying the second set of characteristics, which would seem to refer to the central elements of democracy. Consequently, it is important to keep in mind as we look at elites and leaders in pluralistic systems that we are not necessarily talking about democratic societies.

The second system type we refer to as *highly structured* systems. For some readers, this may seem like a euphemism for dictatorship. Not only is this usage not intended, but it would be substantially misleading. The concept of dictatorship has been applied so loosely and broadly, and with such a pejorative connotation, that it has lost a great deal of whatever communicative significance it might once have had. Highly structured systems have certain identifiable features, only some of which are consistent with traditional notions of dictatorship. Highly structured systems are hierarchical: There is a clear chain of authority from top to bottom in the political structure. Similarly, hierarchical systems exhibit a pyramidal distribution of political influence: Persons at the top have a good deal more influence than those at the bottom. Furthermore, in highly structured systems the flow of political influence tends to be primarily from the top down. This does not mean that contending points of view are not articulated from lower levels of the system, but it does suggest that the critical decisions are made by relatively small numbers of persons operating at or near the top of this hierarchically structured pyramid.

Highly structured systems also exhibit a wide scope of governmental activity, often much wider than that which characterizes pluralistic systems. That is, government is involved in a substantial proportion of the activities that affect the daily lives of human beings. In addition, the political organizations that are critical for the distribution of societal resources usually are linked in a very firm way to the dominant political party. Highly structured systems are not necessarily one-party systems, but they normally are characterized by the existence of one party that is significantly stronger than its competitors. It is not necessary that a single party dominate the political scene over a long period of time; some highly structured systems have been characterized by alternating party dominance. The most important point is that whatever political organization is dominant operates in a hierarchical way, and through a pyramidal form of political activity.

Our third system type is the *transitional* system. The dominant feature in such systems is change. Often this change is of relatively recent origin, and is painfully disruptive of traditional forms of social, economic, and political organization. Transitional systems are moving away from the dominance of institutions such as landholding, the family, and the church. But one of their principal characteristics is that secular institutions have not developed sufficiently to accept the burdens of responsibility that were previously carried by more traditional institutions. Thus there is a kind of vacuum of legitimacy characterizing the transitional system. Political activity consequently often seems unpatterned, and the political scene highly volatile. Great fluctuations are observed in the occupancy of political elite positions: swings from the ideological left to the ideological right, from civilian to military regimes, and among allegiances to the major international groupings.

Use of the term "transitional" might seem to imply movement from one point to another. It is important to stress that our use of the concept of transitional systems implies only that these systems are moving *away from* a particular configuration of political activity; we do *not* imply that they are moving *toward* any particular set of political conditions. The uncertain and volatile character of politics in these systems renders it unwise to project the future directions of their development. Nor is such a projection necessary in order to classify these systems. Some may move in the direction of pluralistic systems; others may become increasingly highly structured. Still others may develop systemic characteristics not subsumed under either the "pluralistic" or the "highly structured" label. For our purposes, the important distinguishing features are those conditions of traditional politics *away from which* these societies now appear to be moving.

Perhaps we can sharpen our focus on the distinctions among these three system types by abstracting from the foregoing discussion a list of the critical dimensions along which types of political systems vary. These dimensions, presented in table 4–1, are:

1. The *breadth of representation* of different societal groups with *independent resources* and *bases of influence.*
2. The extent of *participation in decision making* by nongovernmental groups with independent resources and bases of influence.
3. The degree of *institutionalization* of the participation of such groups.
4. The degree of *competitiveness* that exists among such groups within the system, and between such groups and political organizations that are formally part of the government structure.
5. The extent to which the elite is *permeable;* i.e., open to entry from a variety of groups, including groups not now represented in the elite.
6. The degree of *task specialization* within the elite; that is, the extent to which elite activity has been *specialized* and *functionally separated,*

TABLE 4–1. Classification of Three Types of Political Systems According to
Some Critical Dimensions of Difference

Dimension	Transitional	System Type Highly Structured	Pluralist
1. Breadth of representation of political groups with independent resources	Low	Low	High
2. Extent of participation in decision making by independent nongovernmental groups	Medium	Low	High
3. Degree of institutionalization of participation of independent nongovernmental groups	Low	Low	High
4. Degree of intergroup competitiveness	Medium	Low	High
5. Extent to which political elite is permeable	Medium	Low	High
6. Degree of task specialization within the political elite	Low	Medium	High
7. Extent to which allocational activities of political elites are open to public scrutiny	Low/Medium	Low	High
8. Extent to which the evaluations of elite behaviors by nonelites are relevant to the continuance of elites in power	Medium	Low	High
9. Scope of impact of elite decisions	Medium	High	Medium

such that a variety of functionally identifiable subgroups can be observed within the elite.

7. The extent to which activities of elites that have directly to do with the authoritative allocation of values are open to *continuing public scrutiny.*

8. The extent to which the *evaluations of elite behaviors* by nonelites are relevant to the continuance of elites in power.

9. The *scope of impact* of elite decisions.

Some argument could be given concerning the rough classification presented in table 4–1. But, in general, the distinctions among these system types seem clear enough to permit us to classify essentially any contemporary political system into one of these categories.

CAREER TYPES

In the following chapters we focus on three political career types: executive, legislative, and party. Actually, our third category might more appropriately be called the category of "professional politician." There are some—but not many—political actors who have achieved stations of importance by holding only political-party positions. Nearly all party activists who have become critical in societal decision making have done so at least in part through positions occupied in the executive or legislative branches of government. Consequently, our career categories overlap—in this and other respects. We focus on the principal career channel occupied by each of the elites on whom we subsequently present data. But we recognize that the vast majority of our subjects have held positions in all three of these types of functional political arena.

Similarly, it is well known that the degree of functional differentiation of the political elite differs substantially among societies. The extent to which there is an identifiably distinct executive, legislative, or party elite is very different among systems. Sometimes the overlapping of elites is *structural* in nature, such as when no distinct judicial branch exists and judicial functions are carried out by members of the executive or by the legislature. Sometimes the overlapping is *functional*, as when a legislature exists, but serves only to rubber-stamp decisions already made by the executive. And sometimes the overlapping is *personnel*-based, as when a limited number of persons (usually all members of a single or dominant political party) hold key positions in all political hierarchies. In general, the greatest degree of functional differentiation among elites is in pluralist systems; transitional systems usually exhibit the smallest degree of functional differentiation. However, there are exceptions to this general rule.

Broadly, we can contrast our three career types in terms of a simplified typology of sociopolitical functions.[1] We may say that executive elites are critical in the performance of the *command* function. They operate in a more or less hierarchical environment in which both power and responsibility are dispersed pyramidally through identifiable organizational levels. Although collective decision making is not uncommon within the executive branch, there is nevertheless an identification of decisional authority with a given individual in each functional area of government activity and at each level of the executive branch. Within the legislative career channel, by contrast, the principal activity generally is *bargaining*. Legislative careers are focused on interelite negotiation and compromise. Furthermore, members of legislative institutions have unequal influence, in part on the basis of affiliations they hold outside the legislative institutions. That is, unequal influence distribution within legislatures often corresponds roughly to the distribution of political party membership within the institution. On the basis of legislative position alone, legislators in any given system generally are more or less equal. It is this characteristic that leads to the bargaining/negotiation/compromise character of the legislative process. Careers in political parties—or the careers of professional politicians—are focused on a slightly different sociopolitical function. Here the emphasis is on *competition* and *conflict*, or what Schattschneider has called the "mobilization of bias" within the system.[2] Party elites are responsible for structuring the dimensions of partisanship in the political system. They articulate programs and present candidates that serve to reflect and/or mold the existing and potential cleavages in society in such a way as to promote the interests of their own organization.

We should be careful not to oversimplify. It is undoubtedly the case that each of these sociopolitical functions is performed in part by political elites in each of the three career channels on which these chapters focus. Furthermore, any given individual may emphasize each—or all —of these political functions at one time or another in his career, in part because of the overlapping and temporal shifting of political career channels. At the same time, these basic distinctions among the functional activities of elites in different sectors of political practice serve to identify and contrast the somewhat different contexts in which the holders of political influence operate. And these distinctions may help us to understand some of the differences in social background and career characteristics among the three career channels at which we look in the following chapters.

The general distinctions among elites in terms of system types and career types, as presented in this chapter, are illustrated with reference to the COMPELITE data set, a collection of 16 items of information on each of more than 2,000 elites from seven countries.[3] (This data collection is described in more detail in chapter 8.) The data on pluralistic systems are taken from studies of the Federal Republic of Germany and Japan; the data for highly structured systems are taken from studies of elites in the Soviet Union and Bulgaria; and the data on transitional systems are taken from studies of three Latin American countries: Argentina, Brazil, and Mexico. Generalizing from this small number of cases to the broader category of systems into which they have been placed can be dangerous, since generalizing from a single case, or a limited number of cases, to a general category is always potentially misleading. It is probably true that nearly every specific case fits less than perfectly into any general characterization. There is not much doubt that the systems we look at here fit with reasonable comfort into their general categories. The issue is not their validity as illustrations;

rather, the question is whether it is reasonable to generalize to the parent category from the limited number of cases. To what extent are our subject countries "representative" of the general system types?

Further, the career channels represented in the studies vary somewhat. In general, the studies focus on political groups thought to be particularly important in each society. Thus the studies of the pluralistic systems of Germany and Japan include primarily (but not entirely) legislative elites. The studies of the highly structured systems focus substantially on party elites, although the overlapping of high government and party positions results in the inclusion of a high proportion of executive branch elites as well. And the three Latin American studies include very few legislators, focusing as they do on executive and political party elites.

It is reasonable to argue that the elites studied are generally representative of persons who have held a broad range of political elite positions in these societies in recent years. At the same time, it should be recognized that the criteria for including subjects were different among the studies. These pieces of research, as we indicate in chapter 8, were conducted by different persons at different times for different purposes. They illustrate a compelling problem in comparative cross-national research: The majority of comparative studies, regardless of the care taken in the execution of the research, are not wholly or even substantially comparable with one another. Certain procedures, described in chapter 8, were used to verify the validity of using these somewhat disparate data sets as part of a single cross-national comparative study. In general, the results of these validation efforts were very encouraging, and we can have some confidence that there is a high degree of comparability across studies in the measures used. Nevertheless, the possible limitations of comparability implied by the different orientations of the original pieces of research should be kept in mind.

A total of 16 background, career, and attitudinal/behavioral characteristics for 2,028 elites from seven countries is contained in COMPELITE. These characteristics are summarized in table 4–2. Some of them—year of birth, urban/rural origins, level of formal education, nature of special training—refer to what we usually call social background characteristics. Others—behavior contrary to institutional norms, participatory attitudinal posture, extralegal political behavior, ideological posture toward political issues—refer to dimensions of attitude and behavior. The remainder of the measures—the majority of those contained in COMPELITE—refer to characteristics of the political careers of these elites.

In this chapter we shall glance at a few of the most important differences among our three system types and our three career types along

TABLE 4–2.   Some Characteristics Used in Comparison of Elite
Groups[a]

SOCIAL BACKGROUND CHARACTERISTICS

Year of birth
Age entering elite positions
Urban/rural origins
Level of formal education
Nature of specialized training

CAREER CHARACTERISTICS

Career type: principal career channel
Involvement with nonparty groups
Longevity of political career
Significant subnational career
Professional military involvement
Coopted entry into elite
Positional marginality

ATTITUDES AND BEHAVIORS

Antinorm behavior: contrary to prevailing institutional norms
Participatory attitudinal posture
Extralegal behavior
Ideological orientation

---

[a] Variables included in the COMPELITE data collection.

these dimensions of social background, career characteristics, and attitude and behavior. In looking at the last category, we shall restrict our
attention to two variables: behavior contrary to prevailing norms and
ideological orientation. This is because the other two behavior/attitude
measures are not available for all system types.

DIFFERENCES AMONG SYSTEM TYPES

Social Background Characteristics.   Judging from the nations whose elites
are represented in COMPELITE, there are distinct differences among
system types in the average *age* of occupants of elite positions. Elites
are much younger in transitional systems, and oldest in highly structured systems. Pluralist systems occupy a middle position. As table 4–3
shows, nearly one-fourth of the Latin American elites who constitute
our transitional system subjects were under 40 years of age; the corresponding figure for the pluralist systems is 11 percent and, for the

socialist systems constituting our highly structured subset, about 6 percent. By contrast, only 10 percent of the Latin American elites were over 60 years of age, as compared with 21 percent of the pluralist system elites and 40 percent of the socialist elites.

These differences in elite age structure appear to be related to several important differences among the three system types. First, the younger age of elites in transitional systems is due in considerable part to the fact that traditional bases of political authority in those systems are in decline, and the resulting political situation is volatile and seemingly unpatterned. The opportunities for younger, less experienced persons to move into positions of power are correspondingly greater. We know that the institutionalization of political activity—the establishment of widely accepted and regularized procedures for carrying on the business of governing—tends to remove some of this volatility and absence of pattern. It tends also to lengthen the average tenure of an elite in office, and to keep older and more experienced persons on the political scene.

Second, in highly structured systems there is a tendency for elites to perpetuate themselves in office over relatively long periods of time. This leads to a progressive aging of the political elite—usually from a relatively young revolutionary elite to an increasingly aged elite as the revolution is consolidated and the system moves toward greater stability. The perpetuation of the elite is due to two closely related factors: the absence of institutionalized succession procedures for replacing leading personalities, and the relatively concentrated and encompassing character of political power. In short, it is relatively easy to mobilize the means necessary to suppress opposition, and difficult for the opposition—potential or real—to press for the institution of formal procedures

TABLE 4-3.   Elite Age by System Type (column percentages)

Age (years)	Transitional[a]	System Type Highly Structured[b]	Pluralist[c]	N
40 or less	22.1	5.9	11.2	236
41–60	67.5	53.7	67.7	1,093
more than 60	10.4	40.4	21.1	364
	100.0	100.0	100.0	
N	607	374	712	1,693

[a] In this and subsequent tables, this category includes data from Argentina, Brazil, and Mexico.
[b] Bulgaria and the USSR.
[c] Federal Republic of Germany and Japan.

that might increase their chances of penetrating the existing power distribution. In a related manner, the uncertainties surrounding elite succession encourage caution in handing over power even to trusted lieutenants.

The middle position of pluralist systems on the elite age distribution can be explained in these same contexts. There are conflicting pulls in pluralist systems. The institutionalization of provisions for opposition and for regular elite circulation promote the entry of a certain number of younger elites into office, while the regularity and stability of political activity tend to lead to the retention of a considerable number of older, more experienced political actors.

As table 4–4 indicates, there also appear to be intersystem differences in the *urban/rural origins* of elites. In particular, elites in pluralist systems appear to be much more likely to come from urban places, whereas elites in transitional and highly structured systems are substantially more likely to have rural origins. Although there is little doubt that this generalization holds broadly for countries in our three system categories, the finding does not appear to be related to any systematic difference in the nature of the political process in the respective system types. Rather, the urban origins of pluralist system elites seem to stem from the fact that many pluralist societies are relatively highly industrialized and urbanized. Thus a much higher proportion of the population lives in urban places, making greater the likelihood that any given elite would have urban origins.

This finding may be substantially misleading, for two reasons. First, our two pluralist systems in the COMPELITE data set are even more urban in character than the average pluralist system—a good deal more urban than is the United States, for example. Second, a number of studies have shown that in some pluralist systems (particularly the United States) small towns and rural places are noticeably *overrepresented* among the political elite, especially among elites at subnational levels and in legislative bodies. Thus members of state legislatures in

TABLE 4–4. Urban/Rural Origins of Elites by System Type (column percentages)

Urban/ Rural Origins	Transitional	System Type Highly Structured	Pluralist	N
Rural	63.6	72.6	24.2	593
Urban	36.4	27.4	75.8	773
	100.0	100.0	100.0	
N	396	219	751	1,366

the United States are often somewhat more rural, collectively viewed, than the population of the state itself. Recent court decisions and legislative enactments have reduced the overrepresentation of rural areas in U.S. state legislatures, but the phenomenon still exists.

Some intersystem differences in the level of *formal education* of elites can be observed, as suggested by table 4–5. The difference among systems in the proportion of elites having a higher education is relatively small, although the presence of higher education among the leaders of systems governed by communist parties generally has been lower than in most other systems. Generally, political elites are substantially better educated than the general population, and about half of the elites in all system types have had some postsecondary education. The differences lie in the proportions having completed secondary education. For pluralist systems, this percentage is very high; only 5 percent of the pluralist elites in the COMPELITE study had only an elementary education or less. By contrast, approximately 40 percent of the Latin American and Soviet-East European elites had no more than an elementary education. Thus the formal education variable for the transitional and highly structured system elites exhibits a marked bimodal distribution: It is divided between low and high education levels. In the pluralist systems the overall level of education is higher.

Two factors appear to account for these differences. First, pluralist systems are generally more developed economically, and have the resources to invest in comprehensive education programs. Similarly, economic modernization creates the need and demand for the extension of increasing levels of formal education to increasing numbers of persons. Second, the relative social democratization, and broader opportunities for social mobility, that have characterized some pluralist societies lead to the expectation of at least a modest level of educational attainment for a majority of citizens.

TABLE 4–5. Level of Formal Education of Elites by System Type (column percentages)

Education Level	Transitional	System Type Highly Structured	Pluralist	N
Low	38.3	45.7	5.1	517
Medium	6.8	12.2	44.2	424
High	54.9	42.1	50.7	914
	100.0	100.0	100.0	
N	561	582	712	1,855

We should be careful not to press this argument of socioeconomic determination of elite education levels too far. After all, it is clear that a central characteristic of the European socialist systems, certainly including the Soviet Union and Bulgaria, has been the extension of much broader educational opportunities to the general population; the average education level of the Soviet political elite, in particular, is increasing rapidly. However, an important element of elite recruitment has characterized the East European (including the Soviet) communist parties since early in their respective "Stalinist" periods. The leadership of these parties, notwithstanding the avowedly "proletarian" character of their revolutions and programs of social action, has been drawn disproportionately from rural and small-town sources. In part because these regimes replaced conservative governments presiding over socially hierarchical societies, their leaders have been recruited from segments of society that were not in favor in earlier times—and consequently did not enjoy the likelihood of higher education for their children.

Career Characteristics.   The *longevity* of political officeholding seems to vary a good deal among system types, as indicated in table 4–6. It is low in transitional systems and highest in pluralist systems. Since this finding might seem somewhat inconsistent with some things we have said above—we might have expected that elites in highly structured systems would have the highest longevity—a careful look at these data is in order. The principal difference between the longevity figures for highly structured and pluralist systems lies in the "low" category: 38 percent of the elites in highly structured systems fell here, as opposed to only 22 percent of the pluralist system elites. Entry into political prominence in highly structured systems has been a risky undertaking. The absence of regularized succession procedures, the relatively great importance of personal patronage and loyalties, and the presence of relatively intense interpersonal political competition combine to create

TABLE 4–6.   Career Longevity of Elites by System Type (column percentages)

Career Longevity	Transitional	System Type Highly Structured	Pluralist	N
Low	51.7	37.9	21.9	629
Medium	12.2	29.5	33.7	438
High	36.1	32.6	44.4	672
	100.0	100.0	100.0	
N	607	420	712	1,739

TABLE 4-7.   Significant Subnational Careers by System Type (column percentages)

Subnational Career	Transitional	System Type Highly Structured	Pluralist	N
No	58.0	54.3	42.7	968
Yes	42.0	45.7	57.3	941
	100.0	100.0	100.0	
N	488	670	751	1,909

a substantial number of "meteoric" political careers—rapid ascendance
followed by equally rapid decline. Hence the relatively great number
of elites with low political longevity in highly structured systems. On
the other hand, if we were to look at figures on the *average* length of
stay in political office, especially among national-level elites, it is likely
that highly structured systems would score at least as high as, if not
higher than, pluralist systems. The reason is simple: Those elites in
highly structured systems whose longevity is "high" (and bear in mind
that this is only a very general comparative category) tend to stay for
very long periods of time—much longer than the typical elite in a
pluralist system.

That the longevity of elites in transitional systems should be, on the
average, a good deal lower than that of elites in the other two system
types should not be difficult to understand. The volatility of the political
process—especially the recurrent use of extralegal means of political
accession in two of the Latin American countries on which we have data
—creates and dethrones many "instant elites." In chapter 5 we take a
closer look at some interesting aspects of this persistent use of extralegal
political means in Latin America.

There is one modest, but probably important, intersystem difference
(shown in table 4-7) in the prevalence of *subnational political careers*
among national elites. Elites in pluralist systems are somewhat more
likely to have had significant subnational careers before moving into
positions of national prominence. There is very little difference between transitional and highly structured systems in this regard. The
greater incidence of subnational careers in pluralist systems seems due
largely to the relatively decentralized character of these systems, as
compared with the other two system types. Local and regional administrative units are more important in most pluralist systems, and political
careers in those units are correspondingly more significant. It is not
merely that subnational units—states in the United States, or Länder in

the Federal Republic of Germany, for example—are accorded greater constitutional importance than their counterparts in the other two system types. Nor is it only that traditions of regionalism are able to flourish better in such systems. Pluralist systems by their very character encourage the establishment of bases of influence outside the configuration of currently dominant political forces. Some of these bases of influence are functional in character, as with labor organizations, but others are locational or regional in nature.

It is not surprising that we discover that the presence of professional *military* experience is greatest in the Latin American systems that constitute our subset of transitional systems (see table 4–8). And although the presence of military men may be somewhat higher in Latin American cabinets than in the cabinets of other transitional systems, this general finding seems to hold across that category of systems. At the same time, the percentage of professional military in the leadership of our highly structured systems was not much lower. The noticeable difference is between these two categories and the category of pluralist systems, where the presence of military is far lower. The strict separation of civilian political power and military professionalism that characterizes most pluralist systems is undoubtedly responsible for some of this difference. Similarly, the relatively stable and institutionalized pattern of political activity in most pluralist systems has obviated the necessity of direct military intervention in the political process, as has so often been characteristic of Latin American nations. Prominent military officers have occupied the position of head of state in pluralist systems— General de Gaulle in France and General Eisenhower in the United States would be two recent examples—but the overall representation of professional military men among pluralist system elites has been consistently low. The contrasting implications of the high level of military involvement in transitional system politics, and the low level of military involvement in pluralist system politics, for the political, social,

TABLE 4–8. Professional Military Experience of Elites by System Type (column percentages)

| Military Experience | System Type | | | |
	Transitional	Highly Structured	Pluralist	N
No	78.3	81.0	97.6	1,751
Yes	21.7	19.0	2.4	277
	100.0	100.0	100.0	
N	607	670	751	2,028

TABLE 4-9. Cooptation of Elites by System Type (column percentages)

Cooptation	Transitional	System Type Highly Structured	Pluralist	N
No	28.8	82.4	58.8	1,146
Yes	71.2	17.6	41.2	843
	100.0	100.0	100.0	
N	607	670	712	1,989

and economic development of these societies would appear to be potentially great; in any case, they are beyond the scope of this book. But some recent research[4] has shown that the imposition of military regimes in developing countries has had a substantial political impact, but almost no impact on social and economic change. A good deal more research on this subject is now needed.

Students of political leadership recently have discovered that the extent of *cooptation* present in a political elite may have important ramifications for the attitudes and behaviors exhibited by these elites. As table 4-9 suggests, there are some differences among system types in the extent to which political elites have been coopted from established careers outside politics. The greater the extent of cooptation in the selection of political elites, the lower the numerical preponderance of what we have termed "professional politicians"—persons with long careers in political activity who did not have substantial professional careers in a nonpolitical activity before entering politics. The extent of cooptation varies dramatically; it is 71 percent in the Latin American systems, 41 percent in the pluralist systems, and about 18 percent for the highly structured socialist systems. Again, these findings are useful only if we consider the factors behind them. First, some—but fewer than half—of the coopted Latin American elites were military men. They meet the formal definition of cooptation—established careers outside politics and entry into politics at a relatively advanced career stage —but the sort of cooptation they represent is of a special kind. Functionally, we think of cooptation as a process whereby a system seeks special skills—often technical and managerial—needed to govern an increasingly complex social order by reaching into the upper ranks of nongovernmental professions. Many military elites in Latin America came into office as a result of extralegal power transfers. One may argue that such extralegal rearrangements of elite occupancy represent cooptation as well, but the process is noticeably different from that of encouraging high-ranking managers, engineers, or economists to join legally constituted political administrations. Thus the figures for transitional systems in table 4–9 probably overstate the extent of functional cooptation in those elites.

Second, the figure of about 18 percent coopted elites for highly structured systems is misleadingly low. Cooptation is increasing rapidly as an elite selection procedure in the Soviet Union and in most East European socialist systems; indeed, some students of these systems believe that this is one of the most important elements of change observable there. The figures for highly structured systems in table 4–9 are low for two reasons. First, one of the two socialist systems we deal with is Bulgaria, where cooptation has been used less than in any other East European country, with the possible exception of Albania. Second, the sample of Soviet elites with which we are dealing includes several subsets of specialized elites, i.e., persons of importance in nonpolitical hierarchies such as the legal profession and the military. Many of these people have not had significant political careers, notwithstanding the relatively high degree of overlapping and integration of elite hierarchies in highly structured systems. These specialized elites are thought to have some political influence, but they do not have what could be considered distinct political elite careers. Therefore, they do not show up in the data as having been coopted. A more accurate indication of the extent of cooptation among high-ranking political figures in the Soviet Union probably is provided by Fleron's observation that, as of the late 1960s, more than half of the members of the Central Committee of the Communist party of the Soviet Union were coopted.[5] It is likely that the differences between pluralist and highly structured systems in the use of cooptation for elite selection are now relatively small, and growing smaller. We return to this issue in chapter 6.

Table 4–10 suggests that there are essentially no differences among system types in the average *positional marginality* of elites. This variable measures the likelihood of losing one's position within the first

TABLE 4–10. Positional Marginality of Elites by System Type (column percentages)

Positional Marginality	Transitional	System Type Highly Structured	Pluralist	N
No	71.9	75.2	67.0	1,102
Yes	28.1	24.8	33.0	460
	100.0	100.0	100.0	
N	430	420	712	1,562

normally stipulated term of officeholding. Thus a positionally marginal legislator is one who loses his seat not later than the first election after the one in which he won the seat. Between one-fourth and one-third of the elites being studied here were found to be positionally marginal.

It is instructive to compare the data on positional marginality in table 4–10 with the data on longevity of political career in table 4–6. There were noticeable differences among system types in terms of longevity —the length of one's political career, all positions included—with pluralist systems exhibiting the highest degree of longevity and transitional systems displaying the lowest. One might suppose that positional marginality and career longevity would be strongly and inversely related: where longevity is high, positional marginality would be low, and vice versa. Judging from tables 4–6 and 4–10, this would not seem to be the case; the intersystem differences in positional marginality are much smaller than the intersystem differences in career longevity. However, these tables simply compare the distribution of these career characteristics by system type; to determine whether there is a relationship between the two variables, we need to look at their joint distribution, which we shall do shortly.

First, however, we should note that one explanation for these seemingly inconsistent findings rests in the difference between the two career measures. Positional marginality refers to a *given position;* career longevity refers to the *set of positions* that collectively constitute a political career. It is possible for an elite to hold specific positions for relatively short periods of time, but yet to hold a relatively large number of positions in sequence; both positional marginality and longevity would thus be relatively high. This appears to be the case in pluralist systems, apparently because: (1) there is a relatively large number of elite positions available in pluralist systems; (2) the rate of elite circulation, or turnover, tends to be fairly high; and (3) pluralist systems, to use Seligman's terminology, seem to have a more elaborate set of cushions to soften the decline of persons who lose political office—and these cushions often include other positions with at least ceremonial (and formal) importance.

Furthermore, when we look at the cross-tabulation of career longevity and positional marginality (see table 4–11), we discover that there is a relationship between the two variables when the data are viewed at the individual level. Elites whose career longevity is lowest are most likely to show positional marginality; elites with high career longevity are least likely to exhibit positional marginality. Thus although the patterns of intersystem variation are different for these two career measures, there is an identifiable relationship between career longevity and positional marginality at the individual level.

It is also important to ask whether the nature of the relationship between these two variables might be different in different types of system. That is, there might be an *interactive* relationship in which the link between the two career characteristics would be different for different categories of a third variable—here, system type. As table 4–12 shows, this is precisely the situation in this case. In transitional and pluralist systems the relationship between career longevity and positional marginality takes on the expected inverse form: Marginality is associated with low longevity. But for the highly structured systems the relationship is just the opposite: Elites with low career longevity are unlikely to be positionally marginal, whereas positional marginality is distinctly higher among elites with higher career longevity.

The implication seems clear: In these two socialist systems, shorter careers tend to be characterized by a very small number of positions, each held for a relatively substantial length of time. Longer political careers are typified by frequent movement among a large number of positions, each occupied for a relatively short time. Precisely why this should be the case is unclear, but the implication of this finding for the conduct of political careers in socialist systems is noteworthy: If career success is measured by longevity, then success may be enhanced by a willingness to accept a high level of positional mobility and, by implication, job uncertainty.

TABLE 4–11.   Positional Marginality by Career Longevity (column percentages)

| Positional Marginality | Career Longevity | | | |
	Low	Medium	High	N
No	51.3	71.7	82.7	1,102
Yes	48.7	28.3	17.3	460
	100.0	100.0	100.0	
N	452	438	672	1,562

Attitudes and Behaviors.   As we might expect, one of the most noticeable differences between pluralist systems and transitional and highly structured systems concerns the occurrence of *antinorm behavior*—behavior contrary to prevailing institutional or societal norms—among political elites. As table 4–13 suggests, antinorm behavior is low in pluralist systems (21 percent of the elites exhibited such behavior), but nearly twice as high, about 41 percent, in the other two system categories. The substantially greater degree of institutionalization of political competition and conflict, and the pervasive and largely voluntary acceptance of basic norms of political activity, contribute to the relatively

TABLE 4–12. Positional Marginality by Career Longevity for Three Types of Political Systems (column percentages)

| | Career Longevity | | | | | | | | | | | | |
| | Transitional Systems | | | | Highly Structured Systems | | | | Pluralist Systems | | | | |
Positional Marginality	Low	Medium	High	N	Low	Medium	High	N	Low	Medium	High	N	N
No	50.4	89.2	79.5	309	93.1	63.7	65.0	316	9.6	70.4	92.7	477	1,102
Yes	49.6	10.8	20.5	121	6.9	36.3	35.0	104	90.4	29.6	7.3	235	460
	100.0	100.0	100.0		100.0	100.0	100.0		100.0	100.0	100.0		
N	137	74	219	430	159	124	137	420	156	240	316	712	1,562

TABLE 4–13.   Antinorm Behavior of Elites by System Type (column percentages)

Antinorm Behavior	Transitional	System Type Highly Structured	Pluralist	N
No	59.1	58.7	79.4	1,317
Yes	40.9	41.3	20.6	672
	100.0	100.0	100.0	
N	607	670	712	1,989

low incidence of antinorm behavior in pluralist systems. By contrast, in Latin America it can well be argued that one of the most institutionalized features of politics is the resort to extralegal, often violent, means to effect elite change. We have treated involvement in coups d'état, for example, as an example of antinorm behavior in Latin America. But such a classification is open to challenge; although coups and other "revolutionary" acts are formally proscribed, it may well be that large numbers of people (perhaps especially contending elites) view such acts as not only necessary but even ethically acceptable modes of political practice. We use a formal definition of normatively sanctioned behavior for purposes of analyzing these data, but we do so with a sense of caution.

The relatively high level of antinorm behavior in the two socialist systems whose elites are being studied here requires some elaboration. Nearly all of this antinorm behavior, especially in Bulgaria, took place *before* socialist regimes were established in these countries. That is, these elites participated frequently in illegal activities directed toward the elimination of the previous regimes. Thus they exhibited a willingness to engage in antinorm behavior, but not within the context of the socialist system. This finding consequently must be viewed quite differently from the corresponding figure for the three Latin American countries.

A final attitudinal dimension on which some intersystem difference can be observed is the presence of an *ideological orientation* toward political issues (see table 4–14). An ideological orientation was most characteristic of the Latin American elites studied (59 percent had such an orientation), and least characteristic of the pluralist system elites (about 38 percent). The socialist elites occupied a middle position on this measure; 47 percent were categorized as ideologically oriented.

Findings that seem to link pluralist polities with a relatively pragmatic political style are common. The evidence seems persuasive that, in general, societal problem solving proceeds in a somewhat less doctrinal vein in systems in which political influence is more dispersed (a circumstance requiring negotiation, bargaining, and compromise), and in which reasonably effective conflict-management procedures are institutionalized. Politics is, of necessity, procedurally complex in most pluralist systems, and these complexities demand a relatively great degree of pragmatism and flexibility. We should qualify this generalization in two respects. First, the elites in Japan and the Federal Republic of Germany that comprise our pluralist system subset were by no means wholly nonideological; more than one-third of them were classified as having an ideological orientation. Second, there are a few clear and highly visible exceptions to the generalization; the influence of ideological doctrine on politics in Italy and France, for example, seems to be somewhat greater than is the case with Germany, Japan, or the United States. Clearly, additional factors other than basic system type affect the role of ideology.

The fact that elites in the two socialist systems studied were collectively less ideological than were elites in the transitional systems of Latin America might seem surprising. Western students of socialist systems have tended to attribute great importance to ideology in discussing the bases of political choice in those systems. This is not surprising, given the overt emphasis placed on ideological doctrine under socialism. However, there is persuasive evidence that the importance of ideology in general, and of notions of ideological orthodoxy in particular, continues to decline in socialist systems. This trend may well be an accompaniment of another change noted above, the increasing use of cooptation as an elite selection mechanism. With the relative decline of the lifelong party bureaucrat, and the increasingly evident ascendance of the technically trained and oriented coopted specialist, the importance of ideological doctrine as a basis for choice taking has diminished. We shall return to this issue in chapter 6.

TABLE 4-14. Ideological Orientation of Elites by System Type (column percentages)

Ideological Orientation	Transitional	System Type Highly Structured	Pluralist	N
No	41.1	52.7	62.2	680
Yes	58.9	47.3	37.8	687
	100.0	100.0	100.0	
N	504	670	193	1,367

DIFFERENCES AMONG CAREER TYPES

Parallel to the differences that can be observed among system types
are some contrasts in elite characteristics that can be associated with
different career channels. That is, we assume that the selection and the
activities of political elites are influenced not only by characteristics of
the systems in which they operate, but also by factors intrinsic to the
elite positions themselves. We can say that differences in system type
amount, in effect, to contrasting elements of social, economic, and political context, or environment. Differences that can be traced to the
career channels themselves may be presumed to correspond to aspects
of organizational structure and of role. That is, if we discover that there
are patterned differences in social backgrounds, career characteristics,
and attitudes and behaviors among occupants of different kinds of elite
position (in our case, executive, legislative, and professional party careers), we can assume that these differences are due in part to characteristics of the organizational settings in which these elites act, and to
the nature of the activities (functions) associated with the performance
of the respective political roles.

Some of the differences we observed among system types in the
preceding section of this chapter may be related in part to differences
among career channels. The elite groups included in the COMPELITE
data base come from varying configurations of formal positions. The
data on pluralistic systems deal primarily with legislative elites, for
example; executive and party elites are emphasized in the Latin American studies. It is quite possible that some of the differences noted among
system types may be traceable to the fact that the elites studied for the
respective system types were drawn from dissimilar positional groupings.

Social Background Characteristics. The differences in *age composition*
among our three career types are not dramatic, but they are still identifiable, as shown in table 4–15. The executive elites have the highest
percentage under 40 years of age (nearly 18 percent, as compared with
about 12 percent for legislative and party elites); legislative elites have
the highest proportion among those 60 years and older (28 percent,
versus 20 percent for party elites and 16 percent for executives). In
general, it appears that executive elites tend to be youngest, followed
by party elites; legislative elites constitute the oldest of the three
groups.

Several factors seem to combine to explain these differences among
career types. First, legislative careers tend to be longer than careers in
the executive branch or in party hierarchies; as we shall see shortly,

TABLE 4–15. Elite Age by Career Type (column percentages)

| Age (in years) | Career Type | | | |
	Executive	Legislative	Professional Party	N
40 or less	17.7	12.6	12.1	236
41–60	66.4	59.6	68.5	1,084
more than 60	15.9	27.8	19.4	360
	100.0	100.0	100.0	
N	521	623	536	1,680

career longevity is highest for legislative elites. Second, a certain number of the executive elites in our subject group are military men who were involved in extralegal accession to power at a relatively young age. Third, the fact that many of the legislators under study are from pluralist systems reinforces the likelihood of their being older, given the relatively greater stability and institutionalization of political activity in those systems.

The *urban/rural origins* of the elites under study here also appear at first to differ according to career type. The executive elites are substantially more likely to be from rural or small-town locations—about 60 percent of the executives had rural origins, as compared with fewer than 40 percent of the legislative and party elites (see table 4–16). However, this apparent difference is due largely to the fact that the majority of the executive elites in the COMPELITE study are from Latin American countries. Indeed, when we look at the relationship between urban/rural origins and career type by system type (table 4–17), we discover that: (1) executive elites are only slightly more rural

TABLE 4–16. Urban/Rural Origins of Elites by Career Type (column percentages)

| Urban/Rural Origins | Career Type | | | |
	Executive	Legislative	Professional Party	N
Rural	59.2	37.8	39.7	588
Urban	40.8	62.2	60.3	731
	100.0	100.0	100.0	
N	387	584	348	1,319

TABLE 4-17. Urban/Rural Origins of Elites by Career Type for Three Types of Political System (column percentages)

| | Career Type | | | | | | | | | | | | |
| | Transitional Systems | | | | Highly Structured Systems | | | | Pluralist Systems | | | | Σ |
Urban/Rural Origins	Exec.	Legis.	Prof. Party	N	Exec.	Legis.	Prof. Party	N	Exec.	Legis.	Prof. Party	N	N
Rural	65.2	62.6	47.8	252	73.5	77.1	66.7	156	16.1	24.4	29.5	180	588
Urban	34.8	37.4	52.2	144	26.5	22.9	33.3	60	83.9	75.6	70.5	527	731
	100.0	100.0	100.0		100.0	100.0	100.0		100.0	100.0	100.0		
N	282	91	23	396	49	83	84	216	56	410	241	707	1,319

than legislators in Latin America; (2) legislators were slightly more rural than executives in the socialist systems; and (3) the most rural subgroup in the pluralist systems was the professional politicians, followed by legislators. In general, when we break down the analysis by country type, the differences in urban/rural origins among career types do not seem very significant.

Levels of formal education show more substantial, and genuine, variation among career types. As table 4–18 indicates, the distributions of low, medium, and high education levels are noticeably different. About 60 percent of both executive and legislative elites had at least some higher education, as compared with fewer than 38 percent of the party elites. However, the incidence of elementary education or less was much lower among legislators (8 percent) than among executives (26 percent) and party elites (nearly 30 percent). The average level of formal education is highest among legislators and lowest among the professional politicians. With some minor variations, this pattern holds for all three system types; it is most accentuated in the transitional systems, where 88 percent of the party elites had an elementary education or less, and 87 percent of the legislators had at least some higher education.

The identification of at least a modest level of education as a channel to, and in some societies as nearly a prerequisite for, a legislative career provides an interesting basis for speculation. We know that, especially in pluralistic systems but to a considerable extent in transitional systems as well, a substantial number of legislators are trained as lawyers. The functional characteristics of the practice of the law and jurisprudence and of legislative roles are generally similar: Both involve advocacy, bargaining, compromise, and a predisposition toward the use of established and agreed-upon procedures in resolving differences of opinion.

TABLE 4–18. Level of Formal Education of Elites by Career Type (column percentages)

Education Level	Career Type			
	Executive	Legislative	Professional Party	N
Low	25.6	8.0	29.5	322
Medium	12.6	32.1	32.9	420
High	61.8	59.9	37.6	858
	100.0	100.0	100.0	
N	500	608	492	1,600

It seems reasonable to suggest that legal training and legislative careers exert mutual and reciprocal attraction; this may contribute a good deal to understanding the higher level of education associated with legislative careers.

By contrast, it is not difficult to understand that higher formal education might not be as important for party and executive careers. The bases of mobility and career success for professional politicians often are local or regional constituencies, or opportune involvement in systems of patronage and political loyalty. Formal education is less critical in such careers. Similarly, the bases of many executive careers would not appear to depend critically on higher education. In a number of pluralistic societies, for example, many cabinet members and national administrators have been coopted from the ranks of the economic elite, as is the case in the United States, the Federal Republic of Germany, and the United Kingdom. The incidence of higher education among American and German corporate executives is increasing, but is still relatively modest. And in transitional systems, many political executives have come from military, business, or landholding career channels, where the incidence of higher education has not been particularly high.

Career Characteristics.   Career types also appear to differ in their average *longevity,* or duration, although we shall discover that these differences are in part a function of differences among system types. Table 4–19 suggests that career longevity generally is somewhat higher among legislative elites and lowest among party politicians. There are important qualifications to this generalization, based on differences among system types, as shown in table 4–20. Short-duration careers characterize party elites most strikingly in the transitional systems of Latin America, where 86 percent of the party elites were classified as having low career longevity. The highest career longevity was exhib-

TABLE 4–19. Career Longevity of Elites by Career Type (column percentages)

Career Longevity	Career Type			
	Executive	Legislative	Professional Party	N
Low	38.0	26.3	45.1	624
Medium	15.3	27.9	32.4	438
High	46.7	45.8	22.5	672
	100.0	100.0	100.0	
N	561	627	546	1,734

TABLE 4-20. Career Longevity of Elites by Career Type for Three Types of Political System (column percentages)

| | Career Type | | | | | | | | | | | | |
| Career Longevity | Transitional Systems | | | | Highly Structured Systems | | | | Pluralist Systems | | | | Σ |
	Exec.	Legis.	Prof. Party	N	Exec.	Legis.	Prof. Party	N	Exec.	Legis.	Prof. Party	N	N
Low	37.5	58.2	86.0	314	49.2	20.2	41.4	159	14.3	20.5	24.5	151	624
Medium	15.0	12.2	4.4	74	12.9	23.5	46.8	124	23.2	32.9	38.2	240	438
High	47.5	29.6	9.6	219	37.9	56.3	11.8	137	63.5	46.6	37.3	316	672
	100.0	100.0	100.0		100.0	100.0	100.0		100.0	100.0	100.0		
N	373	98	136	607	132	119	169	420	56	410	241	707	1,734

ited by executive elites in both pluralistic and transitional systems. In our highly structured socialist systems, by contrast, nearly half of the executive elites had low longevity, while a plurality of party elites were classified as having medium longevity.

These between-system contrasts in career longevity correspond to some important distinctions in the basic political features of these three system types. Party careers of short duration might be expected in Latin American systems, where party systems generally have been highly unstable and where political parties have appeared, disappeared, and undergone substantial ideological and tactical transformations in short periods of time—often as a reflection of changes in the dominant personalities among the parties' adherents. The contrastingly higher career longevity of party elites in the highly structured socialist systems derives in considerable part from the fact that a single political party has been dominant for a relatively long period. The absence of regularized procedures of elite succession, already mentioned, may contribute to somewhat higher career longevity among party elites in these systems. At the same time, the intense interpersonal and interfactional competition that also has characterized these highly structured systems probably accounts for the fact that only just over 10 percent of their party elites were classified as having high career longevity.

We have already discussed the reasons for relatively high executive career longevity in transitional systems—especially reflected in the perpetuation of some military regimes in Latin America over relatively long periods. (The Stroessner regime in Paraguay, still in power in 1978, began in 1951.) The fact that career longevity for executive elites was higher than that for legislative elites in pluralist systems in our COM-PELITE study is more surprising. It may be that Japan and the Federal Republic of Germany are not typical of pluralist systems in this regard; career longevity apparently is higher among legislative elites in the United States, for example.

The incidence of *significant subnational political careers* is distinctly higher among legislative elites than among executives or party politicians. Two-thirds of the legislators in our study had significant subnational careers, as against about 40 percent of the executive elites and 47 percent of the party elites (see table 4–21). This pattern is most noticeable for the transitional systems of Latin America (where 89 percent of the legislators had subnational careers), and holds also—but much less dramatically—for pluralist systems, as table 4–22 shows. (The incidence of significant subnational careers among national elites is generally higher in pluralist systems than in the other two system types, as we noted earlier.) In the highly structured socialist systems, by contrast, subnational careers were slightly more prevalent among executive elites, although the differences among career types were modest.

TABLE 4-21. Significant Subnational Careers by Career Type (column percentages)

Subnational Career	Career Type			
	Executive	Legislative	Professional Party	N
No	60.6	33.8	53.1	778
Yes	39.4	66.2	46.9	837
	100.0	100.0	100.0	
N	551	627	437	1,615

In general, it seems clear that legislative elites have closer and more consistent ties to local and regional constituencies than do executive elites. The structure of the selection process for legislators usually requires that they serve at least nominally as representatives of some geographically defined constituency. By contrast, executive elites may be required to think in terms of national constituencies; this surely is the case with candidates standing for election to national offices, such as the presidency of the United States.

It is somewhat surprising that, in the socialist systems under study here, party elites were the least likely to have significant subnational careers. We know that many Soviet party elites have worked their way into positions of importance by establishing power bases in party organs at the Republic level, or in major cities, and/or by serving lengthy "apprenticeships" in such lower-level organs. Our data suggest, however, that the numerical incidence of this career pattern may not be as high as had been thought, especially in Bulgaria.

As we might expect, the extent of *cooptation* among party elites is much lower than that among legislative and, especially, executive elites, as shown in table 4-23. However, this pattern is not present in the socialist systems in our study, as indicated in table 4-24. Again, both the general pattern and the socialist exception reflect important aspects of the political process in each system type.

It should be remembered that our category of professional party elites includes persons whose careers have been spent primarily in internal party activity. Many of the executive and legislative elites we are studying have been active in political party politics as well, but we have not considered them to be "party elites." Thus the latter category frequently includes persons who have joined a political party at a relatively early age and have continued to work within the party organization over a substantial period. It is not surprising that the incidence of cooptation—selection of political elites from among persons who have

TABLE 4-22. Significant Subnational Careers by Career Type for Three Types of Political System (column percentages)

| | Career Type | | | | | | | | | | | | |
| | Transitional Systems | | | | Highly Structured Systems | | | | Pluralist Systems | | | | Σ |
Subnational Career	Exec.	Legis.	Prof. Party	N	Exec.	Legis.	Prof. Party	N	Exec.	Legis.	Prof. Party	N	N
No	68.6	11.2	85.2	283	46.2	51.3	56.2	217	42.9	34.1	47.3	278	778
Yes	31.4	88.8	14.8	205	53.8	48.7	43.8	203	57.1	65.9	52.7	429	837
	100.0	100.0	100.0		100.0	100.0	100.0		100.0	100.0	100.0		
N	363	98	27	488	132	119	169	420	56	410	241	707	1,615

TABLE 4–23. Cooptation of Elites by Career Type (column percentages)

| | Career Type | | | |
Cooptation	Executive	Legislative	Professional Party	N
No	38.0	45.9	71.4	891
Yes	62.0	54.1	28.6	843
	100.0	100.0	100.0	
N	561	627	546	1,734

established careers outside of politics—would be somewhat lower among party elites. At the same time, we should remember (see table 4–18) that career longevity was lowest overall for party elites, especially in the transitional systems of Latin America. Consequently, it seems unlikely that the low incidence of cooptation among party elites in transitional and pluralist systems can be traced entirely or even substantially to the presence of a number of long-time party functionaries. It appears as if political elites active primarily in party organizations are less likely to have been coopted than their elite counterparts in government positions, at least in transitional and pluralist systems. This is likely due in part to the greater visibility, prestige, and attractiveness of national government posts, as compared with party positions.

The situation is reversed in our highly structured socialist systems, where cooptation is most prevalent among party elites (34 percent of the party elites we are studying were coopted, a figure that probably understates the extent of actual cooptation, as we noted earlier). If one makes the reasonable assumption that the critical loci of power in these systems remain in the Communist party, this finding is not difficult to explain. It is by now generally accepted that neither social and economic development nor political governance have proceeded as efficiently as desired, or as possible, in the socialist systems of Eastern Europe (including the USSR). Part of the blame for these perceived inadequacies of societal development has been placed on the Stalinist emphasis on political and ideological fidelity in elite recruitment and promotion; such fidelity was thought to be much more important than technical or managerial expertise. In the last 15 years the need has been felt to bring more persons with such practical skills into the political elite, and many of these people must come from nonpolitical occupational hierarchies. Given our assumption that the Communist party wishes to retain a monopoly of political influence—and given the relative paucity in the past of party functionaries with technical and mana-

TABLE 4-24. Cooptation of Elites by Career Type for Three Types of Political System (column percentages)

Career Type

Cooptation	Transitional Systems				Highly Structured Systems				Pluralist Systems				Σ
	Exec.	Legis.	Prof. Party	N	Exec.	Legis.	Prof. Party	N	Exec.	Legis.	Prof. Party	N	N
No	19.0	18.4	63.2	175	80.3	71.4	65.7	302	64.3	45.1	80.1	414	891
Yes	81.0	81.6	36.8	432	19.7	28.6	34.3	118	35.7	54.9	19.9	293	843
	100.0	100.0	100.0		100.0	100.0	100.0		100.0	100.0	100.0		
N	373	98	136	607	132	119	169	420	56	410	241	707	1,734

TABLE 4–25.   Positional Marginality of Elites by Career Type (column percentages)

Positional Marginality	Career Type			
	Executive	Legislative	Professional Party	N
No	75.7	71.6	64.3	1,102
Yes	24.3	28.4	35.7	455
	100.0	100.0	100.0	
N	507	588	462	1,557

gerial expertise—it is logical to assume that much of the cooptation would be found first among party elites.

In transitional and in pluralist systems, *positional marginality* is highest among party elites and lowest among executive elites (see tables 4–25 and 4–26); we can assume that this is for the same reasons that explain similar findings concerning career longevity. In the highly structured socialist systems, party elites have the lowest level of positional marginality. However, the differences among career types in socialist systems are only modest; in general, it appears as if positional turnover and/or uncertainty is roughly similar among career types in these systems.

Attitudes and Behaviors.   The presence of *antinorm behavior* appears to vary among career types, as suggested in table 4–27. It is highest among executive elites and lowest among party elites. However, as table 4–28 indicates, these differences largely reflect between-system contrasts. In the transitional systems of Latin America, antinorm behavior (especially including participation in coups) was highest among executive elites, fully one-half of whom engaged in such activities. Antinorm behavior also was highest among executive elites in pluralist systems, but the percentage was a good deal lower (28 percent).

In the highly structured socialist systems, legislative elites were distinctly higher in antinorm behavior. Remembering that the antinorm activity for one of the two socialist countries (Bulgaria) generally took place before the socialist regime came to power, we can infer that a substantial number of older communist militants have pursued legislative careers. This does not account fully for the relatively high incidence of antinorm behavior in our socialist system category, however. It is noteworthy that this high incidence also holds for the Soviet elites under study here, for whom the recorded antinorm activity has taken

TABLE 4-26. Positional Marginality of Elites by Career Type for Three Types of Political System (column percentages)

| | Career Type | | | | | | | | | | | | |
| | Transitional Systems | | | | Highly Structured Systems | | | | Pluralist Systems | | | | Σ |
Positional Marginality	Exec.	Legis.	Prof. Party	N	Exec.	Legis.	Prof. Party	N	Exec.	Legis.	Prof. Party	N	N
No	75.5	71.2	50.0	309	75.8	69.7	78.7	316	76.8	72.2	57.3	477	1,102
Yes	24.5	28.8	50.0	121	24.2	30.3	21.3	104	23.2	27.8	42.7	230	455
	100.0	100.0	100.0		100.0	100.0	100.0		100.0	100.0	100.0		
N	319	59	52	430	132	119	169	420	56	410	241	707	1,557

TABLE 4–27. Antinorm Behavior of Elites by Career Type (column percentages)

| Antinorm Behavior | Career Type | | | |
	Executive	Legislative	Professional Party	N
No	54.0	67.0	76.4	1,140
Yes	46.0	33.0	23.6	594
	100.0	100.0	100.0	
N	561	627	546	1,734

place since the institution of the Bolshevik regime in 1917. Thus it may be inferred that challenges to basic political norms in the Soviet Union may be more likely to emanate from legislative elites than from party or executive elites.

Executive elites also were a good deal more *ideological* in political attitudes than the other two career types, as shown in table 4–29. About 46 percent of the executives were categorized as ideologically oriented, as compared to 41 percent of the party elites and about 38 percent of the legislative elites. Again, however, these apparent differences among career types reflect in part differences among system types, as indicated in table 4–30.

The linking of executives with an ideological posture stems from the strong presence of this relationship in the transitional Latin American systems. In the pluralist systems under study, party elites were the most ideological in orientation. And in the socialist systems there were virtually no differences among career types in extent of ideological orientation.

The finding that party elites constitute the most ideological subset in pluralist systems should not be surprising; we have already noted that one of the principal functions of political parties in these systems is the structuring and promotion of partisanship. And in transitional systems we may assume that the traditional weakness of political parties and the frequently interventionist posture of the military, as reflected in the seizure of power by force, combine to make it likely that political executives would be the principal carriers of expressly ideological postures toward politics. More surprising, however, is the finding that the proportion of ideologically oriented elites does not vary among career types in the socialist systems. It is generally thought that party elites are substantially more ideological than are government elites in these systems, simply by virtue of the expressly ideological character of the party and its societal roles. We have seen above that there has been substan-

TABLE 4-28. Antinorm Behavior of Elites by Career Type for Three Types of Political System (column percentages)

| | Career Type | | | | | | | | | | | | | | Σ |
| | Transitional Systems | | | | Highly Structured Systems | | | | Pluralist Systems | | | | | |
Antinorm Behavior	Exec.	Legis.	Prof. Party	N	Exec.	Legis.	Prof. Party	N	Exec.	Legis.	Prof. Party	N	N
No	50.7	61.2	80.9	359	56.1	36.1	59.8	218	71.4	77.3	85.5	563	1,140
Yes	49.3	38.8	19.1	248	43.9	63.9	40.2	202	28.6	22.7	14.5	144	594
	100.0	100.0	100.0		100.0	100.0	100.0		100.0	100.0	100.0		
N	373	98	136	607	132	119	169	420	56	410	241	707	1,734

tial cooptation into the party elite in the Soviet Union; this may be expected to reduce the proportion of ideologically oriented persons at higher levels of the party apparatus. Our data suggest that this process already may have eliminated or substantially reduced the position of the party as the predominant repository of ideological perspectives.

This chapter has suggested that there are identifiable differences— and some similarities—among transitional, highly structured, and pluralist political systems in the social backgrounds, careers, and attitudes and behaviors of their elites. We also noted some differences among career types, although these differences seem to reflect in part differences among system types.

These general patterns of similarity and difference provide a backdrop for viewing the nature of elites and leadership in each of the three system types, which we do in the following three chapters. It has already been stressed, but bears repeating, that the generalizations presented in this chapter must be taken as tentative, both because they are derived from data on a small number of systems, and because there are uncertainties concerning the cross-national comparability of some of the measures of social background, careers, and, especially, attitudes and behavior. These generalizations seem reasonable and defensible, but they must be examined through closer attention to the more detailed data on elite characteristics presented in the following pages.

TABLE 4–29. Ideological Orientation of Elites by Career Type (column percentages)

Ideological Orientation	Career Type			
	Executive	Legislative	Professional Party	N
No	44.1	62.5	58.9	595
Yes	55.9	37.5	41.1	517
	100.0	100.0	100.0	
N	474	283	355	1,112

TABLE 4-30. Ideological Orientation of Elites by Career Type for Three Types of Political System (column percentages)

Ideological Orientation	Career Type												Σ
	Transitional Systems				Highly Structured Systems				Pluralist Systems				
	Exec.	Legis.	Prof. Party	N	Exec.	Legis.	Prof. Party	N	Exec.	Legis.	Prof. Party	N	N
No	34.6	55.3	51.1	207	64.4	61.3	66.3	270	73.3	72.2	53.2	118	595
Yes	65.4	44.7	48.9	297	35.6	38.7	33.7	150	26.7	27.8	46.8	70	517
	100.0	100.0	100.0		100.0	100.0	100.0		100.0	100.0	100.0		
N	327	85	92	504	132	119	169	420	15	79	94	188	1,112

5

Extralegal Political Behavior among Latin American Political Elites

This chapter examines several social background and career characteristics of Latin American political elites as predictors of their involvement in coups d'état and related "revolutionary" political acts. Our purpose is to illustrate certain important elements of political leadership and to increase our understanding of procedures of political succession in Latin America—procedures that are often viewed as aberrant, yet can be seen as firmly institutionalized phenomena. Indirectly, then, this chapter also deals with the nature of political stability and instability in Latin America.

Students of Latin American politics[1] agree substantially on its central characteristics, especially on the most important features of political leadership. For our purposes, five frequently cited characteristics are especially relevant. First, Latin American elites seem to exhibit a deep-seated "revolutionary commitment" to liberal democracy.[2] This commitment manifests itself in at least three specific ways. One manifestation is an *ideological attachment* to the *symbols* of democracy. Political leadership groups in Latin America appear to have an even more overt ideological commitment to such democratic symbols than the leaders of many political systems that seem to incorporate democratic practices more faithfully in their actual operation. However, at the same time, this Latin American commitment to liberal democracy is sufficiently *revolutionary in nature* that it seems to have facilitated the frequent use of extralegal, and often violent, means in political life. Thus the ideological commitment to democratic symbols and ends has not been matched by a commensurate commitment to nonviolent, regularized *procedures* for achieving these ends. Finally, the overt "constitutionalism" that accompanies a commitment to liberal democracy seems to be rendered essentially meaningless by the countermanding reality of a *lack of respect for political institutions* established in constitutions, as well as for the constitutions themselves. Thus Latin American political leaders seem to attach great importance to constitutional documents as programmatic statements of abstract goals, yet regularly violate the constitutionally stipulated procedures through which the desired goals are supposed to be achieved.[3] Constitutional democracy seems to be esteemed in principle, but generally disregarded in political practice.

A second characteristic of Latin American politics is asserted to be its chronic "instability." The concept of instability has been given a wide variety of meanings by students of comparative politics, and of Latin America in particular.[4] For some, instability is indicated by the presence of recurrent political violence; for others, instability is shown by the repeated constitutional reworkings that have occurred in nearly all Latin American nations throughout their independent histories; and for still others, instability means the absence of patterns or regularities in the processes of political change. There sometimes seems to be a frustrating degree of "randomness" in Latin American political developments.[5]

A third feature of political leadership in Latin America is the dominance of the executive branch over the other branches of government, particularly the dominance of the president of the republic over other leading political actors.[6] Yet although there is nearly universal agreement that the executive is politically dominant, there is considerable implicit disagreement as to how consequential that dominance really is. Some students of Latin American affairs seem to believe that the dominance of the executive branch means that the president and his cabinet play the critical roles in determining political outcomes. Other writers, although agreeing that the executive is politically dominant, feel that the basic character of the political, social, and economic orders is largely determined by factors that cannot be, or are not being, manipulated by any political actors within these systems. In this view, the executive branch dominates the corps, but the corps consists largely of toy soldiers. The principal activity of the political system is thought to be the making and unmaking of governments rather than the shaping of the social and physical environments to facilitate societal development.

A fourth, and related, generalization frequently made about political leadership in Latin America is that this leadership is highly personalistic.[7] This personalism has its roots in the *caudillo* system, but has been sustained and magnified by twentieth-century developments, especially the impact of military and communications technology on the ability of a limited number of individuals to control large numbers of others.[8] Personalism in political leadership manifests itself in numerous ways, but one of the most important for our purposes is the supposed lack of pattern or predictability that it injects into the process of leadership change. Thus patterns of leadership change in Latin America are said to be determined largely by factors peculiar to the personalities and backgrounds of the individuals who are in power, or are contending for power, rather than by characteristics of established political institutions or by prevailing political norms.

Fifth, it is generally agreed that the varying, but usually influential, political roles of military groups in Latin America have a major impact on the nature of politics and on the character of political leadership. Several different typologies of military involvement in Latin American politics have been suggested.[9] For our purposes, the details of these different forms of involvement are not critical. What is important is that the military has played a major role in politics in many of these countries and that a significant number of political leaders in Latin America at any given point in time are likely to be military men, or to have spent substantial time as professional military.

Thus political leadership seems to reflect many of the characteristics of Latin American political life in general. Political leadership appears to be: (1) unstable; (2) substantially ideological in nature; (3) often violent in practice; (4) often extralegal or extraconstitutional in its succession procedures; and (5) often at least superficially unpatterned in terms of the regularity of the change process.

These generalizations are more than a little frustrating for the social scientist; a great number of unanswered questions remain before us, a few of which provide the basis for this chapter. The answers tentatively offered here will be incomplete, because it is sometimes unclear how the questions can best be asked, and because the data available with which to address these questions are not wholly adequate. But the questions are important enough to make some tentative first steps seem necessary.

OVERVIEW OF THE STUDY

This chapter attempts to shed some light on explanations for involvement in coups d'état and related "revolutionary" acts in Latin America. We shall look at certain social background and career characteristics of persons who have held high government and party positions in seven Latin American countries, examining these variables as predictors of extralegal political activity. We will give special attention to the contrast between military and nonmilitary backgrounds and to the nature of political party affiliation, especially contrasting ideological and nonideological parties.

Some recent research suggests that career variables are better predictors of elite attitudes and behaviors than are social background characteristics.[10] More specific to Latin America, existing studies suggest that persons with military backgrounds and persons affiliated with ideologically oriented political parties have been disproportionately involved in coups d'état and other "revolutionary" political activities.[11] The implication is that the likelihood of involvement in these extralegal political activities is greater for persons with military backgrounds and-/or persons identified with ideological political parties. These generalizations have high face validity.

At the same time, most studies have not cast their explanations so as to account for *variance* in the dependent variable, involvement in extralegal political activity. Past studies usually have demonstrated *coincidence* (joint occurrence) but not *covariance* (joint patterns of occurrence and nonoccurrence). These studies have pointed out that, for example, military men are often involved in coups, but the research usually has not asked whether a military background *covaries* significantly with this kind of behavior, i.e., whether the military/nonmilitary career distinction is a useful predictor of the likelihood of involvement in coups. In other words, we must ask not only if many of the persons involved in extralegal political succession are military men or from ideological parties, but also whether nonmilitary individuals and persons from nonideological political organizations tend *not* to be involved in such behaviors. In short, if we learn that a given individual is or is not in the military—or is or is not a member of an ideological political party—how much do we improve our ability to predict accurately whether or not he is likely to engage in extralegal behavior? In a related sense, it is important to ascertain whether military background and affiliation with an ideological political party have independent predictive significance or whether they may be functions of other causative factors.

In this chapter we attempt to move toward formal, variance-based explanatory statements by examining the relative strength of a number of social background and career variables as predictors of involvement in coups d'état and related "revolutionary" activities. It seems important to distinguish between revolutionary behavior in general and involvement in coups d'état in particular. There is considerable doubt as to whether coups d'état constitute "revolutions" in any meaningful sense of that word. The issue has been joined frequently in literature on Latin American politics[12] and need not be explicated again here. Broadly, the argument frequently is made that Latin American coups often are merely means by which new musicians are brought in to play the same old tunes. In any case, it does seem important to distinguish between involvement in political behaviors that are not directed immediately toward the overthrow of a given group of political authorities, and attempted coups whose clear and expressed purpose is to unseat the political authorities in power.

In the research reported here the "revolutionary activities" variable includes essentially all extralegal involvements *not* directed toward the immediate overthrow of a government, e.g., leadership of or participation in general strikes, organized protests, sabotage, political assassinations, and organized street violence. It is reasonable to argue that those who engage in such activities usually have in mind social change substantially more "revolutionary" in nature than the changes envisioned by the perpetrators of coups. Participation in coups is defined broadly to include not only those persons directly involved in the attempts to seize power but also those who accept positions in governments formed immediately as a result of coups. This broad definition seems necessary because it is sometimes difficult to determine precisely who was involved in the coup itself. Moreover, persons who are close enough to the conspirators to move immediately into positions of political importance might well show similar regularities in background or experience to those who are directly involved in the seizure of power.

The independent variables in this study include urban/rural upbringing, age, amount and type of education, occupation, foreign travel and study, nature and number of nonparty organizational affiliations, type and level of government positions, type and level of political party activities, and nature of political party affiliation or identification. For reasons indicated above, we give particular attention to party affiliation and to the military/nonmilitary dimension of training and occupation.

The classification of political parties used in this analysis is three-dimensional.[13] The dimensions are ideological/pragmatic, traditional/-nontraditional, and liberal/conservative. The ideological/pragmatic dimension refers to the nature of the platform statements made by the political parties and the nature of the demands made by the parties upon their members or adherents. Political parties were coded according to the extent to which their platforms and appeals to adherents and supporters were stated in expressly doctrinal, abstract, value-based prescriptions. Those parties ranking high on this dimension were considered ideological; parties that were less doctrinal and did not make ideological demands on their adherents were coded as pragmatic. The traditional/nontraditional dimension refers to the nature of the issues stressed by these political parties. Traditional parties were ones that emphasized issues having to do with the questions that have structured much of the political activity in Latin America for more than a century, and that correspond to traditional social cleavages in these societies: landholding, social class structure, and the relationship between church and state. Nontraditional parties were ones that emphasized other issues that have emerged out of more contemporary political circumstances, including relations with the United States and the extent and distribution of social welfare. The liberal/conservative dimension refers to the substance of the parties' positions on domestic, economic, and social issues. Liberal parties in Latin America are those that tend to favor a greater measure of social welfare, greater redistribution of economic wealth, and greater state involvement in the ownership and/or regulation of productive enterprises. Conservative parties favor the status quo or less involvement in these policy areas.

The three party dimensions were grouped together to form an eight-category typology of political organizations. For purposes of analysis, however, the party dimensions were treated both conjointly and discretely; that is, the relationship of the party variable with the dependent variables of extralegal activity was examined using the three-dimensional classification as well as each of the three dichotomized dimensions. Thus we need to ask not only how well party affiliation as an eight-category polychotomy predicted, e.g., involvement in coups, but also whether there is a distinction between liberals and conservatives with respect to the likelihood of their involvement in coups.

Some brief elaboration of the categories into which the other predictor variables were divided may be helpful. In this study the occupation variable was dichotomized into military and nonmilitary categories. In distinguishing urban from rural origins, a population of 25,000 or more was considered to indicate an urban location. In the absence of evidence to the contrary, persons born in urban locations were assumed to have grown up there, and vice versa; however, where locale of upbringing was known to be different from place of birth, the former was used. The measures dealing with level of government and party activity were dichotomized into national and subnational categories. A person's "level of principal activity" was assumed to be that level of political activity at which he had spent the greatest amount of his time *prior* to entry into the subject population for this study, i.e., prior to assuming a cabinet-level government post or a national party position. The variable of type of government activity similarly refers to that activity in which the person spent most of his time before entry into the national elite; it was divided into categories of executive, legislative, and judicial careers. Type of party activity was divided into two categories: activities centering around the formulation of major lines of party policy and strategy (policy-making positions), and activities dealing with administrative, organizational, and mobilization functions (non-policy-making positions).

The variables describing the number and nature of an elite's *non-party* organizational affiliations (e.g., labor organizations, other professional groups, cultural-educational groups) turned out to be especially important in this study. A good deal more will be said in this chapter about how these variables were handled; however, an initial general comment is in order. There is no doubt that many organizational affiliations of Latin American elites are not reported in the sources used in this study. More than half of our subjects are not known to have had formal nonparty organizational affiliations; this does not seem likely. It is probable that the data we used included information only on organizational affiliations for which an elite's involvement was significant. For convenience, we refer to persons who have "no" formal nonparty affiliations. You should translate this shorthand as indicating a person not having formal nonparty affiliations important enough to be self-reported, or reported in the many secondary sources used in gathering these data.

The parent data collection on which the analysis is based includes 46 variables describing 1,347 persons who held high political office in one of seven Latin American countries between 1935 and 1960. The countries are Argentina, Bolivia, Brazil, Ecuador, Mexico, Paraguay, and Uruguay. The political positions used as a basis for defining the population were cabinet-level positions in the executive branch of government and formal offices at the national level in political parties with parliamentary representation.[14]

As we would expect in a study using data gathered largely from secondary sources, the level of missing data is relatively high; that is, we do not have a complete set of biographical data for every elite being studied. In addition, conservative procedures have been used for excluding cases.[15] As a result, some of our analyses include only about two-thirds of the executive and party elites who held office in the seven countries for the period 1935–1960. For purposes of analysis the 25-year period covered by the study is divided into two segments, 1935–1950 ($N = 564$) and 1951–1960 ($N = 332$). The time span was divided in this way because of the general agreement in the literature on Latin American politics that the 1935–1950 period was substantially different from the later period because of the effects of the worldwide economic depression and of World War II. The use of 1950/1951 as the dividing point for the two periods was arbitrary. This time point coincides with government changes in only a few of the countries, but the use of a common cutting point provides at least some measure of temporal comparability for the data.

In addition to simple bivariate cross-classifications (i.e., cross-tabulations of two variables), the data analysis involves Multiple Classification Analysis (MCA).[16] MCA is an analogue of multiple regression analysis. Such techniques serve two purposes. First, they permit us to determine the extent to which the values of a dependent variable (in our case, extralegal political activity) can be predicted accurately from a knowledge of the values of a set of independent ("predictor") variables. In effect, this is an indication of the extent to which the incidence of the dependent variable is *dependent* on the co-incidence of a certain set of causal factors. We speak of this relationship in terms of *accounting for variance* in the dependent variable, and represent this "explained" variance with the notation R^2. Second, these techniques identify the *independent* contribution made by *each* predictor variable to an understanding of the variance in the dependent variable. That is, the effect of each independent variable on the dependent variable is ascertained, *controlling for the effects of all other independent variables—* as if the other predictor variables were not present. Thus MCA provides an indication of both the collective strength of the predictor variables in accounting for variance in the dependent variable, and the independent contribution made by each predictor variable when controlling for the effects of the other predictors.

EXPLAINING REVOLUTIONARY BEHAVIOR

One category of political behavior we are interested in understanding is what we have called "revolutionary behavior." This variable includes all antiregime or antigovernment behavior other than participation in coups d'état or guerrilla warfare. Revolutionary behavior includes such things as political assassinations, civil violence, and participation in general strikes and public protest. Revolutionary behavior is behavior of political opposition, but it is not immediately or directly aimed at the extralegal overthrow of any given group of political authorities.

We discover that about two-thirds of the variance in revolutionary behavior is accounted for by the 13 independent variables used in this study. Consequently, we should entertain some doubts about the conventional notion that such behavior is unpatterned and, therefore, unpredictable. The R^2 (the amount of variance in revolutionary behavior accounted for by the independent variables) from the MCA run is .60 for the full 25-year period and even higher, .74, for the period 1951–1960. Party affiliation has an ambiguous and apparently changing *simple (bivariate)* relationship with revolutionary behavior. There is a consistently strong positive *bivariate* relationship between a military background and participation in revolutionary acts. Significantly, however, the simple bivariate relationships between military background and party affiliation, on the one hand, and revolutionary behavior, on the other, nearly disappear in the *multivariate* analysis. Indeed, in the MCA, variables having to do with the nature and extent of a person's affiliation with nonparty organizations appear as the best predictors of an inclination toward revolutionary behavior for elites in Latin America. The remainder of this section is devoted to elaborating and explaining these findings.

Because of the widespread common belief in the significance of military background and of affiliation with ideological political parties for an understanding of revolutionary behavior, it seems appropriate to begin with a look at the bivariate ties between these variables and revolutionary behavior. Table 5–1 shows a significant association between a military background and participation in revolutionary acts. (Cross-tabulations for the temporal segments, 1935–1950 and 1951–1960, are not presented here; the relationship is equally significant in both time periods.) Some 26 percent of the military men engaged in revolutionary activity, as compared with 5 percent of the nonmilitary elites. More than half of the "revolutionaries" under study were military men. Consequently, when we examine only the two-way relationship between a military background and revolutionary behavior, the relationship seems positive and strong.

TABLE 5–1. Revolutionary Activity by Occupation (Military/Nonmilitary) (1935–1960)

	Revolutionary Activity							
	No			Yes			Total	
Occupation	N	Column %	Row %	N	Column %	Row %	N	Column %
Nonmilitary	708	(86)	(95)	35	(47)	(05)	743	(83)
Military	113	(14)	(74)	40	(53)	(26)	153	(17)
Total	821	(100)	(92)	75	(100)	(08)	896	(100)
			$X^2 = 73.22; p < .001$					

TABLE 5-2. Revolutionary Activity by Party Affiliation (Pragmatic/Ideological Dimension) (1935-1960)

Party Affiliation	No			Yes			Total	
	N	Column %	Row %	N	Column %	Row %	Fre-quency	Column %
Pragmatic	356	(58)	(95)	18	(26)	(05)	374	(55)
Ideological	255	(42)	(84)	50	(74)	(16)	305	(45)
Total	611	(100)	(90)	68	(100)	(10)	679[a]	(100)

$X^2 = 23.732; p < .001$

[a]217 of the 896 persons on which this analysis focuses had no known political party affiliation.

Table 5-2 conveys a similar picture with regard to the relationship between membership in ideological political parties and revolutionary behavior. The bivariate relationship is strong; 16 percent of the members of ideological parties had engaged in revolutionary behavior, as compared with 5 percent of the members of pragmatic parties. Further, 74 percent of the elites who engaged in revolutionary behavior were members of ideological parties. The cross-tabulations for the two time segments show that the relationship between ideological party affiliation and revolutionary behavior declines in strength in the 1951–1960 period, but is statistically significant in both periods.

Given the thrust of conventional wisdom about Latin American politics, these findings linking military background and ideological party affiliation with revolutionary behavior are expected and comfortable. However, the picture is very different when we look at the results of the MCA, presented in table 5-3. There we discover that party affiliation performs poorly as a predictor of revolutionary behavior, explaining less than 1 percent of the variance. The military/nonmilitary distinction (occupation) performs little better, explaining at best a little more than 2 percent of the variance (for the 1935–1950 time period). In light of the fact that the overall proportion of explained variance in revolutionary behavior is relatively high, the statistical unimportance of these two independent variables is particularly striking.

The two variables that account for an overwhelming proportion of the variance in revolutionary behavior have to do with the nature and extent of an elite's affiliation with nonparty organizations. The organizational affiliations of our subjects can be divided into four categories:

TABLE 5-3. Strength of Predictors of Revolutionary Activity (Multiple Classification Analysis)

Predictor	1935–1960 (N = 896) R^2 = .6030 % of Total Variance	Rank	1935–1950 (N = 564) R^2 = .5776 % of Total Variance	Rank	1951–1960 (N = 332) R^2 = .7363 % of Total Variance	Rank
1. Number of nonparty organizational affiliations	24.55	1	9.23	2	34.65	1
2. Nature of nonparty organizational affiliations	17.51	2	22.53	1	28.55	2
3. Foreign study (number of instances)	4.46	3	4.79	4	0.49	8
4. Foreign travel (number of instances)	4.10	4	2.36	7.5	2.91	4
5. Level of party activity	2.59	5	4.65	5	0.25	10
6. Level of positions held in nonparty organizations	2.30	6	4.86	3	1.25	5
7. Occupation (military/nonmilitary)	1.51	7	2.36	7.5	0.11	13
8. Level of formal education	1.30	8	1.86	9	0.90	6
9. Population of birthplace (urban/rural origins)	1.15	9	2.58	6	0.35	9
10. Party affiliation	0.65	10	0.62	11	0.22	11
11. Level of government activity	0.11	11	0.54	12	0.18	12
12. Type of government career	0.07	12	0.52	13	0.53	7
13. Type of party career	—	13	0.86	10	3.21	3

"organizational marginality" (which describes persons who have no known formal nonparty organizational memberships), professional associations, intellectual/cultural/educational groups, and political agitation groups. This last category includes nonparty groups whose declared purpose is to engage in militant political activity in an attempt to influence government policy. In our analysis, we examined both this *qualitative* variable—nature of nonparty organizational affiliations— and a *quantitative* variable: number of formal nonparty organizational affiliations held.[17]

For the full 25-year period and for 1951–1960, the *number* of nonparty organizational affiliations is the most powerful predictor of revolutionary behavior. Table 5–4 shows the bivariate relationship between number of nonparty organizational affiliations and revolutionary behavior. It appears as if persons with "few" (as opposed to none or "many") nonparty organizational memberships constitute an especially "revolutionary" subset of these Latin American elites. A comment about the initial distribution and subsequent recoding of this variable may help in interpreting table 5–4. The initial distribution of values was trimodal; the three categories in table 5–4 reflect these modes. Many of these elites had no known formal nonparty organizational affiliations; a second mode was at two affiliations; the third mode was much higher at seven affiliations. It was consequently decided to divide the number of affiliations into three categories: none, few (one–three), and many (four or more). The recoding of this variable thus reflects the modes of the initial distribution.

TABLE 5–4. Revolutionary Activity by Number of Nonparty Organizational Affiliations (1935–1960)

	Revolutionary Activity							
	No			Yes			Total	
Number of Affiliations	N	Column %	Row %	N	Column %	Row %	N	Column %
None	546	(67)	(91)	51	(68)	(09)	597	(67)
Few (1–3)	83	(10)	(86)	13	(17)	(14)	96	(10)
Many (4 or more)	192	(23)	(95)	11	(15)	(05)	203	(23)
Total	821	(100)	(92)	75	(100)	(08)	896	(100)

$$X^2 = 5.68; p < .10$$

TABLE 5-5. Revolutionary Activity by Nature of Principal Nonparty Organizational Affiliations (1935-1960)

Nature of Principal Affiliations	Revolutionary Activity							
	No			Yes			Total	
	N	Column %	Row %	N	Column %	Row %	N	Column %
None	546	(67)	(91)	51	(68)	(09)	597	(67)
Professional associations	174	(21)	(94)	11	(15)	(06)	185	(21)
Intellectual/cultural/ educational	88	(11)	(94)	6	(08)	(06)	94	(10)
Political agitation	13	(01)	(65)	7	(09)	(35)	20	(02)
Total	821	(100)	(92)	75	(100)	(08)	896	(100)

$$X^2 = 20.15; p < .001$$

We discover in table 5-4 that elites with few nonparty organizational affiliations (one-three) are more likely to engage in revolutionary behaviors than are elites having either no or many nonparty organizational affiliations. The majority of persons with records of revolutionary behavior had no nonparty organizational affiliations; however, the population under study includes more persons without nonparty organizational affiliations than persons in either of the other two categories. The *row percentages* in table 5-4 are the important ones: The probability of engaging in revolutionary behavior is distinctly higher among the group represented in row two (few nonparty organizational affiliations) than it is for the elites represented in the other two rows in the table.[18] The relationship is especially strong for the period 1935-1950.

The second most important predictor of revolutionary behavior was *nature* of nonparty organizational affiliation. The bivariate relationship between nature of affiliation and revolutionary activity is shown in table 5-5. A look at table 5-5 may help in the interpretation of table 5-4 as well. Keeping in mind that nonaffiliation is a category of both variables, we can use these two tables to understand the two overlapping dimensions of nonparty organizational affiliation.

There seems to be a distinct relationship between the types of nonparty organizational affiliation held by Latin American political elites and their likelihood of being involved in revolutionary activities. Specifically, members of political agitation groups are especially likely to engage in revolutionary activity. The best predictor of militant political protest is membership in nonparty organizations whose aims and orientation are consistent with this sort of protest behavior. Again, the largest single subgroup among our "revolutionaries" consists of persons who have no nonparty organizational affiliations. However, it is among those having affiliations with political agitation groups that the *probability* of revolutionary behavior is highest.[19] Some 35 percent of the members of political agitation groups engaged in revolutionary acts; the percentage was 9 among those with no affiliations, 6 among members of intellectual and related organizations, and 6 among members of professional associations.

At this point we can attempt a summary statement about the most important predictors of revolutionary activity among Latin American political elites. It appears as if the likelihood of revolutionary behavior can be traced to two distinct forms of what might be called "elite marginality." One form is represented by the decision to join organizations devoted to militant political protest. The second consists of a decision to join few nonparty organizations—a decision that might be considered unusual for a person who occupies, or hopes to occupy, a position of societal importance. This elite marginality hypothesis is reinforced by the finding that persons who belong to a *large* number of organizations are disinclined toward revolutionary behavior; only 5 percent of the subjects with many (four or more) nonparty affiliations engaged in revolutionary activity, as compared to 14 percent of the persons with few affiliations and 9 percent of those with no affiliations.

This elite marginality hypothesis might seem uninteresting, perhaps even tautological, but it is neither trivial nor self-obvious. Much of what has been written about Latin American politics suggests that revolutionary behavior has become essentially institutionalized, in considerable part because it has been integrated into the functions of established societal institutions such as the military and ideologically oriented political parties. The data we are examining in this chapter do not support this conventional explanation for the occurrence of revolutionary behavior among Latin American political elites. Rather, they suggest that the best predictors of revolutionary behavior in Latin America are similar to what one would expect to find in societies in which this sort of behavior is not thought to be so substantially institutionalized—namely, either limited organizational links with the political "establishment" or membership in organizations expressly committed to strategies of political agitation. To repeat: Neither military background nor membership in an ideological political party is a useful component of a multivariate model predicting revolutionary behavior among Latin American political elites. If we wish to maximize our ability to predict the likelihood of revolutionary behavior among these elites, we should inquire about the nature and extent of their nonparty organizational affiliations.

Because this finding seems somewhat inconsistent with conventional writing about Latin American politics, we should explain the apparent anomaly in our analysis: How can the bivariate relationships between ideological party affiliation and military background, on the one hand, and revolutionary behavior, on the other, be so strong when the multivariate relationships are so weak? In answering this question we can refine and elaborate our findings concerning the predictors of revolutionary behavior. One of the virtues of multivariate data analysis is that more systematic bases for causal inferences can be provided by determining the extent to which any given variable contributes to explaining variance in a dependent variable *when the effects of other variables are held constant.* When we control for the effects of other variables, the relationships of military background and ideological party affiliation with revolutionary activity decline dramatically. Therefore, these two variables must somehow reflect other, more genuinely causative factors that increase the likelihood of revolutionary behavior. An examination of the bivariate relationships between military background and ideological party affiliation, and of some of the independent variables that emerged as more powerful predictors of revolutionary behavior in the MCA runs, shows this to be the case.

The prototypic, politically active military man in Latin America is a composite of several background and career factors that are positively related to revolutionary behavior. Similarly, *the prototypic member of an ideologically oriented political party in Latin America reflects most of these same characteristics.* It is because military men and members of ideological parties reflect a *composite* of revolution-related personal characteristics more faithfully than any other occupational or functional group that these two groups are disproportionately represented among revolutionaries. The relationships with revolutionary behavior, therefore, derive not from any intrinsic characteristics of the military or of ideological parties as such, but rather from the *agglomeration* of characteristics exhibited by a substantial proportion of their members.

Some specifics will illustrate the argument. As we have just seen, the nature and extent of nonparty organizational affiliations are the best predictors of revolutionary behavior. First, our data show that Latin American military men are underrepresented among the political elites who have substantial nonparty organizational ties in society. Many military men have no known organizational affiliations; those who do belong to organizations tend to belong to only one or two. Thus the overall extent of organizational ties of military men is identifiably lower than that for any of the other occupational groupings examined in this study. Second, there is a positive relationship between rural or small-town origins and revolutionary behavior; our politically active military elites tended to be from small towns or the countryside. Third, elites with less formal education were substantially more inclined than their better-educated counterparts to engage in revolutionary behavior; military men tended to have less formal education than other political elites. Fourth, experiences of study abroad and foreign travel are positively related to revolutionary behavior; the military elites were far more likely to have records of foreign study and foreign travel than the other occupational groupings among the elites studied.

Much the same pattern holds with respect to the characteristics of members of ideologically oriented political parties. First, their members were less likely to have a large number of organizational ties than were members of pragmatic parties. Second, ideological political parties were disproportionately represented among the members of political agitation groups. Third, members of ideological parties were more likely to be from rural areas and, fourth, to have less formal education than members of pragmatic parties. Thus a focus on the immediately visible institutional identifications of these elites may tend to obscure more meaningful explanations for their behavior. It is not so much that military men or political ideologues are "revolutionary" because of their military status or ideological postures; the more important consideration is that these persons tend to exhibit many of the background and career characteristics that seem to contribute to revolutionary behavior.

We should not be too quick, however, to dismiss the importance of the study of ideological political parties or of the military as political institutions in Latin America. These two institutions may provide *frameworks* through which the militant political protest behavior we have been discussing can be manifested. We should entertain the possibility that the existence of such organizations is a *necessary*, but not *sufficient*, condition for the relatively widespread incidence of revolutionary activity in these societies. Such behaviors can best be explained, as our analysis seems to show, with reference to certain elements of the backgrounds and political orientations of people who join the military or who affiliate with ideological parties. The institutions themselves may provide vehicles for the expression of the inclinations held by these persons. Further, it is likely that the nature of the institutions influences the sort of person who is recruited or coopted into membership. Our analysis suggests that revolutionary behavior among political elites in Latin America must be described primarily in terms of the elites' background characteristics, early career experiences, and organizational affiliations, rather than in terms of the characteristics of the institutions with which they tend to be affiliated. At the same time, the characteristics of the institutions may be important in catalyzing this amalgam of background and career elements into concrete political protest behavior.

One other aspect of the relationships among institutional affiliation, career experiences, and revolutionary behavior should be given further attention here. This has to do with the relationships among military background, foreign travel, and foreign study. The relationship between each of these three predictor variables and revolutionary behavior is positive and significant. However, if we remove all military elites from the two-way cross-classifications between foreign study and revolutionary activity, and between foreign travel and revolutionary activity, the relationships disappear. Thus it appears as if military background *interacts* with foreign exposure in producing revolutionary behavior; military men with foreign exposure are a particularly revolutionary subset of the military elites. Most of our military elites, especially those who were abroad between 1935 and 1945, studied in Germany and/or the United States, primarily the former. It is tempting to infer that exposure to the particular brand of revolutionism and militarism present in Germany during this period had an influence on the subsequent behavior of these elites, but there is no way of verifying from our data whether these experiences actually contributed. However, this line of reasoning does suggest the importance of examining more carefully the potentially catalytic effect of foreign exposure on the political perspectives of military elites in Latin America.

EXPLAINING INVOLVEMENT IN COUPS D'ÉTAT

In the previous section we focused on what we called revolutionary behavior—militant protest activity designed to effect major changes in public policy but not meant to unseat particular sets of political authorities. Thus coups d'état were not included in the category of revolutionary behavior. Since a great deal has been made of the significance of the coup d'état as a means of leadership change in Latin America, and because there is considerable debate about whether this behavior should be classified in the same category as other forms of political protest and/or revolution, it is appropriate that we give separate attention to involvement in coups.

Again let us begin by entertaining the two "conventional" hypotheses: (1) that military elites are substantially more inclined than are nonmilitary elites to participate in coups; and (2) that membership in

TABLE 5-6. Involvement in Coups d'État by Occupation (Military/Nonmilitary) (1935-1960)

| | Involvement in Coups | | | | | | | |
| | No | | | Yes | | | Total | |
Occupation	N	Column %	Row %	N	Column %	Row %	N	Column %
Nonmilitary	652	(85)	(88)	91	(71)	(12)	743	(83)
Military	115	(15)	(75)	38	(29)	(25)	153	(17)
Total	767	(100)	(86)	129	(100)	(14)	896	(100)

$$X^2 = 15.309; p < .001$$

ideologically oriented political parties is associated with participation in coups. Table 5-6 shows that there is a significant relationship between a military background and involvement in coups. (The relationship holds more strongly for 1951-1960 than for the earlier period, but is significant in both periods.) The relationship between party affiliation and involvement in coups is more ambiguous. Surprisingly, we discover that for the full 25-year period members of pragmatic political parties are more likely to be involved in coups than are members of ideological parties. Table 5-7 shows that the relationship between party affiliation and involvement in coups is quite strong for both time periods, but that the relationship is reversed between the two periods. During 1935-1950 members of pragmatic parties were more likely than were members of ideological parties to be involved in coups, whereas during 1951-1960 members of ideological parties were substantially more likely than were their pragmatic counterparts to have attempted extralegal accession.

The explanation for this temporal reversal of the relationship between party affiliation and involvement in coups d'état is not clear from the data being examined here. One possibility might have been that the change was associated with another dimension of the political party classification—the conservative-liberal distinction. Given the respective prevailing ideological climates in the seven countries under study in the two time periods, one might have hypothesized that coups during the late 1930s and early 1940s were carried out primarily by conservative pragmatic political groups, whereas coups during the 1950s were associated increasingly with more liberal political parties. However, when we divide the political parties into conservative and liberal categories, and cross-tabulate these two categories with involvement in

TABLE 5–7. Involvement in Coups d'État by Party Affiliation (Pragmatic/Ideological Dimension) for Periods 1935–1950 and 1951–1960

Involvement in Coups

	1935–1950								1951–1960							
	No			Yes			Total		No			Yes			Total	
Party Affiliation	N	Column %	Row %	N	Column %	Row %	N	Column %	N	Column %	Row %	N	Column %	Row %	N	Column %
Pragmatic	216	(55)	(77)	64	(82)	(23)	280	(59)	84	(49)	(91)	8	(22)	(09)	92	(44)
Ideological	177	(45)	(93)	14	(18)	(18)	191	(41)	89	(51)	(76)	28	(78)	(24)	117	(56)
Total	393	(100)	(83)	78	(100)	(17)	471[a]	(100)	173	(100)	(83)	36	(100)	(17)	209[a]	(100)

$X^2 = 18.71; p < .001$ $X^2 = 7.35; p < .01$

[a] 261 of the 896 persons on which this analysis focuses had no known party affiliation.

coups, there is no noticeable relationship in either time period. Consequently, this finding must remain unexplained with reference to the data used in this study.

The results of the MCA done in an effort to predict involvement in coups d'état are equally ambiguous and somewhat discouraging. The MCA results are discouraging not only because military background and party affiliation are not the best predictors of the dependent variable, but also because the amount of variance in involvement in coups accounted for over the 25-year period, and for the period 1935–1950, is so small. As indicated in table 5–8, foreign study emerges as the most powerful predictor of involvement in coups over the 25-year period. However, it accounts for only a very small part (3.55 percent) of the total variance. All of the predictor variables together account for only 17.3 percent of the variance for the 25-year period.

It is worth examining the MCA solution for the period 1951–1960, since here the proportion of variance accounted for (41.63 percent) is respectable.[20] This information also is contained in table 5–8. The explanatory pattern is not unfamiliar; the second and third strongest predictors are the two nonparty organizational affiliation variables. They have the same kind of relationship with involvement in coups d'état as they had with revolutionary behavior; involvement in coups seems to be associated with either: (1) a small number of organizational affiliations, including membership in political agitation groups; or (2) an absence of nonparty organizational ties.

The best predictor (accounting for 10.2 percent of the variance) of involvement in coups between 1951 and 1960 is level of formal education. Education apparently has an impact on involvement in coups different from its effect on revolutionary behavior. *Revolutionary behavior is engaged in by less-educated elites; coups d'état are participated in by better-educated elites.* In this connection, it is also worth noting that urban-born elites were somewhat more likely to be involved in coups than to engage in other types of revolutionary behavior. Thus many coups in Latin America have been carried out by better-educated, urban elites. In contrast, less-educated, rural elites were predominant among those who engaged in revolutionary behavior. This difference highlights the importance of drawing distinctions between coups and other revolutionary acts; it also suggests that we should examine the relationship between revolutionary behavior and involvement in coups for the subjects in our study.

Table 5–9 shows that there is a significant association between revolutionary activity and participation in coups d'état. However, this statistic may be misleading. Nearly three-fourths of the persons who engaged in revolutionary activity were never involved in a coup d'état, and only

TABLE 5-8. Strength of Predictors of Involvement in Coups d'État (Multiple Classification Analysis)

Predictor	1935–1960 (N = 896) R² = .1730 % of Total Variance	Rank	1935–1950 (N = 564) R² = .2345 % of Total Variance	Rank	1951–1960 (N = 332) R² = .4163 % of Total Variance	Rank
1. Foreign study (number of instances)	3.55	1	2.39	5	1.57	11
2. Population of birthplace (urban/rural origins)	2.99	2	3.44	2	3.61	4
3. Occupation (military/nonmilitary)	1.80	3	2.50	4	1.61	10
4. Level of formal education	1.66	4	1.28	9	10.20	1
5. Nature of nonparty organizational affiliations	1.61	5	2.05	6	5.07	2
6. Level of positions held in nonparty organizations	1.33	6	1.50	7.5	2.54	8
7. Number of nonparty organizational affiliations	1.10	7	3.33	3	4.91	3
8. Party affiliation	0.90	8	3.55	1	3.02	7
9. Type of government career	0.71	9.5	0.94	10	3.10	6
10. Foreign travel (number of instances)	0.71	9.5	1.50	7.5	1.73	9
11. Level of government activity	0.66	11	0.12	13	3.46	5
12. Type of party career	0.14	12.5	0.18	12	0.81	12
13. Level of party activity	0.14	12.5	0.67	11	—	13

TABLE 5–9.   Involvement in Coups d'État by Revolutionary Activities (1935–1960)

Revolutionary Activity	Involvement in Coups						Total	
	No			Yes				
	N	Column %	Row %	N	Column %	Row %	N	Column %
No	712	(93)	(87)	109	(84)	(13)	821	(92)
Yes	55	(07)	(73)	20	(16)	(27)	75	(08)
Total	767	(100)	(86)	129	(100)	(14)	896	(100)

$$X^2 = 8.94; p < .01$$

16 percent of the persons involved in coups had any previous record of revolutionary behavior. Thus, while there is statistical interdependence between the two behaviors among the elites we are studying, only a relatively small proportion of these elites engaged in both behaviors. Of the 184 persons who were involved in revolutionary activity and/or coups d'état, only 20 (11 percent) were involved in both. The implication of this finding is clear. There are distinct differences in the backgrounds of Latin Americans who have participated in coups, and those who have been involved in other revolutionary acts. This constitutes an additional reason for studying these two categories of behavior separately.

ELITES AND REVOLUTION IN LATIN AMERICA

The data examined in this study suggest several important, but tentative, conclusions about the characteristics of political elites and political leadership in Latin America. First, our findings are not consistent with the notion that recent career experiences and political positions are better predictors of elite attitudes and behaviors than are social background characteristics. In fact, in some respects the analysis presented in this chapter implies the opposite: that basic social background characteristics such as urban or rural origins, level of formal education, and extent of study and travel in foreign countries are among the major predictors of inclinations toward revolutionary political behaviors on the part of Latin American political elites.

Second, our findings raise doubts concerning the conventionally assumed significance of military affiliation and identification with an ideologically oriented political party for involvement in revolutionary activity. Although there are simple bivariate links between these two variables and revolutionary behavior, the bivariate relationships disappear in the multivariate analysis. We have argued that the apparent relationships linking a military background and ideological party affiliation with revolutionary behavior probably were due to the fact that members of these two types of institution tended to represent a kind of prototypic amalgam of background characteristics associated with revolutionary activity. The question of whether the military and ideological political parties may be necessary, but not sufficient, transmission belts that catalyze, mold, and implement the inclinations of their members toward revolutionary political behavior cannot be answered with the biographic data we have examined. What is needed is more detailed data on the internal functioning of these institutions, perhaps especially their recruitment/cooptation processes. Such research seems critical to an understanding of revolutionary behavior in Latin America.

Third, in some respects the research reported here suggests a basis for disenchantment with *both* social background *and* career variables as predictors of elite behavior. The most important predictors of involvement in revolutionary activities were variables describing the nature and extent of nonparty organizational affiliations. These kinds of organization affiliations have thus far been given inadequate attention by students of elite attitudes and behaviors. In this chapter we have interpreted these two variables as indicators of *elite marginality*. The finding that elites with no formal nonparty organizational ties, or with ties primarily with political agitation groups, are most likely to engage in revolutionary behavior suggests the need of more systematic efforts to make concepts of elite marginality functional. Most of the social background factors found to be positively related to revolutionary behavior also were related to the organizational affiliation variables.

Fourth, the data presented in this chapter underscore the importance of maintaining a distinction between coups d'état and other forms of revolutionary activity. Our biographic data predicted behavior other than involvement in coups much better than involvement in coups. Moreover, the overlap between these two types of behavior was less than might have been expected; relatively few elites were involved in both coups and revolutionary acts. The important predictor variables were somewhat different for the two types of revolutionary activity. For example, the organizational affiliation variables were less important in predicting involvement in coups than in accounting for other forms of revolutionary behavior. Level of formal education and some other social background variables were relatively more important for explaining involvement in coups.

   The differences in the adequacy of our multivariate model for predicting revolutionary behavior and involvement in coups d'état have
implications for future research on the antecedents of coups in Latin
America. When variance in individual behaviors cannot be accounted
for by reference to individual or other within-system factors, we may
need to consider possible causal factors at the system level. Given the
fact that biographic data on individuals generally were unsuccessful in
predicting involvement in coups, it is likely that system-level variables
may be affecting the incidence of coups. Whereas a reasonable part of
the variance in revolutionary behavior can be accounted for by individ-
ual-level characteristics, involvement in coups probably requires an
explanatory model incorporating system-level variables.
   Finally, the findings presented in this chapter suggest the importance
of giving careful attention to possible differences between processes of
elite and mass socialization in Latin America. Our data provide a basis
for inferring a relationship between less-educated, rural/small-town
origins and what we have called revolutionary behavior. Some of these
revolutionary acts are illegal or extralegal (e.g., assassination, leading
general strikes), while others call for fundamental social changes
through legal means. Coups, on the other hand, tend to involve better-
educated persons from urban locations. Although it is debatable
whether coups are institutionalized forms of political succession in
Latin America—and we can assume that this might differ from country
to country—it is clear that coups are not sanctioned in any formal, legal
sense. The question of whether formal education or characteristics of
the social setting (e.g., the urban-rural distinction) are accompanied by
distinct patterns of socialization is a vital one. Similarly, there may be
important differences in the nature of socialization factors affecting
persons in different social-class environments. It may well be that varying values and attitudes toward revolutionary activity are related to
differences in socialization processes. To date, little such socialization
research on Latin America has been done.
   There are numerous respects in which the analysis in this chapter is
flawed and consequently must be qualified. First, the seven countries
on which this study focuses were chosen on the basis of their contrasting
levels and rates of economic development, not with any thought of
controlling for differences among their political systems. Consequently,
it has not been possible to examine the relevance of system-level variables for individual behaviors taking place within those systems. Further, the generalizations from this study might not hold for Latin
American political systems on the whole. Second, the missing-data
problem in this study is substantial; this probably is inevitable when
research covering a considerable time period is done largely from sec-

ondary sources. In addition, the subjects on whom data were gathered were selected because of their political positions, not their political behaviors. Thus the data are not focused on persons who engaged in revolutionary or extralegal behaviors; rather, they deal with a set of political elites, positionally defined. It is possible that different explanations for involvement in revolutionary activities might emerge if a sample of *nonelite* "revolutionaries" were included.[21] Generalizations from the study presented here must be limited to political elites.

Finally, it must be recognized that this kind of research only brings us to the point of being able to ask a number of important questions. Answers to most of them will require both systematic attitudinal data and careful analyses of societal institutions. Our evidence has suggested linkages between certain background characteristics and both aspects of organizational involvement and inclinations toward involvement in revolutionary and/or extralegal political behavior. The data have suggested that the two factors often cited in explaining these political behaviors—a military background and ideological party affiliation— may have less independent explanatory significance than generally has been assumed. We still must try to determine, however, the nature of the crucial *attitudinal* and *institutional channels* through which background and career influences are—or are not—translated into political behavior. Why is it, for example, that foreign study seems to have such a strong, catalytic effect on the inclination of military men to participate in coups? How, if at all, do political socialization processes differ between urban and rural settings? To what extent are institutions such as the military critical to the *expression* of inclinations toward revolutionary behavior? Is military recruitment enhanced by a perceived opportunity to use military institutions to work around constitutional limitations in gaining access to, and the use of, political power?

We might be inclined to guess ("infer" is the more dignified term) about some of these questions, but even "educated" guesses in the absence of attitudinal data seem likely to do more harm than good. This is especially true in an area of research in which the temptation to "explain" in the absence of systematic data has been—understandably —great in the past. It seems more appropriate to stress the importance of seeking attitudinal data on Latin American political elites so that more meaningful explanations of these important background/career/ organizational affiliation/attitude/behavior relationships can be achieved.

6

Patterns of Change in Political Leadership in Socialist Systems

The study of political elites and political leadership is especially important in the case of highly structured systems. Because of the nature of these systems, the impact of elite decisions and behaviors is broader in scope (touching most areas of human activity) and is transmitted more directly to affect the lives of individuals (because of the absence of significant intermediate or buffer institutions)[1] than is the case with transitional or pluralist systems. More formally, we can say that elite actions account for a higher proportion of variance in public policy outcomes in highly structured systems than in the other two system categories. Consequently, it is particularly vital that we give careful attention to the characteristics of political leadership and elites in these societies.

In this chapter we look at some of the most important changes that have taken place in the last three decades in the characteristics of elites and leadership in socialist systems. Our focus is primarily on the societies governed by Communist parties in Eastern Europe, including the Soviet Union. We give some attention to political leadership in China as well, especially insofar as the Chinese case deviates from the European socialist pattern.

There seems little doubt that important changes have taken place in the elites and leadership of these political systems in recent years. For many Westerners, the most visible kinds of change have occurred in foreign policy, especially in two areas: (1) the attitudes taken by Communist party leaders toward the United States and other Western nations; and (2) the emergence of genuine and serious disagreements among communist-governed states, especially among the Soviet Union,

China, and Yugoslavia. However, these more visible changes in inter-state and interparty relations appear to result from more fundamental changes observable in internal political circumstances in these societies. These internal changes are observable both in relations among political elites and in relations between elite groups and the broader social system of which they are a part.

These two sets of changes are consistent with one another; it is argua-ble which is the antecedent and which the result—or if both sets of changes may be products of other factors. Many writers, for example, have argued that these changes in political leadership in socialist sys-tems may be traced to one of two kinds of consideration: first, the inevitable pressures toward pragmatism, flexibility, and regard for tech-nical and managerial expertise created by economic and social modern-ization; or second, the conscious grouping of political leadership groups for more effective and efficient means of governance, i.e., the desire to retain cohesive, hierarchical power structures in the face of increasing pressures of a disintegrative and pluralistic character. We shall not attempt to resolve the question of the origins from which these changes in elite characteristics and leadership have emerged; with the evidence we now have at hand, such resolution is probably impossible in any case. More important for our purposes are the *implications* of these changes for the changing character of socialist societies.

In this chapter we shall view changes in political elites as part of three intertwined developments that are frequently asserted to be taking place in socialist systems, especially those in Europe. The first of these has been labeled the emergence of "technocracy" as a type of political leadership system. The second, related trend is toward the bureaucrati-zation and routinization of both intraelite relations and relations be-tween elites and mass. And third, there has been the ever more noticeable transmutation of unstructured and highly intense conflict, especially among elites and potential elites, into forms of political com-petition similar to the kinds observable in pluralist systems. We shall discuss each of these three trends, emphasizing the first, since the coming of "technocracy" may be the key to the permanence of the other two changes. A common thread running throughout this discus-sion will be a concern with changing career patterns within the political elite and how these aggregate career changes are affecting the nature of political leadership.

THE EMERGENCE OF "TECHNOCRACY"

The argument is by now familiar that the European communist sys-tems are moving increasingly toward a new form of political organiza-tion that is technocratic in nature. The changes usually are asserted to stem from the belief that problems of management and governance in industrializing, increasingly modern, and socially complex societies demand technical expertise as well as functional specialization within the political elite. In general, these required changes in the backgrounds and perspectives of those who govern mean that the traditional ideologically based system of elite recruitment, and of elite decision making, must be significantly modified in the direction of greater pragmatism and flexibility.

More specifically, three implications of the move toward technocracy are frequently sketched: (1) increasing use of "rational-technical" criteria in the selection of political elites; (2) a decline in the prescriptive importance of ideological considerations in decision making, and an accompanying change in the role of ideology in the direction of after-the-fact rationalization; and (3) the emergence of a new category of governing elite, usually referred to as a "managerial class" or "technocratic class." We return later in this chapter to the question of the extent to which these implications actually follow from changes in elite career patterns in these societies. At this point, our emphasis is that if such changes are indeed taking place, they imply some fundamental alterations over time in the nature of these highly structured systems.

The evidence is persuasive that the career patterns of communist elites, especially the mechanisms by which they are selected, are changing. Studies of the Soviet Union, the German Democratic Republic, and especially Yugoslavia, for example, seem to demonstrate that technical training and managerial expertise are increasingly important criteria for the selection of elites. According to West German political sociologist Peter Ludz, East Germany has seen a shift from a regime emphasis on political control to an emphasis on economic modernization. This has required the cooptation into the elite of a relatively large number of technically trained experts, and the development of a more pragmatic and flexible "operating ideology."[2] Ludz characterizes some of the new entrants into the political elite as "professionally and economically trained," and suggests that they may well be rapidly becoming a "technocratic elite." Central to the perspectives of this "technocratic elite" is the notion that objective, scientifically based decision procedures are the key to meeting the dynamic challenges of technical progress.

In the Soviet Union, it seems generally agreed that the significance of managerial and technical skills in elite selection is growing, whereas the importance of patronage and political loyalty has declined. Some of the most impressive evidence concerning changes in elite career patterns has been marshaled by one of the leading students of communist elites, Frederic J. Fleron, Jr. Fleron demonstrates that, in the membership of the Central Committee of the Communist party of the Soviet

Union, cooptation of persons with established professional and technical careers has increased dramatically since the early 1950s. For example, looking only at the ten-year period from 1952 to 1961, Fleron discovers that the proportion of coopted professional persons brought into the Central Committee at Party Congresses increased from 22 percent to nearly 53 percent[3] (see table 6–1).

The infusion of more specialized professionals into positions of political importance has been even more dramatic in Yugoslavia. The nature of the Yugoslav system, especially its emphasis on the development of self-management techniques and accompanying organizational autonomy at all levels of society, and its much more pragmatic posture toward the role of ideological doctrine, makes these developments more likely. According to a leading Yugoslav social scientist, Radomir Lukić, education has replaced ideological orthodoxy as "the key instrument of mobility" for aspiring elites.[4] The self-managing model of socialism that Yugoslavia is now approximating embraces a certain amount of what a distinguished Yugoslav sociologist, Rudi Supek, calls "technical autonomy"—that is, relative freedom for technically trained specialists who operate with a minimum of political interference in making at least middle-level policy decisions. The roles of economic specialists and other intellectuals are significant in Yugoslavia, and the kind of task specialization that their roles reflect seems already to be effectively institutionalized.

The apparent Chinese deviation from this pattern of evolving "technocracy" in socialist systems is fascinating. Several studies have effectively documented that there has been no substantial influx of younger, technically trained elites above the lower or middle echelons of the

TABLE 6–1. Recruitment and Cooptation into the Central Committee, CPSU

		New Central Committee Members	
		%	N
1952	Recruited	78.0	39
	Coopted	22.0	11
1956	Recruited	70.6	60
	Coopted	29.4	25
1961	Recruited	47.2	60
	Coopted	52.8	67

Adapted from Frederic J. Fleron, Jr., "System Attributes and Career Attributes: The Soviet Political Leadership System, 1952 to 1965," in Carl Beck, et al., Comparative Communist Political Leadership (New York: David McKay, 1973), p. 59.

party in China. In the view of Derek Waller, "the absence of any sizeable body of elite members with technical education or with scientific-technical career patterns in post-revolution China seems to reflect the top elites' lack of appreciation of problems of administering a complex, industrializing society."[5] Leaving aside the issue of why the influx of technically trained specialists has been so meager in China, the evidence that such is the case seems persuasive. Even into the 1970s it seems clear that more orthodox career patterns, usually based on long records of party service and exhibiting an absence of technical or professional training, continued to dominate in the Chinese party elite.

The influx of technically trained people may be significantly greater at subnational levels in China, a development that may be critical to effective political and economic management in that society. Although the fact is not widely known or appreciated in the West, there was a substantial decentralization of governmental administration in China after 1958. According to one student of Chinese affairs, Victor C. Falkenheim, this decentralization process was accompanied by a substantial "differentiation and specialization" of elite activities at the provincial level.[6] Even if the level of technical training of these provincial cadres is not always high, it does appear that they at least develop substantial on-the-job experience in specialized policy activities. In addition, Falkenheim's research shows that during the 1950s most of the party functionaries who remained at the provincial level did not change their areas of specialization. That is, they appeared to remain in functionally similar jobs and, presumably, developed an increasing degree of experience and professionalism. Thus it may be that the career patterns of national party elites, and those of subnational government and party elites, are moving in divergent directions in China. The possible implications of such a development for future political conflict in that society —a society that has already been racked by violence and severe intraelite conflict in recent years—are significant.

If there is a trend in most socialist systems, certainly those in Europe, toward the emergence of a significant technocratic element in the political elite, we should consider more carefully how this change is coming about. In general, there are two methods by which rational-technical criteria can be inserted into elite selection and promotion procedures: *cooptation* and career reorientation, or *adaptation*. We have already defined cooptation as a process by which persons with established professional careers in nonpolitical areas are brought into the political elite to provide specialized skills, usually technical or managerial, that are important to governance. Career reorientation, or adaptation, consists of retraining, or functionally reorienting the tasks of, existing political elites. Thus a society that is adaptive in a technocratic direction would be one in which a number of elites with nontechnical backgrounds and ideological orientations are provided with technical training and/or are placed in positions in which their roles require that they acquire an increasing level of technical expertise.

Fleron has used these two methods of elite selection and promotion as a basis for distinguishing two basic types of leadership system: the *cooptative system* and the *adaptive-monocratic* system.[7] In the latter system type, the traditional political elite is said to resist the notion of sharing power with the new technocratic elite; rather, it chooses to attempt to acquire within its own membership the skills necessary to govern an increasingly complex social and economic order. In a cooptative system, by contrast, the political elite brings into its membership persons from outside who already have the skills considered to be critical. Naturally this second approach entails dangers; the risk is always present that the coopted specialized elites will press for an increasing degree of participation in the political decision-making process. To that extent, the very character of the system may be changed, and the amount of influence exercised by the traditional, ideologically oriented party elite may be identifiably circumscribed. Thus these two methods of elite recruitment and promotion, cooptation and career reorientation, are distinctly different, and would appear to have different implications for the future of the political system.

It might be useful to consider the distinction between two socialist systems, the Soviet Union and Bulgaria, that appear to have blended cooptation and adaptation in differing degrees in adapting to the requirements of governing a modern society. Both cooptation and adaptation have been used in both of these systems; however, cooptation seems more prevalent in the Soviet Union. There the degree of cooptation at all levels of government, and at least as high as the level of the Central Committee in the Communist party, has been increasing and is already substantial. Well over half of the members of the Central Committee can reasonably be classified as coopted elites. Further, the economic and political changes that have taken place in the Soviet Union in the last 20 years clearly suggest that there have been changes in the points of view that exert influence on political outcomes. The use of terror has been sharply reduced, the degree of intraelite intrigue appears to have declined dramatically, and the society generally exhibits a greater degree of stability. Further, important economic reforms have been undertaken that apparently have set aside forever some of the classic concepts of collectivist economic organization. Profit is again a respectable word in the Soviet Union, and the command character of the economy has been measurably softened through some administrative decentralization and through the institution of some market-type features.

However, the use of cooptation in the selection of Central Committee members has not been matched at the level of the Politburo and the Secretariat, the executive arms of the Central Committee. In fact, Fleron demonstrates that during the period in which the proportion of coopted Central Committee members more than doubled, there was essentially no change in the proportion of coopted individuals in the Politburo.[8] Fleron uses the concept of institutionalized advantage to describe this situation; he argues that the professional party elite, which is distinctly more ideologically oriented than the younger, technically trained coopted elites, enjoys an institutionalized advantage in the sense that the broad currents of change affecting lower levels of the party organization have not had a significant impact on the highest party bodies. Nevertheless, viewing the Soviet political elite in reasonably broad terms, the use of cooptation as a selection and promotion mechanism has increased significantly.

In Bulgaria, by contrast, cooptation has remained at a relatively low level. The preponderance of members of the Central Committee of the party, as well as the Politburo, must still be classified as recruited party professionals. However, in the Bulgarian case adaptation has been used more frequently. Thus we may suggest that, using Fleron's distinctions among leadership system types, Bulgaria still is clearly an adaptative-monocratic system, whereas the Soviet Union is moving rapidly in the direction of a cooptative system.

The Bulgarian situation is especially interesting because it demonstrates the sometimes complex relationships that can exist among the three processes of recruitment, cooptation, and adaptation. Several possibilities suggest themselves. First, adaptation might be used as a substitute for cooptation, as Fleron suggests would be the case for the prototypic adaptative-monocratic system. In this event, there would be substantial career reorientation in order to avoid having to open up the political elite to newcomers whose ideological orientations may be thought questionable. Second, within the constraints imposed by the natural aging of any group of elites, adaptation might also be used as a substitute for recruitment. Within limits, the stability of a political elite could be increased substantially, at least in terms of personnel turnover, simply by declining to bring in new members except when necessitated by the death of current members of the elite. Changing functional needs would then be met by career reorientations. Third, adaptation might be used as a device to prevent the entrenchment of coopted elites in positions of genuine political power. That is, the traditional party elite might force repeated changes of functional specialization on the part of coopted elites to prevent them from acquiring institutional bases of power. The extent to which career reorientation is used as a mechanism of elite change may modify significantly both the relationship between cooptation and recruitment, and the potential impact of cooptation on the nature of the political leadership system.

Another important possibility is that different types of functional specialization within the elite might be characterized by different selection and promotion procedures. For example, we discover in Bulgaria that planning and managerial specializations have been manned increasingly by coopted, and to a lesser extent by newly recruited, elites, whereas specializations in industry, construction, and manpower and labor activities have been almost entirely adaptative in nature for a number of years. That is, persons already in the elite reoriented their careers toward this latter set of functional activities. Insofar as persons selected from different career channels, and through different procedures, have contrasting political perspectives, these distinctions among procedures of selection and promotion for different sets of elite specialization may provide clues to the emergence of potential conflicts within the elite.

One other important finding from recent research[9] on elite career reorientation in Bulgaria illustrates how this approach can illuminate critical trends in the nature of the political leadership system, and in society as a whole. By looking simultaneously at recruitment, cooptation, and adaptation processes, we can identify those functional specializations that are *ascendant* within the elite—specializations that seem to be receiving increasing emphasis in the selection and placement of elites. More formally, we say that a specialization is ascendant if: (a) the number of persons being recruited or coopted into that specialization exceeds the number of specialists in that function who leave the elite; and (b) among elites remaining in power, the number of persons entering the specialization exceeds the number leaving.

In Bulgaria since 1966, two functional specializations have been ascendant: the control function (internal security) and agriculture. The latter does not seem surprising. It testifies to the importance of the problems of the 1950s and 1960s in agriculture, and to the revamping of agricultural planning undertaken since the mid-1960s. That the control specialization has been increasing substantially in importance since 1966 is a good deal more intriguing. Although Bulgaria generally is thought to be one of the most orthodox of the East European systems, in terms of both loyalty to the Soviet Union and internal political policy, it is generally accepted that the domestic "loosening up" that has characterized most East European countries has been observable in Bulgaria as well. But notwithstanding this modest internal "liberalization," the political elite still contains a substantial and increasing number of persons whose principal functional specialization appears to be in the area of political control and internal security.

BUREAUCRATIZATION AND ROUTINIZATION

It is apparent that one of the most important changes that has taken place in East European socialist systems since their inceptions has been the decline of *personalism,* and the rise of *bureaucratization* and *routinization,* as bases for both intraelite and elite-mass relationships. Such a development does not mean that a small number of individuals do not exercise preponderant influence on most of the major policy decisions made in these societies. But it does suggest a modest circumscription of the latitude enjoyed by the top leadership, as well as the existence of a complex set of filters up through which information must pass to the top, and down through which dicta emanating from the top leadership must be transmitted to those whose responsibility it is to implement policy. Because this argument about the bureaucratization of communist systems is so frequently expressed, and also because it is so easily misunderstood, it bears closer examination.

It is fascinating that common images of the most prominent, and apparently best understood, political dictatorships of the twentieth century hold that these systems have been characterized by a high degree of personalism, especially within the upper ranks of the leadership. Thus personalism, and accompanying capriciousness of political choice, are regularly asserted as central characteristics of Hitler's Germany, Mussolini's Italy, Mao's China, and Stalin's Soviet Union. Contemporary historians tend to define the basic characteristics of these systems in terms of the ideological and other political positions taken by the dictator. Further, the notion is widely accepted that, notwithstanding the size of the administrative bureaucracy in these societies, some of the most important defining features of bureaucracy—especially the reasonably routine and consistent application of rules in choice taking— were consistently violated. Thus to suggest that the socialist systems in Eastern Europe are moving away from personalism, and toward more "conventional" notions of highly bureaucratized systems, is to suggest that something is happening in the Soviet Union and Eastern Europe that did not happen in previous highly structured political systems of the twentieth century.

To understand this argument, and to assess its possible significance as well as its validity, we need to look more carefully at the notion of bureaucratization. One of the leading American students of bureaucracy, Anthony Downs,[10] suggests that bureaucracies must at a minimum exhibit four characteristics:

1. Bureaucracies are large. They employ relatively large portions of the population, directly or indirectly, and there is relatively little face-to-face contact between persons working at different levels of the organization.
2. Most or all of the members of a bureaucracy are full-time workers. Most have worked their way up through the bureaucracy, or are in the process of doing so; as a result, most of them have at least a pragmatic personal commitment to the organization's existence.
3. The initial hiring of personnel, their promotion within the organization, and their retention are based at least in part upon some type of assessment of the way in which they have performed, or can be expected to perform, their assigned roles. This means that ascribed characteristics (such as ethnicity, class, family connections, age, or sex), or selection and review procedures by any constituency outside of the bureaucracy, generally are not important in personnel selection or advancement.
4. The major portion of the output of a bureaucracy is not directly or indirectly evaluated in any arenas (in Downs's terms, "markets") outside of the organization itself. In short, a bureaucracy is not directly accountable to any outside constituency.

According to Downs, these are the defining characteristics of bureaucracies. In addition, bureaucracies have certain internal procedures and functions that necessarily follow from these four basic characteristics. These internal operating features also should be spelled out, since an understanding of them is central to our argument about the nature of change in contemporary socialist systems. According to Downs,[11] there are seven such internal operating characteristics:

1. A hierarchical structure of formal authority. We have already mentioned the particular form of hierarchical organization used in the socialist systems of Eastern Europe and the Soviet Union, namely, the Leninist conception of democratic centralism.
2. Hierarchical formal communications networks. As we have already noted, information is to flow routinely upward through a series of predetermined levels before it reaches the top. Similarly, the flow of information downward is to pass through the same levels.
3. Extensive systems of formal rules. One of the most important characteristics of highly structured systems has been the existence of sets of procedural guidelines constraining the behavior of middle- and lower-level bureaucrats to the point where they frequently find it impossible to function effectively. These rules are often inconsistent among themselves, providing a source of particular frustration among economic functionaries in centrally planned economies.
4. An informal structure of authority. It can be argued that the three characteristics just listed necessitate an informal structure of authority

that exists alongside, and usually partly in conflict with, the hierarchical structure of formal authority. That is, the sheer size of the bureaucracy, the likelihood of partial and sometimes substantial isolation of top leaders from lower-level policy functionaries, the burdensome procedures for moving information up and down through the communications network, and the extraordinarily pervasive and constraining sets of formal rules, collectively lead to conditions of near-paralysis if efforts are made to follow them precisely as they are set down. The result tends to be the development of authority relationships outside the formal network.

5.   Related to the preceding characteristic, the emergence of informal and personal communications networks, designed to ease the often critical pressures created on specific individuals within the bureaucracy by the cumbersome nature of the formal communications network.

6.   Formal impersonality of operations. If bureaucracies operated precisely as it is stipulated that they should, the principles governing individual behavior within the bureaucracy would always be independent of the personalities or other idiosyncratic features of persons occupying positions in the organization. Bureaucracies, by definition, are to embody the rule of law, not the rule of specific individuals, and guidelines are to be carried out in an even-handed and uniform way, without regard to personal characteristics either of those implementing policy guidelines or of those to whom the guidelines are being applied.

7.   The emergence of patterns of personal loyalty and personal career attachment among officials, especially at the highest ranks of the hierarchy. This is in contradistinction to the formally impersonal characteristic of bureaucracies. Over time, however, the importance of personal loyalties and attachments seems to recede into a smaller segment of the structure, almost invariably at the top. That is, the formal requirement of impersonality of operations becomes more characteristic of the functioning of the bureaucracy at its lower and middle levels, whereas personal loyalty factors remain important for a decreasing subset of individuals at the top. One of the implications of this point is that bureaucratic structures in the socialist systems of Eastern Europe are more genuinely "bureaucratized" at the local and regional levels than at the national level.

Thus if Downs's characterization of bureaucracy is accurate, and if this development is in fact taking place in the Soviet Union and Eastern Europe, certain critical changes are implied in the nature of those political systems. In particular, we may cite the following implications:

1.   Formal rules, rather than subjective factors (including partisan political factors), are likely to be increasingly important in the making of policy decisions, particularly below the national level of politics. The influence of doctrinaire ideological postures in choice taking may be expected to decline correspondingly.

2.   Informal networks of communication and authority are likely to continue to develop alongside those that are formally constituted. It should

not be inferred that these informal communications and authority networks always serve to undermine the formal ones; on the contrary, it may be that these informal networks develop to make practical what was not feasible under the formal rules. A further point to stress about these informal networks is that they are *networks,* implying a reasonable degree of regularity and predictability, despite their extralegal origins. One of the most important implications of the development of such networks is that they may serve as alternative bases of authority for some individuals who may find access to top elite positions more difficult through formal channels. Such individuals may include, for example, members of the policy-oriented intellectual elite. To the extent to which this takes place, the development of such informal networks would constitute modest challenges to the existing system of formal authority.

3. A substantial routinization of tasks within government and within the party apparatus is implied by the process of bureaucratization. Division of labor becomes more specific and specialized; individuals are assigned to increasingly narrowly defined tasks. Such a system, among other things, makes it more difficult for persons anywhere other than at the top of the bureaucracy to have a sufficiently wide grasp of the workings of the organization to be able to manipulate the organizational structure for their own purposes, or to direct the organization's behavior in directions contrary to the wishes of the top leadership. Thus task routinization seems to have conflicting thrusts: It implies less arbitrariness and capriciousness on the part of supervisors, while at the same time it implies a reduced capability for persons not already in positions of substantial authority to affect the character of the system.

What are some of the reasons for the bureaucratization and task routinization that seem to be taking place in the socialist systems of the Soviet Union and Eastern Europe? Some of the sources of bureaucratization seem to be inherent in the necessity of organizing to govern. This fundamental argument has been articulated by many students of social change, perhaps most notably the German sociologist Max Weber.[12] But some of the apparent causes of this change in socialist systems are not necessarily generalizable to all political environments, and consequently should be treated here.

First, the very notion of routinization seems inherent in the process of *consolidation of political power* by a revolutionary movement. In the Soviet Union, the Bolshevik seizure of power in 1917 occurred under the guidance of a substantial blueprint for the remaking of Russian society. Much of this same blueprint, with some noticeable modifications, was applied in the initial stages of takeover by Communist parties in Eastern Europe after World War II. This revolutionary blueprint, however, was the product of a revolutionary *movement.* As Hannah Arendt[13] and others have argued, there is an enormous difference between a revolutionary movement while it is in revolutionary opposition, and that same movement when it is confronted with the necessity of governing in a reasonably stable manner. The desire for rapid change, and the willingness to undertake dramatic changes in direction, fade quickly in the face of the necessity for consolidation of authority and stability of governmental practice. More generally, we can argue that the longer a regime is in power, the greater the tendency for persistent patterns of governance to institutionalize themselves. The very character of governing for any regime, regardless of the size of its governing bureaucracy, tends to lead to a certain degree of routinization and thus predictability of political practices. Government is, by definition, a form of organization, and a principal purpose of organization is to impose consistent order in place of randomness or capricious arbitrariness.

Second, it is reasonable to argue that the more hierarchical the political management structure that is set up, the greater the degree of routinization and bureaucratization that is required to keep that management system operating effectively. That is, hierarchical structures by definition separate organizational levels in a strict way while at the same time requiring what should ostensibly be a thorough and effective flow of communications both up and down the hierarchy. This can be accomplished only if there are strict guidelines defining the ways in which authority and communication must flow.

Third, and related, the pervasiveness of the roles assigned to state structures in these societies facilitates the growth of bureaucracy. The nature of the system is all-encompassing. For many years the most common characterization by Western students of Soviet and East European systems was "totalitarian." This conception is used much less frequently today, and for good reason, since many of the changes that have taken place in these systems make their classification as totalitarian highly dubious. At the same time, the business of the state is defined substantially more broadly in these societies than in most other contemporary political systems. If a significant proportion of the individual affairs of citizens is to be regulated, or at least monitored, by the state, a large bureaucracy is required.

Fourth, the growth of bureaucracy has been cultivated in socialist systems in part because it tends to develop a personal identification with the state among a relatively large number of persons. This in turn may be seen as a source of reasonably stable support for the regime. In a society with a large bureaucracy, a relatively large proportion of the population is dependent on that bureaucracy for its livelihood.

Fifth, there appear to be psychological factors contributing to the routinization of political activity in these societies. There is considerable evidence that organizational effectiveness requires a certain amount of predictability, as well as humaneness, in the ways in which an organization handles its members. There is acute and poignant testimony to the drastic impact on the Soviet bureaucracy during the 1930s of the essentially random use of terror directed inward against itself by the party apparatus. The Soviet leadership seems to have learned a good deal from that aspect of the Stalinist experience, and it understands that effective organizational structures cannot be sustained in the face of arbitrary and inhumane treatment of those individuals whose activities are critical to governance.

Similarly, sixth, there is a factor frequently overlooked by Western students of socialist systems: the importance of the humanistic ethic in classic communist thought. The late American sociologist C. Wright Mills argued effectively[14] that Westerners, if they wish to understand both the appeal and the operating principles of Marxism, must try to separate out the several components of this body of doctrine. Mills distinguished among the *ideology,* the *theory,* the *ethic,* and the blueprints for *action* embodied in classic Marxism. A review of these distinctions does not seem critical to our argument here. But we should note that the ethic of communism—an emphasis on an abstract ideal of the ultimate dignity of individuals—has been a major aspect of the appeal of the doctrine to many of those who have followed, notwithstanding the clearly incomplete realization of this ideal where Marxist-oriented regimes are in place. Further, there has been a reemergence of identifiable concern for this humanistic ethic of communism, especially in Eastern Europe, during the past two decades. The work of the Yugoslav theoretician Milovan Djilas,[15] or of the Polish philosopher and social scientist Adam Schaff (who has been called the leading living Marxist theoretician[16]), is but illustrative of a more general concern that has emerged among intellectuals—many of them highly placed politically —for an attempt to return to humanistic elements that were an important part of the original writings of Karl Marx.

We can also identify at least three practical political reasons for the bureaucratization and routinization of tasks that seem increasingly to characterize these systems. Seventh, we note that task routinization is apparently more established in the state bureaucracy than in the party apparatus. This is not surprising, since ideological and personalistic considerations are likely to be emphasized more within the party. What is significant is that some elites (and potential elites) have attempted to develop a measure of autonomy for the state apparatus precisely because it embodies a lesser degree of personalism and ideologism in choice taking. In some cases, aspiring elites have used the state apparatus as a power base in an effort to move upward in the party hierarchy. Related to this, it has been widely and increasingly recognized in socialist systems that there is a need for persons with rational-technical skills to operate and manage the more complex socioeconomic system. We have outlined this argument above. It seems to have been a good deal easier to implement these rational-technical criteria as bases for elite selection and promotion in the state apparatus rather than in the party. Thus the state apparatus has become the principal repository for these "technocrats."

Eighth, we should note the increasing evidence that recent political roles have a decisive impact on the issue positions of elites in socialist systems.[17] Studies from Yugoslavia, the Soviet Union, and the German Democratic Republic, in particular, suggest that social background, early education, and early political training are less decisive factors in shaping political attitudes than are the kinds of position recently occupied by decision makers. The point is that the exercise of political power tends to influence the way in which that power will be exercised by the same persons in the future. The ways in which policy makers have met the compelling and practical problems of governance in the recent past exert a great deal of influence on the postures that they will take toward similar issues in the future.

Finally, there is a good deal of interesting speculation concerning the possible *phases,* or *stages,* of development through which socialist systems may be passing. The argument is that most rapidly modernizing socialist systems pass through a similar, and sequential, set of developmental stages. Broadly, periods of revolutionary excess tend to be followed by conservatizing factors, especially the impact of consolidation of power, stability, the need for control, and the comforting effect of being able to exercise power successfully over an increasing period of time. These phases of development also may be defined in terms of the socioeconomic complexity of society. Some writers believe that ultimately it will be the modernization of the socioeconomic structure of the Soviet Union and its Eastern European allies that will bring about the demise of personalism, and the declining significance of ideology in choice taking, in these political systems. There is good reason to be cautious about accepting such a line of argument, and there are additional logical reasons for taking any stage theory of political or economic development with a grain of salt. At the same time, the argument is worth considering, since, for example, it is persuasively contended that Mainland China in the late 1970s is experiencing some of the political and social changes and upheavals that characterized the Soviet Union at approximately the same chronological point in the latter's political history.

THE TRANSMUTATION OF CONFLICT INTO COMPETITION

One of the most striking changes that seems to have characterized the socialist systems of Eastern Europe in the last 20 years is the replacement of unstructured, intense intraelite conflict by more stable and less disruptive forms of political competition. Struggles among contenders for political authority still appear to be conducted substantially outside formal decisional arenas, with a shifting variety of means of influence. Still, the declining intensity of such conflict, and the increasing degree to which it is eventually handled within and institutionalized into the existing political structure, represent a change of enormous importance.

To be sure, it cannot responsibly be argued that the political competition emerging in the Soviet Union is anything akin to that observed in pluralistic systems. If this transmuted form of conflict is viewed as support for the "convergence" theory—which posits gradually increasing similarities between pluralistic and highly structured systems—the support it lends is modest. At the same time, the importance of this change must be assessed from the baseline of previously existing circumstances. During the 1930s and 1940s, and into the 1950s, the conflict within the political elite, and between the existing elite and principal contenders, was pervasive, unstructured, and intense. It is difficult to describe the paralyzing impact of the Great Purges on the intraelite environment, on the way in which individuals related to one another, and thus on the way in which the Soviet Union was ruled. Earlier in this book we discussed Lester Seligman's distinction between high-risk and low-risk systems, and his accompanying notions of the existence of varying degrees of "cushions" for unsuccessful competitors for elite positions. There is no doubt that the Soviet Union and most of the socialist systems of Eastern Europe have been high-risk systems until the recent past. In comparison with the industrialized nations of Western Europe and North America, they remain high-risk in nature. Nevertheless, the fact that more stable and less disruptive forms of political competition have emerged has changed the distance between these two categories of system on the dimension of risk.

One of the most important aspects of this change in socialist systems has been the development of more systematic and widespread cushions, both for those who are unsuccessful in efforts to achieve positions of political importance and for those who fall from such positions. Contrast, for example, the handling of Lavrenti P. Beria (who attempted to seize political power on Stalin's death in 1953) with the handling of Nikita Khrushchev (ousted from party and government leadership in 1964) or Nikolai Podgorny (ousted from his formal position as head of state as well as his position on the Politburo of the party in mid-1977). Beria was hustled through a quick trial and executed; Khrushchev and Podgorny were put out to pasture with comfortable apartments in Moscow and summer dachas in which to enjoy their remaining years. Nor are these examples of individuals displaced from the top unrepresentative of the handling of the less fortunate at middle levels of the bureaucracy. There is ample evidence that the punishment for inappropriate ambition and/or inappropriate performance has become substantially less severe, though no less consistently meted out.

But perhaps one of the most effective ways for us to understand the emergence of a new form of political competition in the Soviet Union and Eastern Europe is to look at two other developments that have taken place since the early 1960s. The first of these is the emergence of acknowledged and distinct differences of opinion among various elite groups in the Soviet Union with regard to policy questions of importance. The second is the emergence of a modest but still symbolically important degree of competition for local and regional government and party offices in certain Eastern European countries, particularly Hungary and Poland.

The research of the American political scientist Milton Lodge has demonstrated effectively the extent of disagreement between functionaries in the party apparatus and representatives of various specialized elite groups (the military, the literary elite, the legal elite, the economic elite) on a variety of important policy questions.[18] (see table 6–2). In general, Lodge finds that Soviet specialist elites are substantially more instrumental (and less ideological) and substantially more participatory (and less hierarchical) than are their counterparts in the party *apparat*. The situation with respect to some party-specialist relations is yet more complex; the comparisons differ depending on the level of party structure at which one analyzes these relationships. For example, the greatest differences between specialists and party elites are at the national and republican levels; at the local and regional levels such differences of opinion are slight. Indeed, Lodge characterizes *apparat*-specialist relations at the local level as "accommodating." Significantly, this lack of difference between specialists and party functionaries at the lower levels of political activity seems to reflect the fact that local party *apparatchiki* are more participatory and instrumental than their counterparts in the central party apparatus. That is, the local party people are more similar to the specialist elites in their orientation. The pioneering work done by Lodge in identifying these differences of perspective on a variety of substantive policy questions —and especially on issues concerning the extent to which specialist elites *should be* participating in policy making—has made a significant

TABLE 6-2. Party *Apparatchiki* and Specialist Elite Attitudes toward Participation in Policy Making and Decision Making (from Milton Lodge, "Attitudinal Cleavages within the Soviet Political Leadership," in Carl Beck, *et al., Comparative Communist Political Leadership,* p. 206)

Elite	Who Should Make Policy	Who Does Make Policy	Who Should Make Decisions	Who Does Make Decisions	Authority Sources	All Participatory Categories Combined
Apparatchiki (N = 70)	2.1	2.3	3.5	3.3	2.9	2.7
Economic (N = 54)	2.1	2.4	4.4	4.6	2.9	3.2
Legal (N = 47)	2.6	2.8	4.3	4.3	3.1	3.1
Military (N = 52)	2.7	2.4	3.8	3.9	2.2	3.1
Literary (N = 36)	3.0	2.4	4.4	4.4	2.8	3.4

Mean Scores

1.0 party participation solely
2.0 party participation primarily
3.0 joint party-specialist coparticipation
4.0 specialist participation primarily
5.0 specialist participation solely

Underlined mean scores are those that show statistically significant differences (*t*-tests, *p* < .01) between the *apparatchiki* and the individual specialist elites.

contribution to our understanding of the emerging forms of political competition that are tolerated in the Soviet Union.

The other critical development has been the cautious acceptance, particularly in Hungary, of competition for local- and regional-level government and party positions. To be sure, the number of posts for which there is competition within the party is relatively small, and the number of occasions on which nonparty persons are permitted to contest for positions held by party persons is even smaller. At the same time, it seems not insignificant that such competition does exist; perhaps even more important is the fact that the outcomes of these contests are not always what we might predict. Candidates on the party's official slate triumph in no more than approximately 60 percent of the cases in which they are contested at the local level in Hungary, and occasionally the party nominee even loses to a nonparty person in general elections. Circumstances of this kind have been extant in Yugoslavia for more than 20 years, but their gradual emergence in Hungary, and to a lesser extent in Poland, represents a factor of great potential significance that bears watching in the next few years. It is probably not accidental that the emergence of this phenomenon in Hungary has been coincident with a modest decentralization of the structures of both government and party as a result of the social and economic reforms begun in 1968. That is, the emergence of more stable and genuinely competitive forms of political controversy seems to have accompanied an effort to provide a slightly enlarged range of autonomy for lower-level party and government units.

A good deal of systematic research has been done on leadership in socialist systems in the last few years, and this chapter has summarized that work only in the most general way. This research area is one of the most important in the field of political science, and it merits considerably increased attention from students of political leadership in the next few years. In summarizing this research here, we have tried to suggest that three closely related developments have affected the nature of political leadership in the socialist systems of Eastern Europe and the Soviet Union. First, the political leadership system seems to be evolving in the direction of what some people have called a "technocracy." Such a system is characterized by the increasing use of less political, and more technical, criteria in selecting and promoting political elites, by a decline in the prescriptive importance of ideology in choice taking, and by a growing group consciousness on the part of persons with more substantial higher and technical education that they constitute a collective force that may be important in changing the character of these societies.

Second, these systems have exhibited over a substantial period of time a process of bureaucratization and routinization of tasks within the elite. In turn, this bureaucratization has affected elite-mass relationships. Broadly, the process of bureaucratization and routinization has reduced the importance of personal loyalties and personal career connections, except at the highest levels of the political elite. It has led to greater predictability and stability in the functioning of both the government and party apparatuses. The process also led to initial inefficiency because of the inordinate size and excessively hierarchical operating principles of the bureaucracy; there has been a resulting emergence of informal channels of communication and authority, which in some cases may serve as alternative power bases for competing elites. Finally, the earlier unstructured, intense conflict within the elite has been transmuted into more stable and less disruptive forms of political competition. This development has had an enormous impact on the character of interpersonal relationships within the political leadership groups in these societies, and leads us to classify them as being less high-risk systems than had previously been the case.

It cannot be stressed too strongly that these three related developments do not signal the departure of the Soviet or East European systems from the category of highly structured, subject-participant political cultures. Nor do the changes necessarily imply that these societies are more pluralistic, or that they are "converging" with societies that we have classified as pluralistic. These changes do, however, seem to argue that the character of the socialist systems of the Soviet Union and Eastern Europe has moderated, and that the nature of political leadership is of a different order than was the case less than two decades ago. The changes may be too recent to assess their probable long-run impact on, for example, relations between these socialist systems and nonsocialist systems in Europe and North America. But the likelihood that some such changes in international relations will occur as a result of leadership changes under socialism bears close attention.

7

Elite-Mass Relations in Pluralist Systems

In chapter 4 we noted some of the characteristics of pluralist systems, especially the fact that political power is dispersed both across space (that is, among several groups or sources at any given point in time) and across time (in the sense that the same groups or sources of power are not dominant to the exclusion of all others for long periods). In addition, we noted that some of the groups that compete for political positions and political influence are independent of current political authorities, and that the competition among groups in pluralist systems is institutionalized and generally nonviolent.

In most pluralist systems, too, the linkages between the political leadership and the politically interested and articulate citizenry are relatively important and well established. It is not merely that the actions of the political leadership are generally open to public scrutiny. There is some commitment to the notion of *accountability*—the political leadership's performance is to be judged by a broader group of citizens, and the continuation of the leadership in office is dependent on an essentially favorable evaluation.

Such a system is sustained in part by a commitment to the notion of "rule of law, not of men." The implication is clear: There is a widespread and firm commitment to a given set of values, a commitment that transcends the popularity or personal rule of any given set of public officials. The values themselves may vary somewhat. What is important is that men—including political leaders—are judged by basic laws, rather than these basic laws being subject to suspension or substantial interpretation through the whims of individuals, no matter how exalted their positions or the esteem in which they are held.[1] It is therefore not surprising that students of political elites and leadership generally believe that the nature of political leadership in pluralist systems is substantially shaped by the nature of the political system—especially the political culture. This is in contrast to highly structured systems, in which the nature of the system sometimes can be substantially shaped by the political leadership. In short, the nature of political leadership is thought to be *systemically constrained* to a much greater degree in pluralist systems than is the case in highly structured systems.

At the same time, these constraints may be as much potential as real. It is by now well established that the level of political interest and political information, even in advanced pluralist systems, is relatively low, and that the bases on which those persons who care enough to participate in the political process make decisions frequently seem less than fully rational. In addition, the enormous complexity of contemporary government, and of the issues that require public resolution, makes it extremely difficult for even the most attentive of citizens to be fully aware of the decisions taken by their leaders, and especially of the procedures through which those choices were made. We should remind ourselves that, although the systemic constraints on leadership in pluralist systems are potentially substantial, these are relatively low-risk, high-opportunity political environments. The systemic cushions that exist to ease the impact of unsuccessful seeking of office, or inadequate performance in office, are much greater in pluralist systems than elsewhere. Thus there are respects in which political leaders have substantial latitude in what they do and how they do it, even in pluralist societies.

A great deal has been written about political elites and political leadership in pluralist systems, and these pages cannot hope to summarize even the most important of this work. Rather, we choose to focus primarily on one pluralist society—the United States—with some comparative commentary on three other advanced pluralist systems—the United Kingdom, Canada, and the Federal Republic of Germany. We also limit the scope of our comments by focusing on three kinds of issues having to do with the roles of leaders and elites in such societies. First we discuss the concept of the "representativeness" of elites and leaders in pluralist systems. Second, we consider certain aspects of elite-mass linkages in these systems, giving particular attention to how elected representatives of the people relate to their constituencies, and to how political culture and public opinion shape public attitudes toward elites and leaders. Third, we take a brief look at some recent research that attempts to identify the most useful predictors of elite attitudes in the United States, Germany, and France.

THE "REPRESENTATIVENESS" OF ELITES AND LEADERS IN PLURALIST SYSTEMS

In systems in which systemic constraints on leadership are greater and the leadership is more directly and regularly accountable to a relatively broad constituency, it might be expected that this leadership would be more representative of its constituency. Before we examine the available evidence, we shall attempt to clarify the concept of representativeness. There are at least three distinct senses in which this term can be used. First, we may say that elites and leaders are representative of their constituents, or of the general public, if they "look like" those constituents; that is, if, taken collectively, the political leadership has roughly the same characteristics as the general population in terms of social background, education, and training characteristics. More precisely, we might expect a genuinely representative political leadership in this first sense to exhibit (over some reasonable period of time) approximately the same proportion of certain salient personal characteristics as did the general population. For example, if about half of the population is female, 20 percent is black, and 20 percent is between the ages of 25 and 35, we would expect the political leadership to approximate those same proportions. Second, we may speak of representativeness in terms of the extent to which political leaders do what they believe their constituents want them to do, or what they believe their constituents would do themselves if they occupied leadership positions. Under such a conception of representation, leaders are "transmission belts" for conveying the wishes of those whom they represent. Third, the notion of representation has also been extended to the case in which the political leader does what he or she believes is best for his or her constituency, as defined subjectively by the political leader. Under this posture, the expressed wishes of an articulate and concerned majority of constituents could be contrary to those of the political leader, but that leader could still claim to be representative of the constituency if he felt confident that his actions were in the best interest of those individuals, their own (incorrect) views to the contrary notwithstanding. This third conception of representativeness represents a substantially looser linkage between elite and mass.

The available evidence lends little support to the notion that pluralist elites are representative of the polity in terms of either of the first two conceptions of representativeness. We can examine the characteristics of persons who have held formal governmental positions at the national and state levels in the United States to demonstrate that the personal backgrounds of political leaders and elites bear little resemblance to those of the general population. (Our examples are at an aggregate, national level; some specific constituencies may exhibit somewhat more "representativeness," in terms of similarity of backgrounds between constituents and their representatives.)

In the United States, as in most other countries, the most flagrant lack of representation in this sense has been with regard to sex. Although the status of women in public affairs has improved distinctly in the past 20 years, it remains astoundingly disadvantaged. For example, fewer than 3 percent of the persons who have served as members of the Senate or House of Representatives in this century have been women. Only about 2 percent of the federal judges in the United States are women, and no woman has ever been a justice of the United States Supreme Court. The median civil service grade held by women federal employees is approximately three grades below the average for men. Indeed, at the highest civil service levels, only about 1 percent of the occupants of positions are women. And needless to say, no woman has ever served as president or vice president of the United States.[2]

Political leadership in the United States is also not particularly representative on the dimension of age. In general, younger age groups are significantly underrepresented among the political leadership, whereas the age range between 55 and 70 is overrepresented. This has led some analysts, perhaps only somewhat tongue-in-cheek, to characterize the American political leadership as a gerontocracy. There have been some identifiable differences among recent political administrations; the leadership of the Kennedy and Carter administrations, for example, has been of a younger average age than those of other recent presidents. In general, however, the average public official is well over 50. Especially in the Congress, some of the most important positions, such as committee chairmanships, are seldom achieved by persons under the age of 60, and not infrequently have been held by persons of 70 or older. The average age of a number of categories of elected officials has been higher in the middle of the twentieth century than at any other time in the history of the United States. Prior to 1875, 56 percent of the Speakers of the House of Representatives were younger than 40 at the time of their election, while only one speaker was over 65. During the twentieth century the *median* age of the Speaker of the House has been over 65 years.[3]

Our purpose here is not to debate the relative merits of a younger or older political leadership, but simply to document the extent to which the leadership is not representative of the general population in terms of age. Of course, a reasonable case can be made for having persons of greater experience in positions of public leadership. One would hardly expect the same proportion of the political leadership to be under the age of 25 as is the case with the general population (approximately one-half). Thus the question, stated as a matter of political contention, is not whether the political leadership appropriately is older than the population as a whole, but whether the *extent* of this overrepresentation of older persons is appropriate. A number of important implications follow from a political system having a relatively old leadership, other than that experience is present in critical decision-making positions. One of these implications is that persons who have served in positions of political importance are able to provide guidance and counsel to their successors only for relatively short periods of time after they leave office. A substantial number of high-level elected public officials die in office, or within ten years after leaving office, thereby circumscribing their opportunity to pass along their accumulated experience and wisdom to others currently in leadership roles.

That the political leadership of the United States has not been representative of the population of the country in terms of race and national background hardly needs to be documented. Again, although blacks have made important strides at both state and national levels in the last 20 years, their representation in the highest councils of government could not be construed to be more than one-eighth to one-tenth of their representation in the general population. The representation of blacks in the Senate and House of Representatives, for example, has been extraordinarily low. There was a period of almost 90 years between Reconstruction and the middle of the twentieth century during which there was not a single black serving in the United States Senate. Between the Reconstruction period and the 1960s, there were 17 Congresses without a single black representative, and the largest number of blacks in any single Congress during this period was three.

More generally, as recently as 35 years ago more than 90 percent of the blacks employed by the federal government were in custodial work. The initial impetus to the rise of blacks to positions above this menial level was World War II, when a number of black professionals were brought into war service appointments, most of which unfortunately were lost in the postwar personnel cutbacks.[4] The increases in black representation in national elective bodies have been significant (about tenfold) in the past 20 years. However, the extent of underrepresentation of blacks in American political leadership positions remains embarrassingly high.

Members of most immigrant groups have also been unlikely to appear in high governmental offices in the United States. One study[5] presents a statistical summary of the nationality backgrounds of 9,618 men and women who served in the United States Congress during a period of 160 years. Only 373 of these persons were foreign born, and with only one exception foreign-born congressmen were white and usually of Western European or Canadian origin. Five-sixths of all foreign-born congressmen came from Ireland, England, Canada, Germany, or Scotland.[6]

Members of the two largest minority religious groups in the United States—the Roman Catholics and the Jews—are also statistically under-represented in top governmental posts. There are distinct differences in this regard between the Democratic and Republican parties, in that the Democratic party has consistently exhibited a higher level of representation of both ethnic and religious minorities.[7] Overall, Protestants have been strongly overrepresented, representing between 85 and 88 percent of the members of the Senate and 80 to 84 percent of the House since World War II.

In some respects the overrepresentation of certain religious groups is merely a reflection of the overrepresentation of certain social-class elements in political leadership positions. Thus Matthews notes that the distortion in the religious composition of the American political leadership is in the direction of the "religious views of the upper and middle classes."[8] That is, the majority of elected public officials in the United States have been Presbyterian, Episcopal, or Methodist in religious affiliation, and these denominations tend to be concentrated among upper- and upper-middle-class segments of the population.

These two social strata, along with relatively well-to-do farm families, have comprised the social base from which most American political leadership has been drawn. The three groups that are most dramatically underrepresented in the political leadership are the urban laboring class, middle-class white-collar workers, and the rural lower class. As is by now well known, social class tends to be measured in terms of a combination of income, occupational status, and education. In each of these categories the American political leadership has stood substantially above the national median. Our political leaders have tended to come from relatively high-income families, and to be the sons of professionals, proprietors, governmental officials, or large farmers. Most have themselves been professionals (especially lawyers) or engaged in large-scale business enterprises. They have had, almost without exception, at least some higher education, and many have held advanced professional degrees. Again, it can be argued that such a situation should be expected where enlightenment is a value positively associated with leadership. We do not wish to imply the inappropriateness of such a value judgment. Our point is simply that the political leadership, on almost any significant social dimension that one might wish to examine, does not look like the general population. Thus whatever affinity of view might be encountered between the general population and the political leadership would have to be due to influences of common mass political socialization, and/or a commitment to certain basic values of the political culture.

This important subject is dealt with elsewhere, including two companion volumes published in the Basic Concepts Series.[9] It is beyond the scope of this book to entertain these issues. Suffice it to say that what we know about political socialization in the United States suggests two generalizations critical to an interpretation of the evidence presented above. First, there is in the United States what seems in comparative perspective to be a surprisingly deep and widely shared commitment to certain *symbols* of democratic political practice. Second, at the same time, these attachments to symbols are of a very general nature, and the vast majority of Americans—including many who occupy positions of political importance—are unable to articulate in specific terms what the general symbols of democracy mean, or how the democratic goals to which they refer can best be protected. In addition, many Americans hold views on specific political issues that seem to be inconsistent with the general values for which they articulate support. For example, many persons who express support for the concept of freedom of speech also urge that persons holding certain political views thought to be "radical," or having sexual preferences not common in the society, should not be permitted to teach in public classrooms, or otherwise to advance their points of view in public forums.[10]

The socialization process in the United States apparently still reinforces some of the nonrepresentative characteristics of the political elite. For example, Jaros traces the fact that women in the United States are less politically active and less participatory than men to elements of political socialization and political culture. According to Jaros, "contrary to many persons' beliefs this does not, in general, stem from restrictions imposed on women—e.g., being tied to the home by responsibility for children. It results in large part from a set of norms that women hold: that they should not be as participatory as men; that politics is a man's game."[11] Jaros argues that there is strong evidence that girls are socialized to these nonparticipatory orientations as children, and that such differences are evident as early as the fourth grade. "Despite increased efforts to involve women in the political world, despite all the recent attention, there is a cultural tradition of feminine nonparticipation transmitted in childhood."[12] In the opinion of another writer, differences in political participation between the sexes "are unlikely to vanish soon."[13] Similar findings have been generated concerning the socialization of working-class youth into political participation.

ELITE-MASS LINKAGES

It can be argued that the effective functioning of pluralist systems would not be compromised by the existence of a political leadership that was unrepresentative in terms of social backgrounds, as long as certain appropriate attitudes toward the notion of representation were held by these political leaders. In the next few pages we shall explore some evidence concerning the postures of elected representatives in two countries—the United States and the Federal Republic of Germany —toward the representation of their constituencies. We shall then look at the development of public opinion toward elites and leaders, and try to ascertain the extent to which public opinion and political culture in Western pluralist systems affect the behavior of political leaders who have as one of their responsibilities the representation of large numbers of other citizens.

Representatives and Their Constituencies. Earlier we discussed three notions of representativeness. The second and third of these, along with a combination of those two, have been described by Wahlke et al.[14] as the three principal representational roles assumed by legislators in pluralist systems. The *trustee* role refers to our third sense of representativeness. The trustee does not feel himself bound by a mandate because his decisions are to be his own considered judgments based on an assessment of the facts in each case, his understanding of all the problems and angles involved, and his thoughtful appraisal of the sides at issue.[15] The *delegate* role corresponds to the second sense of representation discussed above. Delegates are generally agreed that they should not use their independent judgments or principled convictions as decision-making premises. Delegates may not be instructed, in any formal sense, but they believe they know what their constituents want, and they act that way. In the view of Wahlke and his colleagues, one of the striking things about the posture of legislators who take delegate roles, in contrast to those who assume trustee roles, is the failure of delegates to elaborate the issues surrounding why representatives should or should not follow specific instructions, or attempt to mirror the views of constituents, in their decision-making behavior. "Delegates, it seems, have a simpler, more mechanical conception of the political process and the function of representation in legislative behavior."[16]

A third representational role suggested in this research is that of the *politico*. Wahlke et al. determined that the simplistic dichotomization of independent judgment (the trustee) and mandate (the delegate) did not cover all of the empirical cases they observed. Specifically, they discovered that these two role orientations need not be fully exclusive

—a representative may hold one role orientation at one time and a different one at another time, or some representatives may attempt to justify decisions simultaneously in terms of both kinds of role. In short, the world does not divide simply between delegates and trustees, and Wahlke and his colleagues chose the term "politico" to describe persons whose postures toward their relationship with their constituents seemed to overlap the two more clearly defined roles.

What is fascinating about the work done by researchers who have investigated the orientations of representatives in the United States is that the representational posture most commonly found is the one that would tie the representative to his constituency least firmly. That is, a considerable majority of the members of state legislatures whose representational role orientations have been studied assume the trustee posture. Thus not only are American legislators not representative of their constituencies in terms of background and training, they also do not tend to view their roles as involving a faithful transmission of the views of the constituency into the decision-making process. There is some evidence that American legislators may conform to different representative traditions according to the type of issue or policy involved; on policy matters where they perceive the impact of public action on their constituents to be greatest, they are more inclined to accept a delegate posture.[17]

Evidence from research on state legislators in the Federal Republic of Germany further supports the apparent preponderance of the trustee role. Gunlicks[18] interviewed 100 local councillors in the *Land* of Lower Saxony, asking them the extent to which they approved or disapproved of each of four types of representative role. The roles were based on the primary influence of: (1) the voters and other characteristics of the district represented; (2) the views of the leadership of the party of which the councillor was a member; (3) the views of influential interest groups in the councillor's constituency; and (4) the councillor's general conception of the "common good." Gunlicks discovered that only the fourth role orientation, that toward the "common good," was approved by a majority of the respondents. Only about one-fourth of the respondents gave unqualified approval under any circumstances to any of the other three roles. There were some differences observed on the basis of party membership; members of the Social Democratic party were somewhat more likely to accept delegate-type roles based on characteristics of the constituency or views of the party leadership than were members of the Christian Democratic party or the Free Democrats. These interparty differences, however, were not substantial. There also is evidence suggesting that the trustee role, rather than the delegate orientation, is more common both in the United Kingdom and in France. Its generality thus seems relatively well established across the major Western pluralist systems.

If political elites tend not to be representative of their constituencies in terms of personal characteristics, and if they are not generally disposed to attempt to reflect the points of view of that constituency in making policy choices, it is appropriate—and indeed, for the future of representative government, critical—to ask how the process of representation actually *does* work. Through what mechanisms are the concerns and points of view of the mass citizenry in pluralist systems communicated to, and through, their chosen representatives? Similarly, what are the mechanisms by which a reasonable level of accountability of public officials to the citizenry is sustained?

The essence of the system of accountability in pluralist systems is, of course, the election of public officials. Elections represent opportunities for universal participation in maintaining a linkage between the policy views of citizens and the substance of policy formulated by public officials. Broadly speaking, the electoral mechanism may imply one or both of two links between mass views and elite behavior. First, elections may provide officials with a mandate to enact into policy views they have supported, or have heard widely supported, during the course of the campaign. Second, elections may serve to legitimize the policy behavior most recently carried out by successful candidates for reelection.

Elections, however, are held relatively infrequently. Further, it is by now well known that even the best-informed electorates are not very well informed at all. They do not have carefully thought out, consistent, or firmly held positions on most matters of public policy, and they do not invest the necessary time and effort in learning the extent to which given candidates for public office reflect citizen views. Thus the electoral process itself, although critical to maintaining elite accountability, is not only imperfect but—in and of itself—patently inadequate.

In a sense, then, the core of the process of representation is the communication to governmental actors on a continuing basis of interests held by citizens. Students of this process generally believe that there are two principal mechanisms through which this communication of interests takes place. First, citizen concerns may be communicated through a process generally called "constituency influence," i.e., the communication of aggregated individual views by constituents to their representatives. (The term "representatives" is used here in a broad sense, to include not only members of legislative bodies but all individuals serving in elected public office.) Second, the communication of citizen concerns may occur through pressure-group or lobbying activities. To view this as a form of representation requires that we conceive of lobbyists as group agents who are intermediaries between aggregates of citizens and elected representatives.

It appears as if the second of these representational mechanisms has considerably greater impact on political outcomes in pluralist systems. That is, the pressure-group system seems to have relatively great impact on the positions taken by public officials, whereas constituency influence—though its importance is debated among political scientists —is probably of less significance. One of the classic, and still most effective, statements of the importance of pressure-group activity in the United States was made by the American political scientist E. E. Schattschneider.[19] He characterized the basis of this system as "the mobilization of bias," and argued that only a small proportion of the population is represented by those lobbyists who appear to have the most substantial impact on the behavior of public officials. Conversely, large proportions of the population are ineffectively represented, or not represented at all, in the pressure-group system.

Substantial constituency influence, especially over the lower house of Congress, is commonly thought to be a basic normative principle of American government.[20] Whether it is an accurate characterization of how the process of representation functions is another matter. Let us be clear on one point: There seems little doubt that most congressmen *feel* "pressure" from their home constituencies. Similarly, to broaden the scope of our argument, it seems equally clear that other elected public officials at the national and state levels attempt to remain sensitive to the concerns of their constituencies, and exhibit private and public concern when the positions they take are contrary to positions they believe to be held by a majority of articulate and concerned citizens. At issue, however, is how substantially the behavior of elected public officials conforms to the points of view held by those constituents. The evidence is mixed; there are not straightforward or easy conclusions to be drawn.

We can marshal some facts to help us understand the difficulties in this representational process:

1. Relatively few citizens conceptualize interests that clearly represent policy demands or policy expectations.
2. In the view of most political scientists, it is doubtful that policy demands are entertained by citizens even in the form of broad orientations, outlooks, or belief systems.
3. Large proportions of citizens lack the instrumental knowledge about political structures, processes, and actors that they would need to communicate policy demands even if they had any.
4. Relatively few citizens ever communicate directly with their representatives.

5. In general, citizens are not particularly interested in, or informed about, the policy-making activities of their representatives, or of other public officials.
6. Relatively few citizens have any clear notion that they are making policy demands or policy choices when they cast votes.[21]

In the face of this information, one could reasonably wonder how any constituency influence could ever be effectively applied in pluralist systems. The issue is real; the response—and it is only partial—is that voters, consciously or subconsciously, identify what they believe to be the salient characteristics of opposing candidates for office through *political party labels.* Unfortunately, there are difficulties even with this simplified approach to cue giving and cue taking. In the first place, party programs in the United States tend to be vague and relatively similar to one another, at least in the view of the majority of the electorate. Furthermore, there are adequate signs of voter failure to respond appropriately to whatever such cues are provided by party platforms, or by outcomes of elections expressed in terms of party success or failure. For example, Wahlke[22] notes that in one state (Washington) less than half of the public knew which party controlled either house of the state legislature at its most recent session. Shortly after the 1966 election in the United States, 31 percent of the electorate did not know (or was wrong about) which party had a majority in Congress just before the election; more striking still, 34 percent did not know which party had won the most seats in that election. Further, Warren E. Miller and Donald E. Stokes have demonstrated[23] that party symbols are almost devoid of policy content at the national level for most American voters. Yet there is ample evidence that party identification has been the single most stable factor in determining selections among opposing candidates for American voters since World War II.[24]

The situation is not much less chaotic in pluralist systems where the "responsible party model"[25] supposedly is more operative. Thus, in the United Kingdom, the facts about connections between voting and policy preferences of British voters are nearly as disturbing. In one survey, on only one-fourth of the questions concerning political ends or party traits were as many as two-thirds of the sample able to attribute a clear-cut goal to either of the major parties (Labour or Conservative). Where distinctions were drawn, they tended to be stated not in policy terms, but in social group (usually class) terms. On most of the remaining three-fourths of the questionnaire items, between one-third and one-half of the British voters sampled were unable to identify significant differences between the parties. Finally, the evidence in Britain is similar to that in the United States concerning the origins of party

identification. That is, party identification tends to be strongly influenced by familial traditions of political activity, and by other factors
of marginal policy relevance.

The last few paragraphs raise some serious doubts about the effectiveness with which representational government works, even in pluralist
systems with relatively informed electorates. Yet studies of constituency influence in the American Congress suggest that there are some
sets of issues on which representatives appear to be genuinely concerned about, and inclined to follow, the views of their constituents.
The instrumentalist interpretation of this finding would suggest that
congressmen follow their constituency's concerns when they believe
that those concerns will be remembered at the next election. The
evidence on motivation is sufficiently unclear to make it unwise to
speculate. But motivation aside, the correlations between constituency
opinion and the voting behavior of congressmen are rather high in
certain policy areas. The most prominent example of this in the United
States Congress is in the area of civil rights.[26] By contrast, in the area
of foreign policy it appears as if the typical American congressman looks
elsewhere than to his district in making up his mind. He relies in part
on his own judgment, and in part on the president and relevant members of the administration for a calculation of where the public interest
lies. In the last ten years or so, many members of Congress have asserted
a renewed role for legislative bodies in the formulation of foreign policy. It is too soon to tell whether this reassertion of congressional rights
will have some impact on the process by which foreign policy is made,
or on the substance of foreign policy. There seems little doubt, however, that the changing American conception of its role in Southeast
Asia, for example, has been influenced by a reinvigorated congressional
posture of opposition to the positions taken by the Johnson and Nixon
administrations.

The general point we wish to make is that constituency influence on
the behavior of representatives varies among policy issues. In some
issue areas congressmen tend to take delegate positions; in other areas
they tend to take a trustee posture. In some areas they appear to be
substantially influenced by party considerations, which might place
them into the "politico" model mentioned above. In essence, regardless
of the fact that most representatives assert in the abstract that they tend
to follow their own consciences in making policy choices, the empirical
evidence suggests that their views are frequently similar to those held
by a majority of the articulate and concerned members of their constituencies. There may be some uncertainty as to which is cause and which
is effect. Indeed, the relationship between constituency and representative is very complex, as one might reasonably expect in societies that
are socially and economically heterogeneous and complex.

Public Opinion, Political Culture, and Political Leadership. A slightly different way to view the linkages between elites and mass in pluralist systems is to ask what sorts of opinion are held about political leaders and
elites by the mass public, and to inquire how basic features of the
political culture affect the postures that citizens take toward elites.
Initially, we should distinguish briefly between the concepts of public
opinion and political culture. When we talk about public opinion, we
are referring to the way individuals and groups are oriented toward
contemporary issues, actors, and events in civic life. The concept of
political culture refers to the complex of citizen orientations toward the
fundamental political institutions and processes of their political system.[27] We make this distinction because we want to be able to separate
those citizen sentiments that are fundamental or basic to defining the
relationship between the citizen and his political environment from
reactions citizens have to political circumstances or personalities of the
moment. We should also recognize that there can be a levels-of-analysis
distinction between the two terms. Both public opinion and political
culture can be viewed as aggregate, or collective, concepts. At the same
time, we can also speak of the opinions of specific individuals; it is not
possible to speak of the political culture of an individual. We can, however, describe the values and beliefs that comprise the posture taken
by a given individual toward his political environment.

As a practical matter, one of the major differences between public
opinion and political culture is that most citizens in pluralist systems can
express (at least in general terms) a set of basic values and beliefs that,
taken collectively, comprise the political culture of that system. By
contrast, many of these same citizens do not have opinions on a significant number of contemporary political issues and personalities. Consequently, a considerable part of the relationship between elite and mass
in pluralist systems appears to be defined by the political culture, rather
than by contemporary currents of public opinion. In the United States,
the United Kingdom, and the Federal Republic of Germany, there
appears to exist a relatively stable and widespread pool of *diffuse support* for the basic political rules of the game, and thus for political
administrations that operate generally within the bounds of those rules.
This substantial reservoir of latent and/or poorly specified support: (a)
can be mobilized in times of crisis; and (b) tends to obviate the necessity
of citizens' taking specific positions on many matters of transitory importance.

In short, it is the shared, integrative, and generally supportive character of the political culture that seems to make the absence of highly
informed public opinion on specific issues a less-than-critical defect in
the functioning of these systems. Those specific political controversies
that have a substantial impact on the course of the political system

apparently do so because they are perceived as being relevant to more fundamental values that comprise the political culture. The Watergate crisis, which brought down the administration of Richard M. Nixon, would be an example of such a specific, transitory event that had a profound effect upon American politics because it revealed the violation by persons in high places of fundamental tenets of American political culture.

We can demonstrate the importance of the existence of shared, but vaguely defined, political values to the stability of a political order by looking at the remarkable lack of information possessed by Americans on specific political events and personalities. For example, over a period of approximately 30 years the National Opinion Research Center has polled a national cross-section of American adults concerning their knowledge about current political leaders. More than one-third of American adults apparently cannot name both U.S. senators from their own state. (To be sure, this is an improvement from the 47 percent who could not name *either* senator in 1944.[28]) A relatively consistent 50 percent of the population over the past 30 years has been unable to identify the presidential succession procedure in the United States, beyond knowing that the vice president succeeds the president in the event of the latter's death or incapacity in office. And notwithstanding the fact that party affiliation appears to be an important cue on the basis of which citizens decide whether or not to support given political candidates, fewer than 40 percent of the nation's voters regularly claim to have read any part of the political party platforms formulated in national election years. Countless examples of what might seem initially to be shocking levels of lack of information or misinformation within the American public, and that of the other pluralist systems, could be provided.

We all recognize that there is a difference between *mass* publics and *attentive* publics. All pluralist systems contain subsets of the general population that show a consistent interest in politics, and develop reasonably well-thought-out views based on a substantial amount of factual information. This subset we refer to as the *attentive* public. The mass public is composed of both the lethargic, apathetic, essentially uninformed sectors of the population, and the so-called *attention groups* (usually racial or ethnic) who, though not necessarily well informed, are extremely sensitive to words and symbols with which they have been indoctrinated and who respond quickly and generally unthinkingly to such symbols.[29] The attentive public is estimated at between 10 and 25 percent of the adult population in the United States.

Within the attentive public, as well as the attention groups that comprise part of the mass public, there are *opinion leaders* who serve to sort out, simplify, and transmit cues to others. These opinion leaders probably constitute not more than 2 or 3 percent of the American adult population. Their influence, however, can be considerable, particularly with respect to the formation of public opinion on questions that are both emotive in content and relatively technical or complex in character. Broadly, however, the information content of public opinion is low, even in pluralist systems, and the extent to which public opinions are formulated in such a way that they can provide guidance for the policy behavior of elites is slight.

The policy guidance that can be derived from public opinion does vary between issues, as we suggested above. This variation may be due in part to the distribution, or shape, of public opinion on the issue. Students of public opinion frequently distinguish among three varieties of opinion curves, each of which may have different implications for the impact of opinion on elite behavior. First, there is the J-curve opinion distribution, which describes distributions of opinion where a high degree of consensus exists. It should be kept in mind, however, that consensus may have any of several different substantive thrusts. Consensus may be *negative* or *restrictive* on the policy maker; it might be *supportive* of a particular policy position; it might be *permissive* in the sense of being malleable at the discretion of policy makers; or it might be *directive* or *decisive*, in the sense of appearing to mandate specific actions to correct critical circumstances.[30]

Public opinion may also assume the form of a U-shaped curve, which suggests that most people hold one or the other of two sharply opposing views, and that the remainder of those holding opinions are scattered thinly across the attitude scale between. This U-shaped, or bimodal, opinion distribution may indicate a potentially explosive political situation. Third, another conflict pattern may be reflected in a W-shaped curve, where opinions are grouped around three or more views, each constituting a fairly clear minority position. Such opinion distributions suggest a basis for fragmentation within the political system. They have been less common on central political issues in the United States, but more common, for example, in contemporary France.

It is also important to distinguish between two *forms* of opinion consensus: *consensus of views* and *consensus of intensities.*[31] The existence of a consensus of intensities suggests that a majority of the public (or perhaps only of the attentive public) believes that certain issues are more important than others, and should constitute the principal items on the agenda of policy action. A consensus of views suggests that a majority of the public (or attentive public) agrees essentially on *what should be done* about those most important issues. Thus the first form of consensus refers to agenda setting, whereas the second form refers to substantive preferences on specific issues. Anthony Downs has argued persuasively[32] that the impact of public opinion on policy formation by elites is consistently strong only in circumstances where there exists *both* a consensus of views and a consensus of intensities, at least among the attentive public (or what Downs calls the "articulate and concerned majority"). It is Downs's argument that fragmentation on questions either of agenda setting or of substantive policy preferences can be manipulated by elites who would choose to do so. Downs does not argue that such elite disregard for public opinion necessarily will take place, only that the circumstances just described would permit it.

In short, the character of public opinion and the shape of its impact on the behavior of elites and leaders in pluralist systems are very complex. To understand the substantial stability that most Western pluralist societies have exhibited over a relatively long period of time we must therefore look briefly at the underlying tenets of political culture that, as we argued above, seem to have more continuing and decisive effects on the relationship between elite and mass.

An examination of critical elements of political culture in three stable pluralist systems—the United States, the United Kingdom, and the Federal Republic of Germany—suggests as many differences as similarities. There are important similarities, to be sure, perhaps the most pervasive being the widely acknowledged commitment of most political leaders to basic democratic norms, to the nonviolent resolution of conflict, and to genuine efforts to define and pursue a collective good. Similarly, political elites share a mass commitment to the concept of accountability, such that elites accept collective public judgments of their behavior without attempting to manipulate the institutions of the political system in such a way as to change the results of the public judgments. The procedural norms underlying this basic political culture have been frequently discussed, and need only be listed here: equality, basic individual freedom and dignity, the right to political participation, and the rule of law, rather than of man. The imperfect realization of each of these procedural norms in pluralist societies notwithstanding, their relative accomplishment in a global perspective seems clear.

In addition, these three Western pluralist systems have *integrated* political cultures.[33] There is a strong sense of national identity, reinforced in practical terms by what appear to be workable political relationships between national and constituent governments, and by the existence of common cultural origins, common language, and extensive communication and transportation networks that have long since created national economies and national mobility structures.

Some differences begin to emerge when we look at certain other aspects of the political culture. For example, we know that evidence about political socialization in the three countries suggests that the commitment to democratic values on the part of German children is substantially lower than that observed in the other two pluralist systems. A recent investigation of 9 to 15-year-old schoolchildren in four countries (including Italy) revealed an apparent impact of the somewhat more authoritarian, father-dominated family structure in Germany. On political efficacy items, German children were noticeably less democratic than their counterparts elsewhere. Children in the United States were highest, British children second, Italian children third, and the German children lowest at every age level.[34] A similar difference was revealed on questions having to do with tolerance of minorities or tolerance of criticism of the government. The authors of this study concluded that "the political socialization of German children to tolerance of dissent is not assured."[35]

There also are some differences among pluralist Western systems in the extent of mass deference to elite positions and behavior. In particular, deference toward political elites appears to be a good deal higher in Great Britain than in either Germany or the United States; it is lowest in the U.S., with the exception of attitudes toward the presidency. According to the British political scientist Richard Rose, "leaders in [British] political life are expected to be uncommon men and enjoy deference on that basis. National politics is primarily for those who have been born to a high station in life, or who have qualified for a high station by youthful educational achievement."[36] One consequence of this deference is that most Britons have felt no particular obligation to participate actively in public life. It also has meant that the British do not necessarily gauge the acceptability of government policy by the extent to which it results from systematic interaction between rulers and ruled. Politics, in short, has been considered the appropriate vocation of a privileged few, with the occasional participation of the many. This is an attitude that probably would be untenable in a system without a high degree of traditional trust.[37] A study by Butler and Stokes revealed that over half of British citizens believed that the government often pays little attention to public opinion, but that this attitude neither surprised nor irritated most of the citizen respondents.[38]

In the United States there is less general deference toward political figures; indeed, there is some evidence that politics is still considered a "dirty game" by a substantial number of Americans, most of whom state that they would prefer that their children never be involved in public life. At the same time, it also seems clear that our institutions of political socialization tend to develop in American citizens a kind of generalized trust of the basic functioning of the political order as a whole—a diffuse form of support that tends to be transferred to specific officials or institutions in given situations. This is particularly noticeable in the case of the presidency, where public identification with the office as a symbol of the nation—an identification carefully and continually cultivated from earliest childhood—endows the incumbent president with enormous prestige to place in the service of those viewpoints he wishes his countrymen to adopt.[39]

We can gain an interesting perspective on public attitudes toward top executive leaders in three pluralist systems—the United States, Canada, and the United Kingdom—from a study by Erwin C. Hargrove.[40] Particularly interesting is Hargrove's characterization of the skills and resources that are expected of, and valued in, a president or prime minister. In the United States, "Presidents are pushed to reinterpret the American experience and American ideals for the nation and to solve problems in these terms." Hargrove contends that Americans still hold some vague image of "an American dream" to which a president must relate. Similarly, the presidency is responded to as a symbol of national unity. In addition, strong presidents, and usually the most respected, are those who seek to lead public opinion rather than play a passive role. The American president is seen as an individual who must exert strong leadership, and yet recognize the constraints that a pluralist, diverse society and its operative political values place upon him.

In Canada there is more emphasis on the prime minister as a successful political manager, someone who can effectively dampen internal party strife and who can move the country progressively forward in the face of deep ethnic and cultural divisions. Thus the Canadian prime minister must be a pragmatist, "a manager of majorities, not a man inspired by visions."[41] Canadian prime ministers have seen as their major tasks the promotion of a national unity that, for the most part, has already existed in the United States. The polarities with which Canadians have had to deal have been primarily cultural rather than politico-ideological.

In Great Britain, according to Hargrove, there is substantial nationalism, but of a kind a good deal more diffuse and nonideological than that present in the United States or Germany. During periods of external threat, this form of nationalism has been an enormous source of strength and stability for Britain. However, it has been much more difficult to mobilize at other times—including times of internal economic decline. The British prime minister still is viewed by citizens as one who must be able, in a pragmatic way, to interpret and put into practice the abstract ideals of a "good society"—critical limitations on available resources notwithstanding. In Hargrove's view, "the national political myth in Britain seems to be more about procedures than about substance. Tradition, pragmatism, flexibility, corporativism"—these are the sources of strength in British political culture, which must be translated into concrete action by prime ministers. There can be no doubt that Great Britain has moved into a period of malaise, and the demands on political leadership now are concentrated on that leadership's ability to find innovative solutions that will redirect the course of social and economic development in Britain without violating these traditional procedural values that are so widely shared, and so highly regarded.

In one major respect, we can draw a common thread through these vignettes describing elite-mass relationships in Western pluralist systems. This thread is the image of systems in which there is a democratized elite and an ambivalent mass.[42] Perhaps it is ironic that a greater commitment to abstract democratic values, and a greater ability to translate these values into concrete proposals for political action, exists among elites than with the mass public. Elites in pluralist systems are not simply better informed, more active, or more interested in civic affairs; more closely than do the masses, they approximate the ideal modern democratic citizen in basic political attitudes. The typical American, West German, or Canadian is an ambivalent democrat, irresolute in his dedication to democratic values and somewhat erratic when applying democratic norms to concrete situations—where the real test of such values might be expected to be made.[43] One of the implications of this combination of an apparently committed democratized elite and an ambivalent mass is that dramatic increases in the extent of political participation by the mass citizenry could produce a substantial increase in political instability in these societies. That possibility must remain an open question. But it is reasonably clear that the mode of accommodation that has evolved in the relationship between elite and mass in pluralist systems is, at least for the present, remarkably stable, particularly in comparison with similar relationships in other types of political system.

PREDICTORS OF THE ATTITUDES OF ELITES AND LEADERS

One thrust of the arguments presented so far in this chapter is that the sustenance of the basic character of pluralist systems may depend in considerable part on the maintenance of a given set of political values, beliefs, and attitudes on the part of the political leadership in these societies. It is therefore appropriate to conclude this chapter with a brief look at some recent evidence concerning the factors that appear to predict what political leaders think about basic policy questions.

In examining the relationships between factors such as social background and career characteristics and political attitudes,[44] it is important to consider both the *scope* and the *strength* of the antecedent factors. That is, we need to be concerned first about the *range of different attitudes* to which given background and career factors are relevant; this we refer to as *scope.* Second, we need to inquire about the *strength* of the relationship between each background and career factor and each attitude—that is, the accuracy with which we can predict a specific attitude by knowing a given background or career characteristic. Some background and career factors may be powerful predictors of a few attitudes, whereas other factors may be relatively weak predictors, but have at least some impact on a wide scope of attitudes.

Research conducted by Edinger and Searing[45] and by Searing[46] provides a basis for summarizing a good deal of what we know about these linkages between the backgrounds and careers of leaders and what they think about contemporary political issues. We can draw from this research several interesting observations concerning elites in the United States, the Federal Republic of Germany, and France.

First, studies of United States state legislators reveal that the most powerful predictors of their political attitudes were variables having to do with their *geographic origins,* or with the *characteristics of the districts they represented.* The state from which they came was the single most important predictor, followed by such factors as geographical location, population, and urban/rural breakdown of the district. These were followed in importance by political party affiliation.

Equally interesting was the discovery that the number of attributes necessary to predict a reasonable range of attitudes among American state legislators was very great. Searing examined a set of 91 attitudes. He discovered that only two predictors—the state from which a representative came and the geographical location of the district—predicted with strength as many as half of the 91 attitudes. The third most useful factor, population of the representative's district, was relevant to only 33 percent of the attitudes examined. Nearly half of the 56 background factors looked at were relevant to 10 percent or fewer of the attitudes studied. In short, the sources of attitudes among United States state legislators were so diverse that a reasonably concise predictive model could not be constructed.

Searing also discovered that the relative importance of similar background factors for elite attitudinal sets varied widely from one political system to another.[47] The background categories most frequently used in efforts to forecast political attitudes of elites—occupation, education, age, region of birth, religion—showed different predictive scopes in different systems. Age was relevant to 18 percent of the political attitudes in the U.S., but to only 3 percent in France. Level of education was relevant to 22 percent of political attitudes in the U.S., but only 5 percent in France. Region of birth was relevant for 21 percent of the political attitudes in the U.S., but only 8 percent in Germany. Thus it appears that some of the most commonly used social background variables "do not identify sufficiently similar environmental conditions and experiences to permit consistent forecasting of diverse attitudinal distributions in cross-national research."[48]

In the work done by Edinger and Searing, one conclusion emerged as the most critical: Recently held career positions are, with some consistency, better predictors of elite attitudes than are social background factors. Edinger and Searing examined data on elites from France and the Federal Republic of Germany in reaching this conclusion. There were some modest exceptions to the generalization, but the conclusion holds with considerable firmness. (Similar findings have been generated for several socialist systems.) It appears as if the demands of role performance in carrying out specific sets of tasks, even over a relatively short period of time, have a greater impact on the political perspectives held by elites than do background factors or earlier career experiences.

This finding is not inconsistent with the notion that social backgrounds and early career experiences may exert *indirect* influence on the perspective of political elites. It may be that the recruitment and self-selection of specific individuals into given political elite roles are affected by their backgrounds and early careers. Thus persons of given backgrounds might be expected to be found more frequently in particular political roles, with the result that their subsequent political attitudes would reflect not only the *direct* impact of recent career activity, but also the *indirect* impact of those background factors that influenced their career channels. A good deal more research is needed to clarify this possible indirect impact of social background on the political orientations of elites.

We can conclude that cultural and other location-specific factors appear to have great value in understanding the development of attitudes by political elites. There is sufficient variation among locations in the best predictors of elite attitudes that it seems unwise to attempt to postulate any "universal" set of factors that would explain why elites think and behave as they do. Nor would it be wise for us to conclude that the locales from which elites come, and the constituencies resident there, are unimportant in shaping elite attitudes and behaviors.

In this chapter we have barely scratched the surface of the many important issues, and significant recent research, dealing with relations between political leadership and mass citizenry in pluralist systems. It is not begging the question to say that these relationships are extraordinarily complex, as indeed might be expected from the complex character of the societies at which we have been looking. Classic, "idealist" conceptions of elite-mass linkage have never been operative in pluralist systems, and certainly do not exist today. Elites are not personally or attitudinally "representative" of the mass citizenry, nor is the framework of accountability procedures in these societies adequate to guarantee a high degree of responsiveness of elites to public concerns.

The conception of these relationships in the context of a combination of a democratized elite and an ambivalent mass is perhaps the single most useful perspective in attempting to understand how pluralist systems operate. This, in turn, should lead us to focus on two additional kinds of inquiry in the future. First, more systematic attention must be given to the origins of elite attitudes, particularly to the process of political socialization through which elites pass. Second, we need to know more about the formulation of public opinion toward elites and political leadership, and about the conditions under which the extent of public participation in selecting, and reviewing the behavior of, elites might increase.

8

Blending Substance and Method: Some Issues in Research on Leaders and Elites

One of the most important messages of this book has been that there is a close relationship between *how* we learn and *what* we know. We have tried to suggest that the substance of conclusions we draw about subjects as important as political leadership depend considerably on the thoroughness and care with which we conduct the research that provides a basis for our conclusions. The purpose of this concluding chapter is to outline some of the important methodological problems confronting students of political leadership and elites.

TAKE ME TO YOUR LEADER: PROBLEMS IN IDENTIFYING POLITICAL ELITES AND LEADERS

One basic and troublesome problem concerns the gap between our conceptual and our operational definitions of "eliteness" or "leadership." We have suggested at several points that these two concepts need to be kept distinct, because of the focus of "eliteness" on hierarchical position and the contrasting focus of "leadership" on relations between leaders and followers.

More generally, however, these two concepts themselves frequently are not carefully measured, even when the distinction between elites and leaders has been kept in mind. For example, there is a strong tendency to define elites conceptually in a functional way, but to operationalize—that is, to measure—eliteness on the basis of institutional position. Most students of elites probably would accept the Beck and

Malloy formulation that political elites can be identified through their continuing involvement in a set of functional relationships that surrounds the process by which resources and values are allocated for a social unit.[1] In other words, the best way to find political elites is to identify those functions in society that result in the allocation of resources for whole social units. Elites are persons who are involved in such activities. However, most studies measure eliteness on the basis of an institutional, or structural, definition. For example, it is common to identify elites as persons who are members of prominent institutional bodies, such as cabinets, legislatures, high courts, or executive committees of political parties. These studies permit legal prescription, or formality, to endow political office with influence in the value-allocating process. We tend to assume that persons who occupy important positions actually participate in the functions that are critical to the management of society.

This tendency to equate functional and positional eliteness may be misleading. It seems dubious to assume that any individual who holds membership in a prominent decision-making body actually exercises influence on political outcomes. His colleagues may be influential, but it does not necessarily follow that he is. We know that many persons are elevated to positions of prominence for symbolic or propagandistic reasons. They are there to placate dissident elements, or to symbolize the openness of access to the political elite for minority groups. Similarly, the recent history of political change in communist systems implies the periodic existence within major decisional bodies of isolated cliques, or subgroups, whose members appear to have little or no influence on decisions taken by the group as a whole. In short, elites may occupy formal positions for "nonfunctional" reasons, if by "functionality" we mean influence on the decision-making processes that are the central responsibilities of that unit.

Thus there is an important distinction between functional and positional eliteness; one of our greatest difficulties is deciding how to distinguish these two types of eliteness in practice. It is easy to determine who holds important positions; it is more difficult to discern whether a given individual who holds such a position is functionally significant in decision-making activity. In the face of the operational difficulty of making this distinction, there is a tendency to assume that functional and positional eliteness are the same.

The situation is not totally hopeless. For example, there is some basis for assuming that functional eliteness can be measured by comparing individual positions with decisions taken by whole units. Thus one approach to defining functional eliteness is to assume that persons whose positions are reflected with some consistency in the decisions made by groups of which they are a part have functional eliteness. Those persons who seem nearly always to be at odds with the collective decisions would be assumed to have positional, but not functional, eliteness. Naturally such an inference is indirect, and therefore problematic. Dissenters within decision-making bodies might consistently modify the views of the majority, even though the basic substance of their views is uniformly rejected. Members of a decisional minority who nevertheless soften the positions taken by the majority might reasonably be thought to have functional eliteness.

There has been some effort on the part of students of community power structure in the United States to move away from positional definitions of eliteness. In contrast to research designs that simply attribute significance to persons who hold high formal positions, some researchers have opted for a *reputational* definition of eliteness. They believe that eliteness can best be identified by interviewing a substantial number of elites and subelites, or perhaps a sample of the general population. Such an approach is based on the assumption that a sufficient number of careful inquiries will identify the people who *really* count, often including many persons who do not occupy important formal positions in government or political parties.

The notion of "kingmakers," powerful men behind the scenes, has been used for hundreds of years in describing the structure of political power. In pursuing a slight variation of this concept of kingmaking, Bachrach and Baratz have discussed what they call "the two faces of power."[2] They argue that power that is exercised openly (frequently by occupants of formal elite positions) is only one of the two important types of power present in modern societies. The other type, which is often more decisive, is the power of *issue-determination*, or *agenda-setting*. The most powerful individuals might well be those who are able to determine whether a given potential issue shall ever come up for resolution by formal decision-making bodies. Such persons operating outside public scrutiny in effect determine the agenda of political issues acted upon by formal elite groups. In many respects, then, this secretive "face of power" is determining, since it circumscribes the range of activity in which public figures may engage. In the United States, for example, powerful interest groups, acting through their representatives on congressional committees, may sometimes determine the agenda upon which congressional action shall be taken. Similarly, large corporations and interest groups may influence the formulation of policy alternatives at the highest levels of the executive branch of government.

Thus there are several problems involved in identifying the persons who should be studied in an inquiry into political eliteness or leadership. First, we must decide whether to focus on eliteness or on the relational characteristics associated with leadership. As we have suggested throughout this book, the kinds of question to be asked and the sorts of data to be gathered vary depending on which focus is selected. Second, research on elites and leaders demands close congruence between conceptual and operational definitions of central concepts. In particular, we need to be careful about the attribution of functional eliteness, or leadership, to persons whose only claim to such functional importance would seem to be the occupancy of high positions. Finally, we need to decide what kind of functional significance to focus on, with particular attention to the distinction between agenda-setting power and direct participation in resource allocation. Depending on which focus we decide to use, our questions and research procedures are likely to be different.

PROBLEMS OF CROSS-NATIONAL COMPARISON

The need for a comparative, cross-national perspective has been suggested at several places in this book. A general understanding of political leadership as a contemporary phenomenon is dependent upon the study of leadership in the wide variety of circumstances in which it exists. Further, explaining the salient features of leadership in any specific case requires an understanding of how the characteristics of that case are both similar to, and different from, other cases. The basic reason for the critical importance of comparison is that explanation and understanding are based on the notion of variance.[3] We understand the reasons for instability in elite turnover, for example, by discovering what other social, economic, cultural, and political factors *covary* with unstable elite turnover—what other variables have high values when elite turnover is high, and vice versa. And we explain the level of elite turnover in a given society by locating that society within the general patterns of relationships that we have identified by studying elite turnover and other social variables in many societies.

Cross-national comparative research is not easy to do. There is a growing literature dealing with the problems that must be confronted in such research,[4] some of which have to do with the differential *availability* of data, including access to the subjects being studied. Other problems concern the *comparability* of the data that are available. These questions of comparability deserve some comment here.

In the previous section of this chapter we suggested that the most appropriate way to define "eliteness" is on a functional, rather than an institutional, basis. One of the reasons for a functional definition is that we want our concepts, such as eliteness, to be defined in *functionally equivalent* ways across locations—we want them to have comparable "meaning" in each environment in which they are used. This comparability refers to both the qualitative and the quantitative dimensions of the concept: Not only do we hope that our indicators of "representativeness" tap similar aspects of elite-mass relationships in each respective society, but we also feel that classifications of "high," "medium," and "low" representativeness should be sensitive to intersocietal differences in the possible range of elite representativeness. A level of representativeness considered "high" in one society might be "low" in another.

Concepts themselves are not "equivalent"; it is the *measures*, or indicators, of the concepts that must show functional equivalence. The task of identifying equivalent measures of a concept for several different societies is difficult. It is not always clear what is the most valid measure of a concept such as representativeness for any given society. When research is extended across national boundaries, the problem acquires a new dimension; not only must the measure used for each society be valid for that case, the respective measures must also be comparable with one another.

Precisely how this cross-national equivalence of measures should be established and evaluated is not at all clear. One promising approach was suggested recently by Adam Przeworski and Henry Teune.[5] Przeworski and Teune contend that functional equivalence of measures is established by viewing those measures within the pattern of their relationships with other relevant social variables. If our respective measures of representativeness, for example, show similar relationships in each society with other social variables—e.g., educational level of the population, level of economic development, degree of political competitiveness—then we would have some basis for concluding that our measures were functionally comparable across societies.

When we talk about establishing functional equivalence of measures, it is well to keep in mind that we often must work with data gathered by several different researchers, usually for distinctly different purposes. Few students of politics are fortunate enough to be involved in cross-national research projects[6] in which measures designed to be functionally equivalent are sought for several societies. Most cross-national studies involve *secondary* analysis of data already gathered in each of the involved countries. Obviously, in such research we have no control over the nature of the data; we have to work with what is available, and to bring to it the highest possible degree of cross-national comparability.

The notion of functional equivalence, and the procedures and problems involved in determining it, can be illustrated with reference to the development of a cross-national data base for a computer-assisted learning package on political elites.[7] The task was to blend data from a number of different studies on elites into a coherent data collection based on a single list of concepts, and operationalized by a set of measures that were functionally equivalent, but not identical, across the several studies.

The COMPELITE data base (discussed in chapter 4) contains 16 items of information ("variables") on each of more than 2,000 elites from seven countries. The data were gathered in five different research projects.[8] The countries included are Argentina, Brazil, Bulgaria, the Federal Republic of Germany, Japan, Mexico, and the Soviet Union. The studies of the Latin American countries and of Bulgaria emphasized elites in the executive branch of government, and political party leaders. The research on Japan and Germany focused on legislative elites. The study on the Soviet Union dealt both with party leaders and with four specialized elites—economic, legal, literary, and military leaders. The data include social background information, career data, and measures of attitudes and behaviors.

These studies were done at different times, by different researchers, using different approaches, asking different questions, and using different data-gathering techniques. The studies focus on overlapping, but still not identical, elite groups. Consequently, they are not strictly comparable with one another, and the measures of elite characteristics used in the respective studies are far from identical. Putting the COMPELITE data base together was, therefore, a major task.

In order to obtain what could reasonably be thought of as "comparable"—i.e., functionally equivalent—measures of major concepts, considerable modification was necessary of the ways in which data had been coded in each study. Two basic types of problems of comparability had to be confronted.

The simpler case is that in which both the concept and its basic dimension of measurement were identical across the several studies, but the *categories* of the variable had to be defined differently. The variable of urban/rural origins (in COMPELITE this is labeled URBRURAL) provides a good example. URBRURAL was present in the several studies, and its measurement generally was based on the population of the place in which an elite was born and/or raised. However, the dividing line for distinguishing "urban" from "rural" places could not be identical for all studies because of differences in demographic structure among the societies being studied. A population size that is "urban" in one society is not necessarily "urban" in another; measurement must be sensitive to social context. Thus it was ultimately decided that a population level of 5,000 persons would distinguish "urban" from "rural" places in Latin America and Bulgaria, but that a population of 10,000 would be used for the other countries.[9] The choice of what were thought to be functionally equivalent, rather than identical, measures was based on an important premise about the nature of social measures: We are interested in the set of *functional characteristics* assumed to be indexed by our measure, rather than the measure itself. In the example of URBRURAL we attempt to distinguish "rural" from "urban" localities because we believe that the two categories correspond to different kinds of social and cultural environment, which might be expected to affect the lives of their members in different ways. These functional differences might be expected to be associated with different population levels in different places. Ideally, we might wish to have data dealing directly with some of these functional characteristics (e.g., patterns of interpersonal interaction), but such detailed data are not available for every locality in every country we are interested in studying. Consequently, we have to make use of indicators such as population size in the belief that they provide indirect measurement of social and cultural conditions.

A second, and more troublesome, problem of comparability is raised when the analyst wants to investigate a general concept of political activity for which the dimensions of measurement themselves must be different in the several data sets. For example, one of the behavioral concepts on which COMPELITE focuses is antinorm political behavior (ANTINORM)—behavior considered inconsistent with basic norms of the society and/or political organizations and institutions of which a person is a member. The concept of antinorm behavior was not used in any of the original studies on which COMPELITE is based; obviously, then, there were not identical measures available in the several data collections on which to predicate a study of antinorm behavior.

Lacking even a common measurement dimension (for example, population of place of birth for URBRURAL), it was necessary to identify functionally equivalent measures of ANTINORM on the basis of a rather disparate set of variables. The problem of comparability was complex. First, the notion of "political norms" is very broad; there are many different elements of the structure of such norms in all modern societies. Second, the content of political norms obviously varies from society to society; behaviors that are normatively proscribed in some places are common and ethically tolerable in others. Third, the types of elite behavior studied in the several research projects varied a good deal. Thus relatively "obvious" measures of antinorm behavior—e.g., participation in revolutionary acts—were available for some countries, but not for others. Finally, some of the studies on which COMPELITE was based focused implicity on locating elites in their broader *societal* context, whereas other studies emphasized more specific *organizational* contexts, such as roles within legislative institutions. Thus the norms to which antinorm behavior is relevant are operative at distinctly different societal levels. The substantive content of the norms may differ as a result; the specific behaviors that must be studied in relation to these norms surely will vary across countries as well. In some cases it was necessary to consider norms at *both* the societal and organizational levels, since it cannot be assumed that these two sets of norms are congruent in any given society, or that individual behaviors are related to these two sets of norms in similar ways.

Ultimately, the specific measures used for antinorm behavior were far from identical across studies. For Latin America, antinorm behavior at the societal level was measured by participation in coups d'état or other revolutionary acts directed against persons in power. At the organizational level, an absence of any formal affiliations with politically relevant groups other than parties was considered to index antinorm behavior. For Bulgarian elites, antinorm behavior included participation in revolutionary or armed resistance movements. Thus the measures used for the Latin American countries and for Bulgaria seem to have at least rough correspondence with conventional notions of norm-violating behavior.

For the studies of the Soviet Union, Japan, and Germany, behavior counter to the desires of the political party leadership was the measure of antinorm activity. In the case of the Soviet data, persons who expressed the opinion that the Communist party was "interfering" in the work of nonparty specialists, or who argued for minimum party influence outside directly political matters, were considered to be exhibiting antinorm behavior. For the German study, legislators with records of voting frequently against their party's leadership were considered "antinorm"; similarly, Japanese legislators who said they would be prepared to vote against their party leaders, even in the face of expected sanctions, were treated as "antinorm."

Thus the measures of antinorm behavior exhibited substantial differences across studies. They were designed, however, to be functionally comparable, not identical. And their functional comparability was evaluated by looking at the way each measure fit into the patterns of correlation among relevant variables. In general, the cross-national equivalence of these measures of antinorm behavior tended to show similar correlations with other variables for each country in the study.

It is worth stressing that this procedure amounts to *inferring within-nation validity from a finding of cross-national reliability*. That is, we are inferring that we have meaningful measures of antinorm behavior *in each country* on the basis of our observation that the several measures perform consistently *across countries*. Such inference of validity is obviously indirect, and correspondingly tenuous.

CHANGE, THE ONE GREAT CONSTANT: DIFFICULTIES IN STUDYING CHANGE

Knowing where we are is important—and often not as easy as it might seem. But knowing where we are likely to be going is more important and more interesting. Our ability to anticipate future political circumstances rests fundamentally on our grasp of *processes* of social, economic, cultural, and political *change* that have been taking place. Studies focusing on a single point in time are not likely to provide us with a sound picture of social and political dynamics. This kind of understanding requires a grasp of how we have come to where we are.

The distinction between *cross-sectional* (single time point) and *longitudinal* (over a series of time points) perspectives is roughly analogous to the difference between a single cinematic frame and a substantial segment of a motion picture. A single frame might present interesting information, but it is likely that this single frame would neither be representative of all of the frames in the film, nor able to illustrate the *development* of circumstances and relationships presented in the film. Studies focusing on political events at a single point in time are likely to suffer from the same kinds of limitation: They may well be unrepresentative of contemporary political circumstances, and they offer little promise of illuminating developmental processes.

We can sharpen our focus on this issue by considering a concrete problem of data analysis. As Richard A. Pride has shown, very different conclusions may be generated about the relationships among important social variables, depending upon whether one does cross-sectional or longitudinal analysis. For example, cross-sectional analyses for each of several points in time suggest a strong, positive correlation between industrialization and democratization of societies. However, when we correlate the time series data for these two variables, the correlation is greatly reduced.[10] The reason simply is that during certain periods of time there has been either no correlation between levels of industrialization and levels of democratization, or even a negative correlation between the two (e.g., in the decades of the 1930s and 1940s). The temporal context of politics is neither irrelevant nor unchanging.

The logic of this point warrants elaboration. Some students of politics have argued that cross-sectional studies are adequate for investigating political and economic development. They base their argument on the

premise that cross-sectional variance can be "substituted" for longitudinal variance. The nations of the world even today exhibit enormous
differences along economic and political dimensions. Countries representing a wide range of values can easily be found for almost any
significant social variable. This cross-sectional variance among countries
is then treated as if it represented a longitudinal *process* of development: Less-developed nations represent the "beginning" of the process, and increasingly developed nations are viewed as representing
successive phases, or stages, of development.

Although such an approach might have the virtue of convenience—
reliable and comparable social data often are not available for long time
periods—it can lead to a serious misrepresentation of the development
process. The patterns of relationships among social variables are different at different points in time; the temporal setting changes. The technological environment is vastly different now from what it was a few
decades ago, for example. The prospects for social control and manipulation, and for rapid and wide-ranging communication, have increased
enormously. Further, it is not reasonable to equate low levels of economic development today, for example, with low levels of development
in the past—among other things, the nations that have developed stand
as examples (positive and/or negative) to those developing from lower
economic levels. More-developed nations are both passive and active
examples—passive in that their accomplishments and mistakes are visible for those who would learn from them; active in that they provide
resource and technological aid to developing nations.

Furthermore, change is a *process,* by definition. As such, it has the
elements of all processes: *sequences, directions,* and *rates*. It embodies
the complex interplay of social, cultural, economic, and political factors
over time. Cross-sectional studies cannot give us anything more than
superficial insights into such complex temporal processes. Time series
data are needed.

Unfortunately, it is easier to acknowledge the importance of longitudinal studies than to carry them out. A number of distinct problems
are involved in doing such research. We shall summarize a few of the
major difficulties, focusing on data on leaders and elites.

Data Availability and Comparability.   In general, the most comprehensive biographical and attitudinal data are available on elites who came
into positions of national importance between 5 and 25 years ago. With
the exception of the more industrialized societies of North America and
Western Europe, comprehensive biographical data generally have
been recorded in reasonably accessible form only since about 1950. And
because of the usual time lag between achievement of political promi-

nence and the inclusion of persons in biographical directories, adequate data on newly emergent elites sometimes are not easily obtained. Consequently, cross-nationally comparative studies of political elites are constrained in their usual temporal coverage—unless such studies deal only with industrialized Western systems, a narrowing of focus that would adversely affect the usefulness of the study.

Further, even when biographical data are available for substantial periods of time, the respective data collections may not be entirely comparable, either between countries or for different time periods for the same country. We have discussed the former situation above; the latter circumstance can result not only from increasingly thorough record-keeping practices over time, but also from such things as a change of political regime in which new ideological doctrines define specific aspects of elite backgrounds to be sensitive areas of information, or call for general restrictions on the publication of such political information. Thus the socialist systems of Eastern Europe and the Soviet Union treat data on class backgrounds of elites as being ideologically sensitive (officially, nearly all political leaders in these countries are of "proletarian" origin). They also restrict the publication of career data on prominent public figures.

Periodization of Change.   Although it is possible to view political change as a single, continuous process, we usually divide the political history of a nation into periods. These periods may be seen as the phases, steps, or stages through which political change has proceeded. Similarly, we tend to view leadership change in terms of periods, usually corresponding to the dominance of an individual or political group.

Indeed, there has been a strong tendency to conceive of political change in terms of moving from the era of one leader, or set of leaders, to the era of another. Substantial blocks of time in political development often are endowed with characteristics inferred from the personal styles and political views of dominant leaders. This tendency can be misleading to the point of distraction, as with the effects of characterizing Soviet politics between 1924 and 1953 simplistically as "Stalinism." Such oversimplification often obscures major social and economic changes that were essentially unrelated to the identity of the top leadership.

More generally, there has been a tendency to identify the periods, or stages, of political system and political leadership change on an a priori basis. The researcher's impressions about major points of historical demarcation are used to structure his picture of the process of political change. The empirical data he gathers on political change then are forced into whatever predetermined stages, or periods—e.g., "Stalinism"—have been decided on ahead of time. The difficulty with this procedure is that the real-world data may not fit comfortably into these predetermined temporal intervals. It may turn out that the most meaningful changes in elite recruitment, for example, have taken place midway through periods of dominance by a strong leader or political party. This was found to be the case in the Soviet Union; Schueller has identified a watershed in Soviet elite recruitment in 1938.[11] Thus it would seem preferable to identify the stages of political change *inductively*, on the basis of concrete research findings, rather than on the basis of simplistic assumptions about the implications of political dominance by one or a few leaders.

Dimensions of Careers.   Another problem in studying elite change is the tendency to confuse several dimensions of career change. In the first place, there is an obvious difference between changes of elite *personnel* and changes in the *attributes* of elite groups, viewed collectively. Personnel turnover can occur without a corresponding change in the aggregate background and career characteristics of an elite group. Research on the political elite of the People's Republic of China demonstrates a remarkable similarity of basic characteristics between 1930 and 1965,[12] even though there was considerable personnel turnover. Conversely, attitudinal changes may be observed among members of a group whose membership changes very little. This happened with the Soviet leadership after Stalin's death in 1953, for example.

Further, even where there is limited personnel change, and the few new members who are brought in tend to exhibit backgrounds and career experiences similar to those of the old members, it is still possible to observe not only attitudinal, but even career, changes within the elite. In this case, career changes might take the form of professional *reorientation*—a change in the functional area of specialization in which an elite operates. The Bulgarian political elite, for example, seems to have undergone significant career reorientations during the 1960s, notwithstanding the rather slight personnel and attribute changes.[13] Consequently, it is important to examine not only entry into and exit from the elite, but also reorientations of career and attitude that may be taking place *within* the elite.

The "Straw Man" Problem.   Another difficulty in the study of elite change is the possibility that our conceptual categories may "create" a misleading impression of change. The language we use may tend either to obscure or to overstate the extent of change actually taking place. For example, it is common practice to label the Soviet Union as an "ideological" system, and to characterize its leadership structure as ideologically based. For purposes of a static (single time point) description of the Soviet Union today, the term "ideological" seems misleading; it implies that much is still the same as it was during the first three decades of Soviet rule. On the other hand, use of the label "ideological" as a description of earlier periods also can distort our understanding of the Soviet system. Thus Milton Lodge's research[14] suggests that the Soviet leadership system is already more "instrumental" than "ideological." Whether the classification of Soviet leadership as "instrumental" really signifies a significant change in that leadership depends a great deal on the validity of classifying earlier Soviet leadership as "ideological." The central question is: Have things changed in the real world, or are we creating an image of change by using suggestive terminology?

Macro Change and Micro Change.   A final problem in the study of elite and leadership change concerns assumptions linking elite change to broader processes of economic and social change. It is usually assumed that any significant social change—e.g., industrialization—will necessarily be accompanied by changes in political elite groups. The macro-micro relationship usually is assumed to be either causative or one of congruence; either the broader systemic (macro) change causes a (micro) change in political leadership, or the elite change is itself part of the systemic change.

Because linkages between elite change and broader social change are important to understand, many students of political leadership have tended to assume the nature of such linkages, rather than researching them carefully. There is sufficient evidence that these elements of macro and micro change are *not* always related, however, to make such assumptions dubious. Japan, the People's Republic of China, and Iran are three examples of societies in which some substantial social and economic changes were accompanied by only slight modifications in the composition and orientations of political elites. Such relationships need to be carefully established, rather than casually assumed.

DON'T CONFUSE ME WITH THE FACTS; THE USE OF A PRIORI TAXONOMIES

One of the principal arguments of this book has been that understanding requires theory. At the same time, theory sometimes can be a restraint on understanding, rather than an aid. Our unambiguous need for frameworks for handling information sometimes leads us to posit conceptual categories that tend to assume an aura of concrete reality as our research progresses. That is, we may tend to attribute

reality to analytical constructs: "Systems" assume finite physical boundaries, and labels descriptive of *types* of leader become descriptions of
specific persons—e.g., "ideologue," "authoritarian," or "liberal."

Similarly, our data are sometimes "stretched"—"massaged," "recon-
ceptualized," "reinterpreted"—so that they fit more neatly into our
conceptual categories. If we begin with a dichotomous classification of
societies as "capitalist" and "socialist," we do our best to conclude that
whatever societies we study can fit into one category or the other. Or
if we begin by characterizing leadership systems as "pluralistic" or
"elitist," experience suggests that we ultimately will succeed in making
the real world conform to this simplistic, bifurcated imagery—at least
in our own minds. Dichotomous (two-category) classifications are the
worst offenders, but having more than two categories does not necessarily solve the problem.

Not only are such a priori classification schemes frequently oversimplified, and thus misleading, they also tend to be self-confirming. Classifying the United Kingdom or Sweden as a "capitalist" rather than as a
"socialist" country inclines us toward looking for the social and economic features that would justify such a classification. In turn, stressing
those features may lead us to give inadequate attention to the "socialist"
elements in the structures of those systems. There is good reason to
believe that our basic classificatory decisions often are based on gross
criteria, casually chosen and casually applied. Systems may even be
classified on one dimension (e.g., the socioeconomic) on the basis of
their perceived standing on a wholly distinct dimension (e.g., the political). One suspects that such is the case when certain Western European
nations (e.g., the United Kingdom, Sweden) are classified as "capitalist"
(a socioeconomic category) apparently because of their political structure ("democratic"). The crux of such classificatory carelessness is the
tendency common in some Western societies to equate "capitalism"
and "democracy."

JUDGE NOT BY WORDS ALONE: PROBLEMS IN THE USE OF CONTENT ANALYSIS

Chapter 3 stressed the importance of content analysis as a method for
gathering data on elite and leadership orientations. Especially where
direct access to elites is limited, where the validity of given elite statements as indicators of personal orientations may be challengeable, or
where corroborative evidence is needed to supplement interview data,
content analysis is a very useful technique.

Some basic difficulties in using content analysis also were discussed in chapter 3; especially the issues of: (1) the validity of public statements by prominent persons as measures of personal orientations; and (2) the problem of retaining the original context of the word usage. Although these issues will not be analyzed further in this section, some additional problems having to do with content analysis of political materials will be introduced. Broadly, these additional problems are relevant to the *strategy* of the use of content analysis—the researcher's expectations about what kinds of information he can cull from the materials he is looking at.

First, content analysis cannot stand alone as a basis for understanding political leadership; it is useful as one element in a multiple-strategy approach. In a general sense, this is true of any single technique, but it is especially true of a method that focuses on one specific category of evidence. Although the study of elite communications is of great consequence, it is ultimately useful only insofar as these communications are viewed within a framework that includes both the *predictors* and the *consequences* of elite perspectives, e.g., demographic and career attributes and policy outcomes.

Because of its relatively narrow focus, content analysis has the disadvantage—and, in an important sense, the advantage—of forcing the thoughtful researcher to approach its use with an explicit theoretical framework of his own. Too often researchers using content analysis have proceeded from a "let's see what sorts of words are here" posture, or at best with rudimentary theoretical notions. Too often they have fallen victim to the situation described in the old saw, "If you don't know what you're looking for, you're bound to find it." To be sure, there are valid inductive uses of content analysis, especially in terminological mapping of areas of communication in which even the rudimentary dimensions and modes of expression are not known. But for purposes of testing hypotheses in explanatory models, content analysis must be used carefully within the context of systematically developed theory.

The theoretical context of any content analysis application is provided through the content analysis dictionary. As we have noted in chapter 3, the dictionary is especially crucial in computer content analysis. It reflects the researcher's conceptual scheme, his assumptions concerning what references he will find in the data, how these references are to be related to one another, and how they are to be interpreted within his theoretical framework. Dictionary construction is necessarily a tedious and time-consuming process in most content analysis research. But it is necessary—and, it is hoped, creative—tedium, since the ultimate usefulness of the research rests substantially upon the care and imagination with which the dictionary was constructed.

A second issue concerns a fundamental choice that must be made by the content analyst: whether he will examine only *manifest* content, or will also delve into the *latent* dimensions of communications. This is essentially a choice between purely descriptive and descriptive-inferential research designs. Inference has become increasingly important in content analysis research. Extending analysis beyond the lexical attributes of statements usually consists of drawing inferences about the *antecedents* (including the source) and/or the *effects* of the communication; the former category of inference is more common. Researchers who make inferential use of content analysis seem to feel that inferred linkages between the content of a communication and its source require corroborating evidence from independent noncontent data. Holsti divides such corroborative content/noncontent data comparisons into two categories, direct and indirect comparisons.[15] In *direct* comparisons the researcher has an independent behavioral measure of the attribute he wishes to infer from the content of a communication. For example, if content analysis of elite communications were being used to infer the nature of basic education and professional training experienced by the elites, direct corroboration would involve having educational and professional training data on the elites who authored the communications. It could be argued that direct corroboration is less a case of validating inference than of establishing measurement reliability by using more than one indicator. *Indirect* corroboration clearly does involve inferential logic, which can be stated as a syllogism:[16]

> In a given situation, individuals whose behavior patterns are known to be z, z', z'' produce messages with characteristics x, x', x'', respectively. If in similar circumstances a source produces messages with attributes x'', the inference is that it was related to behavior pattern z''.

Thus if elites with varying degrees (low, medium, high) of experience in formal intergovernmental organizations are known to have produced messages with, respectively, low, medium, and high levels of support for the concept of internation integration, subsequent communications evidencing high levels of support for integration might be inferred to come from persons who (among other characteristics) have had a high degree of experience in intergovernmental organizations. (The example is meant to be logically illustrative, not substantively suggestive.) Such inference based on indirect corroboration from noncontent sources obviously requires great caution.

A third set of issues is raised by another choice that must be made by the researcher using content analysis: whether he will focus on the *cognitive* dimension of content, the *affective* dimension of content, or both. This choice has to do with the distinctions among *values, beliefs,* and *attitudes* of elites and leaders. Distinctions among these dimensions of elite orientation have been made in several different ways. According to the view accepted here, the term "values" refers to fundamental "ought"-propositions—positions reflecting positive, neutral, or negative affect toward specified objects. Thus the affective dimension of content analysis involves the study of values. "Beliefs" are "is"-perception propositions—statements indicating how the source of the communication descriptively perceives given objects. Beliefs are therefore nonevaluative, and are handled as part of the cognitive dimension of content. "Attitudes," too, are cognitive in character according to this schema, but they are distinguishable from beliefs. Attitudes are structures for thinking, frameworks within which values and beliefs are set into relation with one another. As such, attitudes have neither affect nor specific descriptive content, but rather are modes of thinking and expression. A particularly salient attitudinal dimension for purposes of research on leaders is the open-closed mind[17] dimension, i.e., the degree of dogmatism with which values and beliefs are held.

Political leaders and elites presumably vary along each of these three dimensions. They have differing values concerning, for example, the proper role of government in social and economic regulation. Different leaders prefer different levels and types of government involvement. They differ in their beliefs about how deeply involved government actually is in societal regulation, and about the likely implications of specific proposed programs of new government activity. And their attitudinal structures are different, in that their values and beliefs are to varying degrees permeable and malleable. Each of these elements of the postures of elites needs to be carefully examined, both discretely and in relation to the other two elements.

A final set of issues in research design for content analysis concerns different ways of looking at either beliefs or values. Parsons, Shils, and Olds[18] have pointed out that social objects may be significant as *complexes of qualities* or as *complexes of performance.* In the former case the object is considered in terms of its attributes, of *what it is;* in the latter the object is seen in terms of its activities, of *what it does.* Values (or beliefs) about qualities and performances of the same object may be congruent, but need not be. For example, statements by Romanian political elites may exhibit positive affect for the Soviet Union or its leadership while showing negative affect toward specific actions or policies being pursued by the Soviet leadership. Or the Soviet leadership may see COMECON as having the attributes necessary for achieving regional economic integration, but perceive that COMECON's performance reflects nonintegrative, or even disintegrative, propensities. It is important to keep this distinction between complexes of qualities and complexes of performance clearly in mind.

THE INTERDEPENDENCE OF METHODS AND CONCLUSIONS: THE EXAMPLE OF COMMUNITY POWER STUDIES

One of the most vigorous disputes waged in the American political science and sociology communities during the 1960s was that between the "elitists" and the "pluralists." Many a professional meeting was enlivened—or, frequently, deadened—with expenditures of emotional energy by proponents of the respective points of view. The debate became such an institutionalized part of the two disciplines that the "elitist" and "puralist" perspectives were dignified by being described as "schools" of thought, and even "models" or "theories."

It would not serve our purposes to review the debate here. But some attention to its implications for the close relationship between *what* we know and *how* we find out—between methods and conclusions—is called for.

As we have seen earlier in this book, the dispute centered around differing interpretations of the extent to which American communities tend to be dominated by small, relatively cohesive, groups of elites. The "elitists" were the social scientists who concluded that American communities tend to be hierarchical, with public affairs substantially controlled by a small number of persons whose dominance is difficult to break. The "pluralists" were those who felt that power in American cities and towns is, more often than not, dispersed among a relatively wide range of social groups and interests.

For our purposes, the interesting element in this debate is the nature of the charges and countercharges made by the two groups. Broadly, the allegations were that:

1. The "elitists" found elitist political structures because they *wanted to* find them; correspondingly, the "pluralists" found pluralistic dispersals of power because they set out to find exactly that.
2. The *methods* used by each group essentially *predetermined* the conclusions of the research.

In short, each side accused the other of having ideological and methodological biases that "created" their conclusions, and rendered it impossible for their research to illuminate the realities of power in American community politics.

It seems unwise to attempt to unravel the complexities of scholarly motivation and ideology. Some "elitists" were widely thought to be pleased to discover highly structured community politics because this finding provided a "legitimate" basis for criticism of existing political arrangements, and for proposals for significant political reforms at the local level. And some "pluralists" might have found their research conclusions to be heartening bases for defending existing political structures. On the other hand, perhaps everyone involved was motivated solely by a scholarly concern for learning as much as possible about local politics. The essential point is that systematic analysis of these personal motivations is not possible—or, at least, was not done—so that such conjectures are best left to the meditations of armchair psychologists.

The second allegation—of methodological bias—can be examined more carefully. Sociologist John Walton has looked at 33 major community power studies done in the United States, dealing with a total of 55 communities.[19] One of the hypotheses he examined was the notion that the *method* used in *identifying* the community elite was significantly correlated with the type of power structure ultimately found. Specifically, it had been suggested that the "reputational" method (which tended to be favored by the "elitists") led to the discovery of pyramidal power structures, in which influence flowed downward from a small group at the top. Conversely, the "decision-making" approach (favored by many "pluralists") was thought to lead often to a finding of more coalitional power structures, in which a variety of interests jostled for predominance. The reputational method involves asking a group of preselected "influentials" to reveal who is "really" influential in the community. The decision-making approach looks at the handling of political issues (allocation of resources and resolution of conflicts) through the formal structures of local government.

Walton concludes that the basic hypothesis is correct; there is a high correlation between the method used and the findings reached. The correlation is sufficiently high that it is unlikely to have occurred by chance. The thrust of his conclusion is important: "The type of power structure identified *by studies that rely on a single method* may well be an artifact of that method."[20] Walton urges that, where possible, a variety of methods—a "multiple-strategy approach"—be used in research on elites and leaders. This is an argument for methodological pluralism, diversity, and comprehensiveness. The message is that a little extra time and care may mean the difference between results that are scholastic artifacts and results that are intellectually sound and socially useful. Walton's point surely is relevant not only to community power studies, but to all inquiry on social questions.

Notes

CHAPTER 1
LEADERS AND ELITES: SOME CLASSICAL AND CONTEMPORARY NOTIONS

1. *Political Leadership,* ed., Glenn Paige, (New York: Free Press, 1972), p. 3.

2. Vilfredo Pareto's best-known work available in English translation is *The Mind and Society,* 4 vols. (New York, 1935). The volumes initially were published in Florence in 1916–1923 under the title *Trattato di Sociologia Generale.* Of Gaetano Mosca's works, the only one translated into English is *The Ruling Class,* trans. Hannah D. Kahn, ed. and rev. Arthur Livingston (New York and London, 1939). *The Ruling Class* was originally published under the title *Elementi di scienza politica* in 1896. A useful collection of essays on Pareto and Mosca is *Pareto and Mosca,* ed., James H. Meisel, (Englewood Cliffs, N.J.: Prentice-Hall, 1965). Also see Meisel, *The Myth of the Ruling Class. Gaetano Mosca and the "Elite,"* 2d ed. (Ann Arbor: University of Michigan Press, 1962). Robert Michels's positions are presented in his *Political Parties* (New York: Dover, 1959). The original German edition appeared in 1911. The ideas of Karl Marx on the nature and role of elites can be found in his *The Eighteenth Brumaire of Louis Bonaparte* (New York: International Publishers, 1926), and in Marx and Friedrich Engels, *Manifesto of the Communist Party* (New York: International Publishers, various editions). Also see C. Wright Mills, *The Marxists* (New York: Dell, 1962).

3. For example, see James S. Coleman, *Power and the Structure of Society* (New York: Norton, 1974), esp. chap. 2; also T. B. Bottomore, *Elites and Society* (Middlesex, Eng.: Penguin, 1966), pp. 115–16.

4. It is a characteristic of increasingly complex social orders that persons outside the formal structure of government exercise influence over political outcomes less consistently, and largely through intermediate, or buffer, institutions. Thus there is an increasingly close relationship between the number of persons who are part of the apparatus of the state and the number who have the opportunity to exert *direct* and *consistent* (though not necessarily decisive) influence on the distribution of societal resources.

5. Mosca, *Ruling Class*, p. 50.

6. E. E. Schattschneider, *The Semi-Sovereign People* (New York: Holt, Rinehart and Winston, 1960).

7. See esp. two studies in the Hoover Institute elite studies series: Maxwell Knight, *The German Executive, 1890–1933* (Stanford, Calif.: Stanford University Press, 1951); and Daniel Lerner, *The Nazi Elite* (Stanford, Calif.: Stanford University Press, 1951).

8. Charles C. Moskos, Jr., "The Social Transformation of the Albanian Elite: The Concept of Elite Generations" (Paper delivered at conference on "Social Science and the Underdeveloped Areas: A Revival of Evolutionary Theory?", Northwestern University, June 1961).

9. C. Wright Mills, *The Power Elite* (New York: Oxford, 1959).

10. Mosca, quoted by Meisel, *Myth of the Ruling Class*, p. 303.

11. Thomas R. Dye and Harmon Ziegler, *The Irony of Democracy* (Belmont, Calif.: Wadsworth, 1970).

12. Michels, *Political Parties.*

13. Bottomore, *Elites and Society*, p. 15.

14. Donald D. Searing, "Models and Images of Man and Society in Leadership Theory," *Journal of Politics* 31, 1 (February 1969), pp. 3–31.

15. Jerzy J. Wiatr, "Political Elites and Political Leadership: Conceptual Problems and Selected Hypotheses for Comparative Research," *Indian Journal of Politics* (December 1973), p. 139.

16. See William A. Welsh, *Studying Politics* (New York: Praeger, 1973), pp. 120–26.

17. Wiatr, "Political Elites and Political Leadership . . . ," pp. 139–40.

18. Ibid., pp. 137–38.

19. Ibid., p. 138.

20. Ibid.

21. Fred E. Fiedler, *Leadership* (Morristown, N.J.: General Learning Press, 1971).

22. Ralph M. Stogdill, *Handbook of Leadership: A Survey of Theory and Research* (New York: Free Press, 1974), pp. 167–69.

CHAPTER 2
APPROACHES AND DATA IN RESEARCH ON LEADERS AND ELITES

1. These volumes were published during the early 1950s. The core volume was Daniel Lerner, Harold D. Lasswell, and C. Easton Rothwell, *The Comparative Study of Elites: An Introduction and Bibliography* (Stanford, Calif.: Stanford University Press, 1951). The series also included: George K. Schueller, *The Politburo* (Stanford, Calif.: Stanford University Press, 1951); Daniel Lerner, *The Nazi Elite* (Stanford, Calif.: Stanford University Press, 1951); Maxwell Knight, *The German Executive, 1890–1933* (Stanford, Calif.: Stanford University Press, 1951); Ithiel de Sola Pool, *Satellite Generals* (Stanford, Calif.: Stanford University Press, 1955) and Robert C. North, *Kuomintang and Chinese Communist Elites* (Stanford, Calif.: Stanford University Press, 1952). Condensed versions of these studies appeared in Lasswell and Lerner, *World Revolutionary Elites* (Cambridge, Mass.: MIT Press, 1965).

2. Lester G. Seligman, *Recruiting Political Elites* (New York: General Learning Press, 1971), p. 16.

3. For example, see Henry J. Abraham, *The Judicial Process*, 3d ed. (New York: Oxford, 1975), pp. 61–64.

4. Interlockingness has been especially characteristic of the Chinese political elite. See North, *Kuomintang and Chinese Communist Elites; Elites in the People's Republic of China*, ed. Robert A. Scalapino, (Seattle: University of Washington Press, 1972).

5. Carl Beck and James Malloy, "Political Elites: A Mode of Analysis" (Paper delivered at the Sixth World Conference, International Political Science Association, Geneva, 1964), pp. 2–3.

6. V. O. Key, *Public Opinion and American Democracy* (New York: Knopf, 1961), p. 540.

7. Beck and Malloy, "Political Elites: A Mode of Analysis," p. 23.

8. Ibid.

9. See esp. Frederic J. Fleron, Jr., "System Attributes and Career Attributes: The Soviet Political Leadership System, 1952–1965," in Carl Beck, Frederic J. Fleron, Jr., Milton Lodge, Derek J. Waller, William A. Welsh, and M. George Zaninovich, *Comparative Communist Political Leadership* (New York: McKay, 1973), pp. 43–85.

10. Ibid., p. 45.

11. Seligman, *Recruiting Political Elites*, op. cit.

12. Ibid., p. 15.

13. See Beck et al., *Comparative Communist Political Leadership*.

CHAPTER 3
METHODS OF ANALYSIS IN RESEARCH
ON POLITICAL LEADERS AND ELITES

1. For a discussion of how studies of small groups can contribute to an understanding of leadership behavior, see Sidney Verba, *Small Groups and Political Behavior: A Study of Leadership* (Princeton, N.J.: Princeton University Press, 1961).

2. For example, see Daniel Lerner and Morton Gorden, *Euratlantica: Changing Perspectives of the European Elites* (Cambridge, Mass.: MIT. Press, 1969).

3. The application of psychoanalytic approaches to the study of political leadership was pioneered by Harold Lasswell. See his *Psychopathology and Politics* (Chicago: University of Chicago Press, 1930) and *Power and Personality* (New York: Norton, 1948). An important illustration of this kind of approach can be found in Erik H. Erikson, *Young Man Luther: A Study in Psychoanalysis and History* (New York: Norton, 1958). For two interesting reviews of Erikson's *Young Man Luther*, see the essays by Lucian W. Pye and Daryl De Bell in *Political Decision-Makers: Recruitment and Performance*, ed. Dwaine Marvick, (New York: Free Press, 1961). On Hitler, see: Alan Bullock, *Hitler* (New York: Harper & Row, 1954); and Erikson, "The Legend of Hitler's Childhood," in Erikson, *Childhood and Society* (New York: Norton, 1963). On Lenin and the Bolsheviks, see David Shub, *Lenin* (New York: New American Library, 1948); and E. Victor Wolfenstein, *The Revolutionary Personality* (Princeton, N.J.: Princeton University Press, 1967). On Stalin, see: Leon Trotsky, *Stalin* (New York: Harper & Row, 1941); and Milovan Djilas, *Conversations with Stalin*, ed. Michael B. Petrovich (New York: Harcourt, 1962).

4. On Churchill, see: Violet Bonham-Carter, *Winston Churchill: An Intimate Portrait* (New York: Harcourt, 1965); Lewis Broad, *Winston Churchill, A Biography*, 2 vols. (London: Sidgwick and Jackson, 1963–1964); Roy Howells, *Churchill's Last Years* (New York: McKay, 1966); Relman Morin, *Churchill: Portrait of Greatness* (Englewood Cliffs, N. J.: Prentice-Hall, 1965); Maxwell Philip Schoenfeld, *Sir Winston Churchill: His Life and Times* (Hinsdale, Ill.: Dryden Press Inc., 1973). On Franklin D. Roosevelt, see: James McGregor Burns, *Roosevelt: The Lion and the Fox* (New York: Harcourt, 1956); Joseph

Gies, *Franklin D. Roosevelt: Portrait of a President* (Garden City, N.Y.: Doubleday, 1971); Edgar E. Robinson, *The Roosevelt Leadership, 1933–1945* (Philadelphia: Lippincott, 1955); Alfred B. Rollins, *Roosevelt and Howe* (New York: Knopf, 1962); Robert E. Sherwood, *Roosevelt and Hopkins: An Intimate History,* rev. ed. (New York: Harper & Row, 1950); Rexford G. Tugwell, *The Democratic Roosevelt: A Biography of Franklin D. Roosevelt* (Baltimore: Penguin, 1969); Tugwell, *FDR: Architect of an Era* (New York: Macmillan, 1967); Tugwell, *In Search of Roosevelt* (Cambridge, Mass.: Harvard University Press, 1972).

5. See Lewis J. Edinger and Donald D. Searing, "Social Background in Elite Analysis: A Methodological Inquiry," *American Political Science Review,* 61 (June 1967): pp. 428–45; Searing, "The Comparative Study of Elite Socialization," *Comparative Political Studies* 1, 4 (January 1969), pp. 471–500; Carl Beck et al., *Comparative Communist Political Leadership* (New York: McKay, 1973).

6. Edward A. Shils, "The Intellectuals and the Powers," *Comparative Studies in Society and History,* 1 (October 1958), pp. 5–22.

7. See William A. Welsh, "Toward a Multiple-Strategy Approach to Comparative Research on Communist Political Elites," in *Communist Studies and the Social Sciences,* ed. Frederic J. Fleron, Jr., (Chicago: Rand McNally, 1969), esp. pp. 319–21; and Welsh, "Methodological Problems in the Study of Political Leadership in Latin America," *Latin American Research Review,* 5, 3 (Fall 1970), esp. p. 4.

8. See esp. Ole R. Holsti, *Content Analysis for the Social Sciences and Humanities* (Reading, Mass.: Addison-Wesley, 1969).

9. For discussions of the strengths and weaknesses of content analysis techniques in investigating various dimensions of human communication, see ibid; and William A. Welsh, "Content Analysis and the Study of Integration in Eastern Europe," in *Regional Integration: Theory and Research on Eastern Europe,* ed. Richard P. Farkas and James A. Kuhlman, (Leiden; Netherlands: A. W. Sijthoff, forthcoming).

10. See Eugene J. Webb, D. T. Campbell, R. T. Schwartz, and L. Sechrest, *Unobtrusive Measures: Nonreactive Research in the Social Sciences* (Chicago: Rand McNally, 1966).

11. Both mass and elite surveys have been done in Kenya, Turkey, and South Korea by associates of the Comparative Legislative Research Center, Department of Political Science, University of Iowa; several interim reports from this recently completed study are available from the center. For reports of recent mass and elite surveys in Yugoslavia, see M. George Zaninovich's chapters in *Political Leadership in Eastern Europe and the Soviet Union,* ed. R. Barry Farrell, (Chicago: Aldine, 1970) and in Beck et al., *Comparative Communist Political Leadership.* Also see *Opinion-Making Elites in Yugoslavia,* ed. Allen H. Barton, Bogdan Denitch, and Charles Kadushin, (New York: Praeger, 1973).

12. Zaninovich in Beck et al., *Comparative Communist Political Leadership.*

13. See Barton, Denitch, and Kadushin, *Opinion-Making Elites in Yugoslavia, op. cit.*

CHAPTER 4
SYSTEM TYPES AND CAREER TYPES

1. See Robert A. Dahl and Charles E. Lindblom, *Politics, Economics, and Welfare* (New York: Harper & Row, 1953), esp. chap. 6–17.

2. E. E. Schattschneider, *The Semi-Sovereign People* (New York: Holt, Rinehart and Winston 1960).

3. COMPELITE is discussed in more detail in Chapter 8. The data set was compiled by William A. Welsh and the staff of the Laboratory for Political Research at the Univer-

sity of Iowa. The data come from research projects conducted by Gerhard Loewenberg, Chong Lim Kim, Milton Lodge, Carl Beck, and William Welsh. The data set, accompanying user's and instructor's manuals, and software written for interactive use on Hewlett-Packard 2000ACCESS and 2000F mini-computers are available from the Laboratory.

CHAPTER 5
EXTRALEGAL POLITICAL BEHAVIOR
AMONG LATIN AMERICAN POLITICAL ELITES

1. For convenience, this chapter adopts the common practice of referring inclusively to "Latin American politics" or "political leadership in Latin America." This practice should not obscure the fact that there are important differences among the polities and the political leadership institutions in Latin America. We should guard against the tendency to refer to Latin America as if the area were essentially homogeneous. See William A. Welsh, "Methodological Problems in the Study of Political Leadership in Latin America," *Latin American Research Review,* 5 (Fall 1970), pp. 3–33.

2. R. A. Gomez, "Latin American Executives: Essence and Variation," *Journal of Inter-American Studies,* 3 (1961), pp. 81–96.

3. Robert J. Alexander, *Latin American Politics and Government* (New York: Harper & Row, 1965), pp. 10–17; J. L. Mecham, "Latin American Constitutions: Nominal and Real," *Journal of Politics,* 21 (1959), pp. 258–75.

4. E. A. Duff and J. F. McCamant, "Measuring Social and Political Requirements for System Stability in Latin America," *American Political Science Review,* 62 (December 1968), pp. 1125–43; Martin C. Needler, *Political Development in Latin America: Instability, Violence, and Evolutionary Change* (New York: Random House, 1968); Arpad Von Lazar, *Latin American Politics: A Primer* (Boston: Allyn and Bacon, 1971), pp. 45–48.

5. Charles W. Anderson, *Politics and Economic Change in Latin America* (Princeton, N.J.: Van Nostrand, 1967), p. 87.

6. Ibid., pp. 18–21; Gomez, "Latin American Executives"; Von Lazar, *Latin American Politics,* pp. 30–36.

7. Kalman H. Silvert, "Leadership Formation and Modernization in Latin America," *Journal of International Affairs,* 20 (1966): 318–32; Von Lazar, *Latin American Politics,* p. 30.

8. Carl J. Friedrich and Zbigniew K. Brzezinski, *Totalitarian Dictatorship and Autocracy,* 2d ed. (New York: Praeger, 1966), pp. 23–27.

9. One of the most useful is by Gino Germani and Kalman H. Silvert, "Politics, Social Structure and Military Intervention in Latin America," *European Journal of Sociology,* 2 (1961), pp. 62–81.

10. Carl Beck et al., *Comparative Communist Political Leadership* (New York: McKay, 1973); Lewis J. Edinger and Donald D. Searing, "Social Background in Elite Analysis: A Methodological Inquiry," *American Political Science Review,* 61 (June 1967), pp. 428–45.

11. Robert J. Alexander, "The Emergence of Modern Political Parties in Latin America," in *The Politics of Change in Latin America,* ed. J. Maier and R. W. Weatherhead (New York: Praeger, 1964), pp. 101–25; Alexander, *Latin American Politics and Government;* T. S. DiTella, "Populism and Reform in Latin America," in *The Dynamics of Change in Latin American Politics,* 2d ed., ed. John D. Martz (Englewood Cliffs, N.J.: Prentice-Hall, 1971), pp. 246–360; Irving L. Horowitz, "The Military Elites," in *Elites in Latin America,* ed. Seymour Martin Lipset and Aldo Solari (New York: Oxford, 1967), pp. 146–89.

12. Horowitz, "Military Elites," pp. 150–53; Needler, *Political Development.*

13. This political party typology was suggested initially by Anna Elizabeth Powell, a graduate assistant working on the early stages of the project. The typology was devised and initial coding of the data begun in 1965. As a result, this typology does not reflect the thoughtful suggestions presented by Peter Ranis, "A Two-Dimensional Typology of Latin American Political Parties," *Journal of Politics,* 30 (1968), pp. 798–832.

14. Data for this study have been collected from a variety of sources. Lists of cabinet members and party leaders were developed from the *Political Handbook and Atlas of the World,* the *Statesman's Yearbook,* the *South American Handbook,* and U. S. Department of State lists. All standard biographic works, including international, regional, and country directories, were examined. Some biographic data were made available through the Pan American Union. Mail questionnaires were sent to both subjects and researchers in Mexico and Uruguay in an effort to improve the data collections for these two countries. Newspaper files were searched by a student research assistant in Buenos Aires to expand the Argentine data. Much of the event-related data was coded from *Facts-on-File, Keesing's Archives,* and the *New York Times Index.* Finally, some biographic data were culled from descriptive scholarly writing.

15. In order to insure comparability among the several multivariate and bivariate analyses, cases were excluded on the following bases: (1) all cases with missing data on any of the three dependent variables were excluded; (2) all cases with missing data on more than three of the thirteen independent variables were excluded; (3) any additional deletions required were handled on a pairwise, analysis-by-analysis basis. Even with these conservative procedures for handling missing data, some of the bivariate cross-classifications that deal with the full 25-year period of this study include fewer than the 896 subjects constituting the basic "sample."

16. F. Andrews, J. Morgan, and S. Sonquist, *Multiple Classification Analysis: A Report on a Computer Program for Multiple Regression Using Categorical Predictors* (Ann Arbor: Institute for Social Research, 1967).

17. While this overlap may be statistically inconvenient, it seems substantively necessary. The decision—especially for a political elite—not to affiliate formally with nonparty organizations would seem to constitute an important qualitative posture toward the organizational environment and cannot be excluded from the variable of "nature of nonparty organizational affiliation."

18. It may be worth underscoring why the row percentages rather than the column percentages reflect the critical explanatory dimensions in many of these two-way tables. Although persons with no nonparty organizational affiliations constituted the most "revolutionary" subset (since most "revolutionaries" had no nonparty organizational affiliations), persons with no such affiliations also constituted a majority of the subjects under study, so that their numerical preponderance in a given category of any other variable was highly likely. For this reason, our focus needs to be on the proportions of persons *within* each category of the nonparty organizational variable who engaged in revolutionary acts, i.e., on the *probability* that a person with, say, many nonparty organizational ties will also exhibit revolutionary behavior. This probability is reflected in the row percentages of the table. A similar way to look at this point is in terms of our ability to predict revolutionary behavior from number of nonparty organizational affiliations. The probability of our being accurate in predicting that a person with few nonparty organizational memberships will be revolutionary is higher than our probability of being accurate in predicting that a person with no affiliations will be revolutionary. The MCA technique proceeds in an analogous way. The association between any given category of a predictor variable and the dependent variable is based on the mean Y (dependent variable) value for cases in that X (predictor variable) category.

19. The independent and dependent variables in question here do not overlap operationally. That is, membership in a political agitation group was not enough to cause a subject to be coded as having engaged in revolutionary activity. Revolutionary activity is a behavioral measure indicated by involvement in specific events. The relationship between membership in political agitation groups and involvement in revolutionary acts or coups is not tautological; some of our elite subjects who were members of such groups did not engage in revolutionary or extralegal behaviors.

20. The judgment as to what proportion of variance in the dependent variable must be explained before the solution is "respectable," or "interesting," is subjective. In a multiple linear regression analysis, both the R^2 and the betas for individual predictors can be evaluated for significance through the use of F-tests. The analogous MCA procedure would be misleading here because of the patterns of interaction in the data.

21. The background and socialization variables that best predict attitudes and behaviors may well differ between elites and mass. Especially persuasive evidence of this observation is presented by M. G. Zaninovich, "Elites and Citizenry in Yugoslav Society: A Study of Value Differentiation," in Beck et al., *Comparative Communist Political Leadership*, pp. 226–97.

CHAPTER 6
PATTERNS OF CHANGE IN POLITICAL LEADERSHIP IN SOCIALIST SYSTEMS

1. See Carl J. Friedrich and Zbigniew K. Brzezinski, *Totalitarian Dictatorship and Autocracy*, 2d ed. rev. (New York: Praeger, 1965), chap. 2.

2. Peter C. Ludz, *The Changing Party Elite in East Germany* (Cambridge, Mass.: MIT Press, 1972), esp. pp. 60–66.

3. Frederic J. Fleron, Jr., "System Attributes and Career Attributes: The Soviet Political Leadership System, 1952–1965," in Carl Beck et al., *Comparative Communist Political Leadership* (New York: McKay, 1973), pp. 58–59.

4. Radomir Lukíc, "Yugoslav Social Structure and the Formation of Public Opinion," in *Opinion-Making Elites in Yugoslavia*, ed. Allen H. Barton, Bogdan Denitch, and Charles Kadushin (New York: Praeger, 1973), chap 3.

5. Derek J. Waller, "The Evolution of the Chinese Communist Political Elite, 1931–56," in *Elites in the People's Republic of China*, ed. Robert A. Scalapino (Seattle: University of Washington Press, 1972), pp. 65–66. The same conclusion is reinforced by Scalapino's research. See his "The Transition in Chinese Party Leadership: A Comparison of the Eighth and Ninth Central Committees," in *Elites in the People's Republic of China*, pp. 67–148.

6. Victor C. Falkenheim, "Provincial Leadership in Fukien: 1949–66," in *Elites in the People's Republic of China*, ed. Scalapino, pp. 199–244.

7. Frederic J. Fleron, Jr., "Toward a Reconceptualization of Political Change in the Soviet Union: The Political Leadership System," in *Communist Studies and the Social Sciences: Essays on Methodology and Empirical Theory*, ed. Fleron (Chicago: Rand McNally, 1969), pp. 222–43.

8. Frederic J. Fleron, Jr., "System Attributes and Career Attributes," in Beck et al., *Comparative Communist Political Leadership*, pp. 58–59.

9. See William A. Welsh, "Stability and Change in the Bulgarian Political Elite, 1944–1971," paper presented at a conference on "Social Stratification and the Role of Political Elites in the Communist States of East-Central Europe," Lawrence, Kan., April 1973.

10. Anthony Downs, *Inside Bureaucracy* (Boston: Little, Brown, 1967), pp. 24–25.

11. Ibid., chap. 6.

12. Max Weber, "Bureaucracy," in *Essays in Sociology,* trans. H. H. Gerth and C. Wright Mills (New York: Oxford, 1962), pp. 196–244.

13. Hannah Arendt, *The Origins of Totalitarianism* (New York: World, 1958), chap. 11, 12.

14. C. Wright Mills, *The Marxists* (New York: Dell, 1962), esp. chap. 1, 2.

15. Especially see Milovan Djilas, *The New Class: An Analysis of the Communist System* (New York: Praeger, 1957); and Djilas, *Conversations with Stalin,* trans. Michael B. Petrovich (New York: Harcourt, 1962).

16. See Adam Schaff, *Marxism and the Human Individual* (New York: McGraw-Hill, 1970). Also see his "Marxism and the Philosophy of Man," in *Socialist Humanism,* ed. Erich Fromm (Garden City, N.Y.: Doubleday, 1965), pp. 141–50.

17. William A. Welsh, "Communist Political Leadership: Conclusions and Overview," in Beck et al., *Comparative Communist Political Leadership,* pp. 298–308.

18. Milton Lodge, "Attitudinal Cleavages Within the Soviet Political Leadership," in Beck et al., *Comparative Communist Political Leadership,* pp. 202–25.

CHAPTER 7
ELITE-MASS RELATIONS IN PLURALIST SYSTEMS

1. Given the fundamental importance to democratic government of a commitment to the rule of law, it is remarkable how public officials can sometimes persuade themselves that their own behavior should not be required to conform to such constraints. Former president Richard M. Nixon's public statements in 1977 to the effect that the president must sometimes be considered beyond the law illustrate this tendency.

2. For data illustrating the extent of male dominance of public leadership positions in the United States, see Wendell Bell, Richard J. Hill, and Charles R. Wright, *Public Leadership* (San Francisco: Chandler, 1961), chap. 3.

3. Bell, Hill, and Wright, *Public Leadership,* p. 58.

4. See Fair Employment Practice Committee, *First Report,* July 1943 to December 1944. (Washington, D. C.: U.S. Government Printing Office, 1945).

5. Murray G. Lawson, "The Foreign-Born in Congress, 1789–1949: A Statistical Summary," *American Political Science Review,* 51 (December 1957), pp. 1183–89.

6. It is worth noting that the situation has been somewhat different in local government, especially in larger urban areas. For example, in an early study Zink found that three-fourths of the city political "bosses" in the United States were either foreign-born or second generation Americans. See Harold Zink, *City Bosses in the United States* (Durham, N.C.: Duke University Press, 1930).

7. Bell, Hill, and Wright, *Public Leadership,* p. 77.

8. Donald R. Matthews, *The Social Background of Political Decision-Makers* (Garden City, N.Y.: Doubleday, 1954), p. 26.

9. See Walter A. Rosenbaum, *Political Culture* (New York: Praeger, 1975); and Dean Jaros, *Socialization to Politics* (New York: Praeger, 1973).

10. This duplicitous posture toward individual freedoms is reflected in the successful campaign against gay rights legislation led by singer Anita Bryant in Florida in 1977.

11. Jaros, *Socialization to Politics,* p. 44.

12. Ibid., pp. 44–45.

13. Fred J. Greenstein, *Children and Politics* (New Haven, Conn.: Yale University Press, 1965), p. 127.

14. John C. Wahlke, Heinz Eulau, William Buchanan, and LeRoy C. Ferguson, *The Legislative System: Explorations in Legislative Behavior* (New York: Wiley, 1962). Also see Eulau, Wahlke, Buchanan, and Ferguson, "The Role of the Representative: Some Empirical Observations on the Theory of Edmund Burke," *American Political Science Review*, 53 (September 1959), pp. 742–56; reprinted in *Political Behavior in America: New Directions*, ed. Heinz Eulau, (New York: Random House, 1966), pp. 24–44. Also see Wahlke et al., "The Roles of Legislators in the Legislative Process," in *Political Leadership*, ed. Glenn D. Paige (New York: Free Press, 1972), pp. 115–31.

15. Eulau et al., "The Role of the Representative," in *Political Behavior in America*, ed. Eulau, p. 34.

16. Wahlke, et al., "The Roles of Legislators . . .," in *Political Leadership*, ed. Paige, p. 119.

17. See James H. Kuklinski and Richard C. Elling, "Representational Role, Constituency Opinion and Legislative Roll-Call Behavior," *American Journal of Political Science*, 21 (1977), 135–147; also see Donald J. McCrone and James H. Kuklinski, "The Delegate Theory of Representation," *American Journal of Political Science*, forthcoming.

18. Arthur B. Gunlicks, "Representative Role Perceptions among Local Councilors in Western Germany," *Journal of Politics*, 31 (1969), pp. 443–64.

19. E. E. Schattschneider, *The Semi-Sovereign People* (New York: Holt, Rinehart and Winston, 1960).

20. See Warren E. Miller and Donald E. Stokes, "Constituency Influence in Congress," *American Political Science Review*, 57 (1963), p. 45.

21. John C. Wahlke, "Policy Demands and System Support: The Role of the Represented," in *Modern Parliaments: Change or Decline?* ed. Gerhard Loewenberg (Chicago: Aldine, 1971), p. 145.

22. Ibid., p. 146.

23. Ibid., pp. 146–47.

24. For example, see Philip E. Converse, "The Nature of Belief Systems in Mass Publics," in *Ideology and Discontent*, ed. David E. Apter, (New York: Free Press, 1964), pp. 206–61.

25. This concept was first articulated by the Committee on Political Parties of the American Political Science Association, "Toward a More Responsible Two-Party System," Supplement, *American Political Science Review* (September 1950).

26. See Miller and Stokes, "Constituency Influence in Congress," pp. 45–56.

27. Rosenbaum, *Political Culture*, p. 119.

28. Bell, Hill, and Wright, *Public Leadership*, p. 126.

29. John C. Wahlke, Alex N. Dragnich, *et al.*, *Government and Politics*, 2d ed. (New York: Random House, 1971), p. 521.

30. Ibid., pp. 522–23.

31. This distinction is developed by Anthony Downs, *An Economic Theory of Democracy* (New York: Harper & Row, 1957).

32. Downs, *An Economic Theory of Democracy*, pp. 67 ff.

33. See Rosenbaum, *Political Culture*, esp. chap. 2, 3.

34. Jack Dennis et al., "Political Socialization to Democratic Orientations in Four Western Systems," *Comparative Political Studies*, 1 (April 1968), p. 81.

35. Ibid., p. 87.

36. Richard Rose, *England* (Boston: Little, Brown, 1964), p. 41.

37. For a discussion of political trust and its significance in the United Kingdom, the United States, the Federal Republic of Germany, Italy, and Mexico, see Gabriel Almond and Sidney Verba, *The Civic Culture* (Princeton University Press, 1963).

38. David Butler and Donald E. Stokes, *Political Change in Britain* (New York: St. Martin's Press, 1969), pp. 32–33.

39. Rosenbaum, *Political Culture*, p. 122.

40. Erwin C. Hargrove, "Popular Leadership in the Anglo-American Democracies," in *Political Leadership in Industrialized Societies: Studies in Comparative Analysis*, ed. Lewis J. Edinger (New York: Wiley, 1967), pp. 182–219.

41. Ibid., p. 198.

42. For an elaboration of this theme, see Rosenbaum, *Political Culture*, pp. 147–51.

43. Rosenbaum, *Political Culture*, p. 149.

44. The term "political attitudes" is used in the following paragraphs because the researchers whose work is summarized used that term. The careful reader will recognize that the subjects are what we have called values and issue orientations. In this book we generally reserve the term "attitude" to refer to a structure, or mode, of thought (e.g., dogmatism).

45. Lewis J. Edinger and Donald D. Searing, "Social Background in Elite Analysis: A Methodological Inquiry," *American Political Science Review*, 61, 2 (June 1967), pp. 428–45.

46. Donald D. Searing, "The Comparative Study of Elite Socialization," *Comparative Political Studies*, 1, 4 (January 1969), pp. 471–500.

47. Ibid., p. 484.

48. Ibid., p. 485.

CHAPTER 8
BLENDING SUBSTANCE AND METHOD: SOME ISSUES IN RESEARCH ON LEADERS AND ELITES

1. Carl Beck and James M. Malloy, "Political Elites: A Mode of Analysis" (Paper presented at the Sixth World Congress of the International Political Science Association, Geneva, September 1964), p. 3.

2. See Peter Bachrach and Morton Baratz, "Two Faces of Power," *American Political Science Review*, 51 (December 1962), pp. 947–52.

3. The reliance of common social science data analysis procedures on covariance as a basis for establishing relationships simplifies reality, and may sometimes be a significant impediment to understanding. In some cases, *constancy* in one variable may be a cause of variation in another. One example would be the impact of *stability* of the West German economy on the *increase* in support for representative institutions in that country between 1949 and 1960. See G. R. Boynton and Gerhard Loewenberg, "Economic Sources of Rising Support for the Regime in Postwar Germany: An Interpretation of a Mathematical Model," paper presented at a conference on "Alienation and System Support," (January 1975, University of Iowa, Iowa City).

4. Two of the most important works are: Adam Przeworski and Henry Teune, *The Logic of Comparative Social Inquiry* (New York: Wiley, 1970); and *The Methodology of Comparative Research*, ed. Robert T. Holt and John E. Turner (New York: Free Press, 1970).

5. See *The Logic of Comparative Social Inquiry*.

6. From the perspective of research design, one of the best such research projects carried out in the last decade was the International Studies of Values in Politics project, which was a study of the relationship between characteristics of local political leadership and the behavior of local governments in India, Poland, the United States, and Yugoslavia. The European Co-ordination Center for Research and Documentation in the Social

Sciences (the "Vienna Center") has coordinated more than 20 such projects since its establishment in 1963.

7. The COMPELITE data set, interactive software, and accompanying manuals are available from the Laboratory for Political Research at the University of Iowa.

8. Most of these studies were done by researchers in the Department of Political Science at the University of Iowa. The German study was done by Gerhard Loewenberg, the study on Japan by Chong Lim Kim, that on the Soviet Union by Milton Lodge (now at the State University of New York at Stony Brook), and the research on Brazil, Argentina, and Mexico by William A. Welsh. Carl Beck of the University of Pittsburgh compiled the data on Bulgaria.

9. The careful reader will note that the definition of "urban" used in the COMPELITE collection is different from that used for some of the same (Latin American) countries in the analysis done in Chapter 5 of this book. The figure of 25,000 population used in Chapter 5 would have rendered the Latin American data incomparable with the data from the other countries included in COMPELITE, especially Bulgaria.

10. Richard A. Pride, "Pattern Analysis: An Alternative Approach to Quantitative Historical Data," *Comparative Political Studies*, 4, 3 (October 1971) pp. 361–369.

11. George K. Schueller, *The Politburo* (Stanford, Calif.: Stanford University Press, 1951).

12. See Derek J. Waller, "The Evolution of the Chinese Communist Political Elite, 1931–56," in *Elites in the People's Republic of China*, ed. Robert A. Scalapino (Seattle: University of Washington Press, 1972), pp. 41–66.

13. See William A. Welsh, "Stability and Change in the Bulgarian Political Elite, 1944–1971," paper presented at a conference on "Social Stratification and the Role of Political Elites in the Communist States of East-Central Europe," Lawrence, Kansas, April 1973.

14. Milton Lodge, "Attitudinal Cleavages Within the Soviet Political Leadership," in Carl Beck et al., *Comparative Communist Political Leadership* (New York: McKay, 1973), pp. 202–25.

15. Ole R. Holsti, *Content Analysis for the Social Sciences and Humanities* (Reading, Mass.: Addison-Wesley, 1969), pp. 33–34.

16. Ibid., p. 34.

17. See Milton Rokeach, *The Open and Closed Mind* (New York: Basic Books, 1960).

18. Talcott Parsons, Edward A. Shils, and J. Olds, "Values, Motives and Systems of Action," in *Toward a General Theory of Action*, ed. T. Parsons and E. A. Shils, (Cambridge, Mass.: Harvard University Press, 1952).

19. John Walton, "Substance and Artifact: The Current Status of Research on Community Power Structure," *American Journal of Sociology*, 71, 4 (January, 1966), pp. 430–38.

20. Ibid., p. 438.

Name Index

Abraham, Henry J., 186
Alexander, Robert J., 189
Almond, Gabriel, 193
Anderson, Charles W., 189
Andrews, Frank, 190
Apter, David E., 193
Arendt, Hannah, 133, 192
Aristotle, 1, 15

Bachrach, Peter, 167, 194
Baratz, Morton, 167, 194
Barton, Allen H., 181, 191
Beck, Carl, 28, 36, 165, 187, 188,
    189, 191, 192, 194, 195
Bell, Wendell, 192, 193
Beria, Lavrenti P., 137, 138
Bonham-Carter, Violet, 187
Bottomore, T. B., 185, 186
Boynton, G. R., 194
Broad, Lewis, 187
Brzezinski, Zbigniew K., 189, 191
Buchanan, William, 193
Bullock, Alan, 187
Burns, James McGregor, 187
Butler, David, 159, 193

Campbell, Donald T., 188
Carter, Jimmy, 145
Churchill, Winston, 48
Coleman, James S., 185
Converse, Philip E., 193

Dahl, Robert A., 188
DeBell, Daryl, 187
de Gaulle, General Charles, 72
de Sola Pool, Ithiel, 186
Denitch, Bogdan, 188, 191
Dennis, Jack, 193
Di Tella, T. S., 189
Djilas, Milovan, 135, 187, 192
Downs, Anthony, 131, 158, 192, 193
Dragnich, Alex N., 193
Duff, E. A., 189
Dye, Thomas R., 186

Edinger, Lewis J., 162, 163, 188,
    189, 194
Eisenhower, General Dwight D., 72
Engels, Friedrich, 185
Erikson, Erik H., 187
Eulau, Heinz, 193

Przeworski, Adam, 169, 194
Pye, Lucian W., 187

Ranis, Peter, 190
Robinson, Edgar E., 187
Rokeach, Milton, 195
Rollins, Alfred B., 187
Roosevelt, Franklin D., 48
Rose, Richard, 159, 193
Rosenbaum, Walter A., 192, 193, 194
Rothwell, C. Easton, 186

Scalapino, Robert A., 187, 191, 195
Schaff, Adam, 135, 192
Schattschneider, E. E., 7, 152, 186, 188, 193
Schoenfeld, Maxwell P., 187
Schueller, George K., 176, 186, 195
Schumpeter, Joseph A., 9
Schwartz, Richard T., 188
Searing, Donald D., 14, 162, 163, 186, 188, 189, 194
Sechrest, Lee, 188
Seligman, Lester, 26, 37, 46, 75, 137, 186, 187
Sherwood, Robert E., 187
Shils, Edward A., 181, 188, 195
Shub, David, 187
Silvert, Kalman H., 189
Solari, Aldo, 189

Sonquist, S., 190
Stalin, Josef, 2, 48, 70, 89, 130, 135, 137, 175, 176
Stogdill, Ralph M., 21, 186
Stokes, Donald E., 153, 159, 193
Stroessner, Gerald Alfred, 86
Supek, Rudi, 125

Tacitus, 1
Teune, Henry, 169, 194
Trotsky, Leon, 187
Tugwell, Rexford G., 187
Turner, John E., 194

Verba, Sidney, 187, 193
Von Lazar, Arpad, 189

Wahlke, John C., 149, 193
Waller, Derek J., 126, 187, 191, 195
Walton, John, 183, 195
Weatherhead, R. W., 189
Webb, Eugene J., 188
Weber, Max, 192
Welsh, William A., 186, 187, 188, 189, 191, 192, 195
Wiatr, Jerzy, 17, 19, 20, 186
Wolfenstein, E. Victor, 187
Wright, Charles R., 192, 193

Zaninovich, M. George, 56, 187, 188, 191
Ziegler, Harmon, 186
Zink, Harold, 192

Subject Index

301.44
WL463l

Welsh, William A.

Leaders and elites

24886